OKLAHOMA CITY COMMUNITY COLLEGE

W9-BSD-620

WITHDRAWN

Coming to Know

WITHDRAWN

WITHDRAWN

Coming to Know

Writing to Learn in the Intermediate Grades

Edited by Nancie Atwell
Bread Loaf School of English
Middlebury College

HEINEMANN
Portsmouth, New Hampshire

IRWIN PUBLISHING
Toronto, Canada

HEINEMANN EDUCATIONAL BOOKS, INC.
361 Hanover Street
Portsmouth, NH 03801
Offices and agents throughout the world

Published simultaneously in Canada by
Irwin Publishing
1800 Steeles Avenue West   Concord, Ontario, Canada L4K 2P3

© 1990 by Heinemann Educational Books, Inc. All rights reserved. No part of this book may be reproduced in any form or by electronic or mechanical means, including information storage and retrieval systems, without permission in writing from the publisher, except by a reviewer, who may quote brief passages in a review.

The publishers and the authors wish to thank the children and their parents or guardians for permission to reproduce the children's work quoted in this book. Every effort has been made to contact the owners of material borrowed for quotation. We regret any oversights that may have occurred and would be happy to rectify them in future printings of this book.

Library of Congress Cataloging-in-Publication Data

Coming to know : writing to learn in the intermediate grades / edited by Nancie Atwell.
    p. cm.
   Includes bibliographies.
   ISBN 0-435-08500-X
    1. Language arts (Elementary)—United States. 2. Language arts—Correlation with content subjects—United States. 3. Report writing. I. Atwell, Nancie.
LB1576.C578 1990
372.6—dc20   89-31483
                                                                              CIP

Canadian Cataloguing in Publication Data

Main entry under title:
Coming to know

Includes bibliographical references.
ISBN 0-7725-1775-4

1. Language arts (Elementary). 2. Language arts—Correlation with content subjects. 3. Report writing. I. Atwell, Nancie.

LB1576.C6 1990   372.6'23   C89-095090-3

Designed by Maria Szmauz.
Interior and front-cover photos by Jo Haney; back-cover photo by Toby McLeod.
Printed in the United States of America.
10 9 8 7 6 5 4

For Dixie Goswami

Contents

Contributors

NANCIE ATWELL   Bread Loaf School of English, Middlebury College, Middlebury, Vermont

MARCIA BLAKE   Boothbay Region Elementary School, Boothbay Harbor, Maine

NANCY CHARD   Lincoln Middle School, Portland, Maine

PATRICIA J. COLLINS   Smith College Campus School, Northampton, Massachusetts

LAURA FARNSWORTH   Howard C. Reiche Community School, Portland, Maine

CINDY GREENLEAF   Boothbay Region Elementary School, Boothbay Harbor, Maine

JO HANEY   Boothbay Region Elementary School, Boothbay Harbor, Maine

JO ANNE LEE   Howard C. Reiche Community School, Portland, Maine

DONNA MAXIM   Boothbay Region Elementary School, Boothbay Harbor, Maine

JANINE PIERPONT   Howard C. Reiche Community School, Portland, Maine

ANNE THOMPSON   Memorial Middle School, South Portland, Maine

CHARLENE LOUGHLIN VAUGHAN   Howard C. Reiche Community School, Portland, Maine

NANCY S. WHEELER   Boothbay Region Elementary School, Boothbay Harbor, Maine

Introduction

NANCIE ATWELL

My unhappiest memory of elementary school involves report writing. I think the assignment was typical: pick a country and write a report about it. Describe its history, system of government, geography, population, major occupations, and natural resources. Include a topographical map, a bibliography, and an illustrated cover. At least twelve pages long. Due in one month, as homework.

Full of Anglophilia and sixth-grade arrogance I put in a bid for Great Britain, which the teacher okayed. This meant I would have to come up with four versions of all the above, one each for England, Ireland, Scotland, and Wales. Never mind that to do even one of the subtopics justice would require at least a book.

Now add a new variable: I am a world-class procrastinator. I think I have finally learned to judge just how long I can stall in the face of a deadline. I have also learned to write on my feet, to mentally rehearse my writing in the midst of doing something else, so that these days, when I do confront a blank page, my mind generally isn't. In sixth grade I had no idea of how to budget my time for a major writing project. If I thought about the report at all, it was to assure myself that I could pull off my usual something at the last minute. I didn't rehearse the report mentally because I was not a writer; thinking about writing, the compulsion that Don Graves (1983) calls "offstage rehearsal," only happens to children who write regularly.

In addition to lacking a writer's habits of mind, I had nothing to think about Great Britain, or at least nothing to think about the topics outlined in the assignment. From my English grandmother, also named Nancie Atwell, I knew about English cooking, gardens, pubs, games, slang, and country life. But what I could teach others or what I wanted to learn were not considerations in the assignment, apart from two essential skills: I was expert in the subtle art of plagiarizing *The World Book*, and I could trace maps.

The weekend before the report was due I finally adjourned to my bedroom and began. By Sunday afternoon I knew I was in deep trouble. I stayed up as late as my mother would allow that night, hardly slept, and went to school empty-handed the next morning. While my classmates bustled around me putting the finishing touches on their illustrated covers, I pretended to be fascinated with the inside of my desk. When the reports were passed up the rows to the front of the room, I held my breath. And the teacher . . .

Never mentioned the missing report. Not that day, not ever. For the remaining three months of the school year I lived, alternately, in dread and anticipation of the moment when she would take me aside and end the torture, a word I don't use lightly. I thought about the report all of the time but had no idea what to do about it now that the deadline was past.

On the last day of sixth grade, in the flurry of cleaning up the room and saying our good-byes, my teacher handed back the social studies reports. I escaped to the girls' room when I saw her come around from behind her desk with a stack of illustrated covers in her arms, and that was that—except for the gnawing at my conscience that has never eased in all of these years.

What I realized in writing about this memory is that my sixth-grade teacher did not discover until the last day of school that I hadn't submitted the report. For the same reason that I had postponed writing it she had postponed grading it: sheer boredom. The reports, as tedious to read as they were to write, informed and entertained no one. I can't blame the teacher. The sixth-grade social studies curriculum required a report on a country, and she had obliged. Then she had procrastinated too, until it was too late for her to bring me to justice.

It did not have to be this way, for her or for me. Writing in the content areas does not have to be a test of reading, a performance for the teacher that demonstrates whether the student located and reassembled someone else's information. From Nancy Martin (1976) we have learned how a teacher might act, instead, as a sympathetic audience who sets students thinking about their own information, as a reader "who will pay real regard to the way it looks through [students'] eyes" (81). Writing in the content areas does not have to be a solitary undertaking. From Donald Murray (1968) and Donald Graves (1983) we have learned about the tremendous benefits to be realized when a teacher and students talk together during class about what a writer has done so far and might do next. And writing in the content areas does not have to fit a format that does not exist in the real world of nonfiction prose. From Janet Emig (1983) we have learned that genuine writing "represents a unique mode of learning—not merely valuable, not merely special, but unique" (123) and that when genuine scholars use writing to learn about their fields, it looks nothing like the empty forms we promote in school assignments.

This book and the project from which it grew are a response to the elementary school's need to help its students, in Jerome Bruner's words, go "beyond the information given" and use writing to find and solve problems in every subject area. Under a grant from the Bread Loaf School of English of Middlebury College, through the generosity of Mr. Bingham's Trust for Charity, I worked for two years with a group of Maine teachers to develop ways that children might use writing to learn throughout their school day. Together, the teachers involved in the Bread Loaf project read books and articles, wrote, and met frequently to discuss what they were learning from the children in their grades 3–8 classrooms. With the encouragement of Paul Cubeta and Dixie Goswami, we discovered what is possible when teachers who understand writing as process ask their students to use writing to learn. We are also indebted to principals Miriam Remar of Howard C. Reiche Community School in Portland and Gloria Walter of Boothbay Region Elementary, and to Tom Morrill and the teachers of the Kingfield Elementary School for the insights we achieved in collaboration with them.

We were careful in this volume to avoid the phrase "teaching writing across the curriculum," which many content-area teachers have interpreted, and rejected, as a call for them to teach English in addition to math or science or history: to assign essays about their subjects and to correct them as an English teacher might. Although I am endlessly interested in the nature of writing instruction that helps young writers grow, I don't believe that teaching students how to write is the responsibility of teachers across the curriculum. We already have plenty of English teachers, and many of us are just now desisting from correcting class sets of essays and, instead, learning how to teach writing. I am suggesting that teachers of every discipline might ask students to think and write as scientists, historians, mathematicians, and literary critics do—to use writing-as-process to discover meaning just as these scholars do when they go about the real, messy business of thinking on paper. As Toby Fulwiler (1987a) has observed, "What *isn't* generally acknowledged is that writing is basic to thinking about, and learning, knowledge *in all fields* as well as to communicating that knowledge" (1).

In the language arts classroom we have started to draw on the writing process theories of Emig and Murray and the writing workshop methods of Graves, Giacobbe, and Calkins to help children learn writing. If students are to be able to use writing to help themselves learn, these theories and methods must find a place in the other disciplines. When content-area teachers know writing from the inside, through reading about how others in their fields have written, observing student writers, and writing themselves, they can begin to tap this most powerful tool for making sense of experience. And they can reject what customarily passes for writing in the content areas: short-answer, fill-in-the-blank, and essay tests and, still the worst offender all these years since my sixth-grade graduation, the written report.

Matthew is an eighth grader of the 1980s. During his language arts class, organized as a writing workshop, Matthew is finding, fine-tuning, and communicating meaning in a range of genres to many audiences. But during science class, Matthew is pretending at something called a report, and so is his teacher (Figure I–1).

"Chromosomes" looks like a report. The teacher, who collects 125 of these each Friday, looks for a five-paragraph format, poly-syllables, and correct spelling. There is no evidence that she read Matthew's report, nor is there evidence that Matthew learned any-thing about the subject at hand, although he did have his suspicions confirmed about his science teacher's method for grading writing.

Report writing, per se, isn't the problem. As Jack Wilde (1988) recently wrote:

> Surely adults are called upon to write reports, so the form has validity. The purpose, though, is different. . . . A business that requires written reports does it . . . to discover something that neither the employee nor the employer knew, nor easily could have come to know without the report. The report is . . . a *coming to know* on the part of both the writer and the readers (179).

The problem with school reports lies in our methods for as-signing them. We need to put the emphasis where it belongs—on meaning—and show students how to investigate questions and communicate their findings, how to go beyond plagiarism to gen-uine expertise and a "coming to know."

One of the main subjects of this volume is alternative methods to the traditional school report. Drawing on the work of classroom teachers Jack Wilde (1988), Carolyn Currier (Giacobbe 1986), Cora Five and Martha Rosen (1985), Linda Rief (1985), and Lynda Chit-tenden (1982), as well as our own research, we have tried to ac-knowledge and accommodate what students need in order to develop reports from which they and others might actually learn something. The basic instructional ingredients have proven to be time, own-ership, and response (Giacobbe 1986).

In designing projects calling for written reports, teachers se-lected appropriate units of study: the particular areas of their cur-ricula that they felt warranted in-depth investigation. Then, they set aside a block of time—four to eight weeks—for the projects and gave their students time in school to carry out research. They also allowed ownership. Within the unit of study children chose their own topics, genres, audiences, and methods. They gathered infor-mation through interviews, books, magazines, site visits, field trips, read-alouds, filmstrips, movies, and guest speakers. And they con-ferred; they had response. While they were gathering data, drafting,

FIGURE I–1 ● MATTHEW'S "SCIENCE REPORT"

Science (A-)

Chromosomes

Chromosomes are tiny thread like structures composed of nucleos? acid rain and chromatin. Chromosomes contain the nucleos acid rain DPX, which is divided into small units called jeans. The jeans sp. determine the skin color and size of the cells. Actually, there are many different kinds of jeans. Dr. Leaky classified some of them Levi, Lee and Calvin Klein. The moment doctor said, nothing gets between you and your Calvin Kleins. While Sedgefield jeans are important for their physical fit, what is really important is that chromosomes are also found in the inside of the body on such regions as the rumpus, shown in the figure above, and along the brain.

Among other sections of a chromasome are the miniature filament and granules called mitochondria

The last section of a cell is cytoplasm, it is used to help protect the chromasomes.

The most important part of my report is that without chromasomes you wouldn't have cytoplasm to protect the chromasomes and jeans for re-production.

genes

and revising their manuscripts, they talked to each other and to their teachers about what they knew and what they wanted to know next. They also received responses from classmates, schoolmates, teachers, siblings, parents, and grandparents who read, saw, or listened to their amazing finished products. Both process and product mattered in writing the reports. Teachers learned to regard report writing as an opportunity for children to lay claim in a formal, permanent way to a body of information that children had generated for themselves.

At the same time, teachers understood that children might not automatically apply process approaches to their research, so they required self-selected topics, drafts, conferences, and portfolios. They encouraged students to focus topics—to narrow down to a manageable subject—and then to expand focus to include all relevant aspects of the subject. In talking with students they used the language of researchers who write: information, organization, validity, references, focus, lead, conclusion, draft, revise, edit. And they helped children understand that the qualities of good writing cut right across the modes. Whatever subject is addressed in a piece of writing, readers want a title that attracts their attention, a lead that captures their interest, specific information presented in a logical, engaging way, clear and graceful language, and conformity with the conventions of spelling and usage. In conferences and minilessons, teachers showed their kids what was possible for them as authors of research.

In the opening chapter of *Coming to Know*, Donna Maxim describes a variety of techniques and tools to introduce to beginning researchers. Donna's third graders, new to content-area research, learn how to take notes in their own words, conduct interviews, differentiate fact from opinion, observe and record their observations, and design simple research projects that demonstrate what they know about a topic. Instead of "expecting students to possess the skills of researchers as if by magic," Donna acts as a guide, planning research activities and modeling what researchers do so that children may approach their initial experiences as researchers with authority and confidence.

Patricia Collins's chapter in the section on researching and reporting describes the process by which sixth-grade students conducted research about the Middle Ages. Pat recognized a gap between the personal-experience narrative prevalent in writing workshop and the informational writing required for content-area study. She devised an approach to report writing that allows children to bring what they know of writing process to a new situation, to produce content-area writing that is as personal and meaningful as children's stories of their own experiences. Perhaps the most important feature of her approach is the range of genres in which her students report their knowledge.

Pat, Donna, and the other contributors to this volume acknowledge that adults learn from information that is embedded in many different kinds of writing—straightforward reports, but also historical novels, interviews and feature articles in magazines and newspapers, how-to manuals, field guides, catalogues, published journals and letters, autobiographies and biographies, recipe books, and our own personal and professional correspondence. We also learn about the world through the specifics presented to us in television and movie scripts—documentaries, but also romances, action-adventures, biographies, comedies, and mysteries. And we learn by reading fiction. I first became aware of scoliosis when I read Judy Blume's painstakingly researched *Deenie* (1973), and I learned as much about life in Thatcher's Britain from Margaret Drabble's novel *The Radiant Way* (1987) as I do from articles in *The New York Times*. Pat's chapter demonstrates that when teachers consider the shape of the writing that students will be asked to produce, they would be wise to remember a dictum from Toby Fulwiler: "Try to assign only that writing which you wish to read." When teachers emphasize information and all the ways that people come by it, form follows function, and students have opportunities to read and to write many different kinds of reports, writing that both informs and engages. We have included as Appendix A a list of the genres that students selected to present their research during the two years of our project.

The second section of *Coming to Know* is devoted to academic journals or *learning logs*. Here we have drawn on the work of Toby Fulwiler (1987a, b), Art Young and Toby Fulwiler (1986), Lucy Calkins (1986), Jana Staton et al. (1982), Ann Berthoff (1981), and Nancy Martin et al. (1976). Logs are spiral-bound notebooks to last a whole school year, one for each subject area. Children's log entries are informal, tentative, first draft, and brief, usually consisting of no more than ten minutes of focused free writing. The teacher poses questions and situations or sets themes that invite students to observe, speculate, list, chart, web, brainstorm, role-play, ask questions, activate prior knowledge, collaborate, correspond, summarize, predict, or shift to a new perspective: in short, to participate in their own learning. After writing, children might read aloud their entries in pairs or small groups, or volunteer to share with the class, with the teacher transcribing their data on an overhead transparency or chart paper. At other times the whole class quickly reads around the room with no comments, in order to get a sense of the group's perceptions and knowledge. Sometimes the teacher collects the logs to skim, perhaps responding in a note to the writer, and some entries are actual letters to the teacher, which receive a letter in reply.

Toby Fulwiler (1987b) cautions that if learning logs are to be vehicles for learning, they cannot be measured as performances, too. Individual entries are never graded or corrected, but they are counted: the student must write something. Students write during class and the teacher usually writes in his or her log, too, so that all may air their thinking on a particular subject. Sometimes the teacher might ask students to write again, after a session of listening to log entries, in response to others' responses and as a chance to think anew (not a test to get it right).

The teachers in this book did not treat the logs as diaries or encourage writing that is highly personal. They were careful to articulate and clarify their intentions before asking any student to write in a log, and they determined early on that their purpose in assigning academic journals was not to counsel their students but to help children think about the relationship between themselves and the worlds of mathematics, literature, social studies, and science —to use journal writing as a tool to generate their own knowledge.

The children's learning logs served this purpose better than we could have hoped. The excerpts included in this book demonstrate powerful thinking across the curriculum—and more. Through the frequent entries they made in their learning logs, students' writing took on greater expression and fluency; they also became more self-directed, more critical, and more willing to take risks. Teachers changed their roles, too—from lecturers to guides, from dispensers of information to observers of children's learning. We know from John Goodlad (1984) that teachers in the United States spend upwards of 90 percent of class time talking at groups of children. Learning logs are one way to break the lecture-listen syndrome and give every student in a class a voice in the discussion.

The Swiss philosopher H. H. Amiel wrote:

> The highest function of the teacher consists not so much in imparting knowledge as in stimulating the pupil in its love and pursuit. To know how to suggest is the art of teaching.

In writing workshop, conferences and minilessons provide occasions for a teacher's suggestions to student writers; in the content-area classroom, learning log prompts are an invaluable way for the teacher to suggest and stimulate. We have included as Appendix B a list, by topic, of prompts that led to successful log entries during the past two years—that is, first-person writing that children both enjoyed and learned from.

In the opening chapter of the section devoted to learning logs, Anne Thompson examines the range of kinds of thinking that turned up in her third graders' logs. Dissatisfied with skill-and-drill methods for teaching critical thinking, Anne noted and began to categorize the instances of rich, contextual thinking evident in children's log entries. In turn, the depth of thoughtfulness of her students' writing evolved because of the questions and situations that Anne posed for them to think about. Her prompts and her students' responses make a convincing case for the use of learning logs by teachers who wish to promote young children's critical thinking as a routine occurrence in the elementary classroom.

Marcia Blake, a fourth-grade teacher, sees the log as a vehicle for helping her students respond to the new intellectual challenges of the upper elementary grades. In her chapter she shows techniques that she has used in science and social studies to help her students adjust to the changing demands of the curriculum—to focus on information, compare it, find patterns, and remember what they have learned. Logs also played an important role in creating a community for learning in her classroom.

Another fourth-grade teacher, Nancy Chard, looks at changes she made in her teaching in light of what she learned from children's learning logs. Nancy shows how logs helped her become more responsive to students as well as bring her social studies curriculum in line with what they know and need to know. Children's learning logs have become an important tool in her classroom for evaluating the effectiveness of the teacher's methods.

The double-entry journal, as developed by Ann Berthoff (1981), has largely been regarded as a method for secondary school and beyond. Charlene Loughlin Vaughan explores its uses in a third-grade classroom and illustrates how she has adapted the technique to her students and how they have used the double-page format to record and organize data and to think about it. As Charlene observes, the physical arrangement of the double-entry journal became a convenient "workplace" for children to focus and extend their knowledge and to visualize connections.

Laura Farnsworth is one of two special education teachers who contributed to this volume. In her chapter she describes a range of daily writing experiences in which she and her students engaged together, in a kind of class log, as a basis for individual students' successful experiences with learning logs and report writing. As Laura notes, the modes of collaborative writing that she sponsored helped special children to focus their attention, to process information more efficiently, and to learn what learners do.

Anne Thompson concludes the section devoted to learning logs. After several months in a new position as a fifth-grade teacher, she reports on an exciting six-week experiment: Anne invited writing in math class, adding a new set of spiral-bound notebooks to those already established for reading, science, and social studies. She and her students started with weekly entries in dialogue journals, and their letters show how writing can help both young mathematicians and their teacher. Anne suggests several other approaches to writing in math class, and she includes examples of math prompts for learning logs in Appendix B.

In recent years the phrase "the reading-writing connection"

has been applied to many contexts. In the third section of *Coming to Know*, two of the contributors examine the role of writing in helping their students learn about and appreciate the literature they read. Both Janine Pierpont and Jo Anne Lee describe approaches in which students choose their own books from well-stocked classroom libraries of children's literature and respond to their reading through writing. Janine asked her fifth graders to correspond with her in literary dialogue journals. When their letters remained plot-bound and impersonal in spite of her gentle nudging, she instituted literature logs in which students responded to open-ended prompts about their reading; many of the questions she asked of readers are included in Appendix B. Over time, the prompted log entries enriched the literary correspondence in students' journals by helping them internalize ways that they might respond on their own in their letters. Janine concludes that both kinds of informal writing are of value to readers and their teachers.

Jo Anne Lee looks at more formal writing in a literature program. Determined to avoid book reports, in which a child's writing is merely a test of reading, Jo Anne asked her fourth graders to create literature projects in the spirit of the books they read. She gave them many options of genre for their projects and followed a process model for writing, from drafting through publication of the finished products. Jo Anne's emphasis on the children's responses to the literature, rather than comprehension skills and record keeping, gave active voice to both the children's writing and their reading.

In a final chapter in the section on reading and writing, Donna Maxim describes how literature—fiction, nonfiction, and poetry—is a cornerstone of her entire curriculum and illustrates ways that she and her students have drawn on literature to learn science and social studies content and to connect what they learn to their own lives. As she observes, no textbook series could ever have the impact of relevant literature across the curriculum. In Appendix C, "Bury Yourself in Books," Donna shares her knowledge of children's literature in a bibliography organized by topic, from ABC books and Ancient Egypt to weather and words, and invites other teachers to develop their own storehouse of favorite books for use in every discipline.

Coming to Know concludes with three articles about the effects of writing to learn on the authors' teaching and professional activity. Nancy Wheeler, a resource room teacher, traces a year and a half in her relationship with a student identified as learning disabled. Both Nancy and Bill wrote in logs to help themselves learn, Bill about dinosaurs and Nancy about her student. She makes a compelling case for writing to learn, both as a staple of a special education program and as a way for a teacher to examine, reflect on, and change her teaching.

In her chapter Jo Haney recalls the development of a new unit for her third-grade science curriculum. Pulling together many of the ideas addressed in this volume, Jo shows how she created a study of puffins that included firsthand experiences, learning log entries, report writing, relevant children's literature, and connections to other disciplines. Excerpts from Jo's own log illustrate the key elements that contributed to the success of her planning; chief among them were her own interest and persistence as a researcher of puffins.

Cindy Greenleaf, a colleague of Jo Haney and Donna Maxim, concludes *Coming to Know* with the story of how the three teachers collaborated as a team in order to take charge of, integrate, and enrich their curriculum. Their roles as teachers changed, from managers of packaged programs to experts in curriculum design. Cindy takes us inside the process and shares excerpts from their group log—the forms that they used to generate and organize resources and coordinate their plans—as well as the weekly conversations in which they negotiated activities, literature selections, budgets, guest speakers, field trips, responsibilities, and prompts for learning log entries across the disciplines. Cindy concludes: "Writing to learn was the key that gave us the freedom to open up our curriculum —to implement an enrichment model and begin to explore connections among the content areas, language arts, and art."

Teachers are constantly writing across the curriculum. We write and record checks, compile shopping lists, dash off notes to colleagues, compose memos to parents, prepare lessons, fill out attendance forms, draft the new student handbook, plan a presentation for open house, complain to mail order companies, keep in touch with distant family and friends, tell others that we love them. Our criteria for writing change as our reasons for writing change: sometimes the act of writing and thinking is more important than the finished product (e.g., a list or a note to a colleague), and other times we craft so that meaning and mechanics will match a reader's expectations (a memo to parents or letter of complaint). As teachers of every subject we can acknowledge that writing is not a singular activity and begin to accommodate the many kinds of writing that exist to help students learn. And we can understand that it is this writing that will prove most valuable to us for the window it provides on our students' minds.

In the best of all possible worlds, language study might no longer be isolated as a separate subject in our curricula. Writing and reading workshop would become redundant because students and teachers would be writing and reading everything all day long: poems, plays, stories, essays, lists, articles, autobiographical sketches, and journals about math, literature, history, the sciences, *life*. In the best of all possible worlds, teachers of all subjects might become not English teachers but experts about the processes of reading and writing, about literature appropriate to the various disciplines, and about students—who they are, what they can do, what they know and need to know. Then the child's day might become a *learning* workshop in which writing and reading are learned in the richest possible context and appreciated as tools of the highest quality for helping children come to know about the world.

REFERENCES

Berthoff, Ann E. 1981. "A Curious Triangle and the Double-Entry Notebook: or, How Theory Can Help Us Teach Reading and Writing." In *The Making of Meaning: Metaphors, Models, and Maxims for Writing Teachers*. Portsmouth, NH: Boynton/Cook.

Blume, Judy. 1973. *Deenie*. New York: Bradbury Press.

Calkins, Lucy. 1986. *The Art of Teaching Writing*. Portsmouth, NH: Heinemann.

Chittenden, Lynda. 1982. "What If All the Whales Are Gone Before We Become Friends?" In *What's Going On? Language/Learning Episodes in British and American Classrooms, Grades 4–13*, ed. Mary Barr, Pat D'Arcy, and Mary K. Healy. Portsmouth, NH: Boynton/Cook.

Drabble, Margaret. 1987. *The Radiant Way*. Toronto: McClelland and Stewart.

Emig, Janet. 1983. "Writing as a Mode of Learning." In *The Web of Meaning: Essays on Writing, Teaching, Learning, and Thinking*, ed. Dixie Goswami and Maureen Butler. Portsmouth, NH: Boynton/Cook.

Five, Cora, and Martha Rosen. 1985. "Children Re-create History in Their Own Voices." In *Breaking Ground: Teachers Relate Reading and Writing in the Elementary School*, ed. Jane Hansen, Thomas Newkirk, and Donald Graves. Portsmouth, NH: Heinemann.

Fulwiler, Toby. 1987a. *Teaching With Writing*. Portsmouth, NH: Boynton/Cook.

Fulwiler, Toby, ed. 1987b. *The Journal Book*. Portsmouth, NH: Boynton/Cook.

Giacobbe, Mary Ellen. 1986. "Learning to Write and Writing to Learn in the Elementary School." In *The Teaching of Writing: Eighty-fifth Yearbook of the National Society for the Study of Education*, ed. Anthony R. Petrosky and David Bartholomae. Chicago: University of Chicago Press.

Goodlad, John. 1984. *A Place Called School*. New York: McGraw-Hill.

Graves, Donald H. 1983. *Writing: Teachers and Children at Work*. Portsmouth, NH: Heinemann.

Martin, Nancy, et al. 1976. *Writing and Learning Across the Curriculum 11–16*. Portsmouth, NH: Boynton/Cook.

Murray, Donald M. 1968. *A Writer Teaches Writing*. Boston: Houghton Mifflin.

Rief, Linda. 1985. "Why Can't We Live Like the Monarch Butterfly?" In *Breaking Ground: Teachers Relate Reading and Writing in the Elementary School*, ed. Jane Hansen, Thomas Newkirk, and Donald Graves. Portsmouth, NH: Heinemann.

Staton, Jana, et al. 1982. *Analysis of Dialogue Journal Writing as a Communicative Event*. NIE-G-80-0122. Washington, DC: Center for Applied Linguistics.

Wilde, Jack. 1988. "The Written Report: Old Wine in New Bottles." In *Understanding Writing: Ways of Observing, Learning, and Teaching*, 2nd ed., ed. Thomas Newkirk and Nancie Atwell. Portsmouth, NH: Heinemann.

Young, Art, and Toby Fulwiler, eds. 1986. *Writing Across the Disciplines: Research into Practice*. Portsmouth, NH: Boynton/Cook.

Researching
and
Reporting

Beginning Researchers

DONNA MAXIM

"My students are so wonderful," Nancy Nash remarked when I stopped by her classroom after school one day. "They've just completed their research projects, and I've learned so much."

"What do you mean?" I asked.

"I remember doing research projects last year, during my student teaching. What a disaster! Now, I can see why some things didn't work. First, I'd chosen the topics. Kids had to write about a U.S. state—the focus of the research had nothing to do with what we had been studying. Then they got out the encyclopedias and started to copy. But this year my students selected their own topics, and their study evolved naturally from our science curriculum. When they went to the library, they didn't rush to the encyclopedias. They looked for resources on the shelves and used the card catalogue subject drawers. It was really exciting. They took notes without copying. And then they . . ."

I smiled as I listened to Nancy talk about her fourth-grade researchers. I knew the work they had done as third graders: all the literature they had read and listened to, all the carefully planned activities that had helped them to succeed in fourth grade. I smiled because it's not often that a third-grade teacher hears words of praise for her former students from an upper-grade colleague, and because I knew that the beginning research techniques that I taught had helped my kids become confident, skilled researchers.

Third graders enter this metamorphic year as hands-on investigators. Over many months they move toward independent research by using reading and writing as vehicles to make new discoveries about themselves and the world around them. But before my third graders ever become involved in independent research projects, I model a variety of procedures used by researchers. I demonstrate, students practice, and we share our discoveries as we investigate new topics across the curriculum. I show them note-taking and interviewing strategies and teach them how to use log entries to predict and then evaluate information brought to the classroom by visiting speakers. I also help them set up individual research notebooks, each complete with a resource list, webs, questions to pursue, and notes. Then they plan final products—not full-blown research papers but manageable formats that beginning researchers can control to display their newfound information. Finally, students discuss what helped them during their research and the discoveries they made during the process.

This chapter is organized around the range of research activities that I sponsored to expose my students to a variety of research principles and procedures and to give them practice in note-taking, observing, interviewing, and questioning. I will also describe project formats that third graders have used to share their new information.

Activities for Beginning Researchers

Early in the fall I introduced methods for note-taking that helped my students avoid both plagiarism and an overreliance on the encyclopedia as a source of information. I began an ocean unit in science by reading aloud the author blurb from the back cover of Vincent Dethier's *Newberry: Life and Times of a Maine Clam* and asking why the information about Dethier's background is important enough to appear on the book jacket. Dethier is a professor of zoology, a person who studies animal life, and although *Newberry* is a fictional story, within it are embedded many facts that he learned through his own research.

During the first read-aloud, the class listed on chart paper the sea creatures they had met and the facts they had learned about each. The following day, after I had read another chapter, I asked children to write down the facts they had heard as individual log entries. During each of the subsequent daily readings, students did the same. After each log entry I also encouraged them to list questions that the story made them wonder about, questions that they might need other resources to answer. In this typical log entry, Dixie has written six facts that she recalled from the story and added two questions that she wondered about.

8:55   10/27

1. Starfish have suction cups.
2. Clams have two shells.
3. Starfish can take their stomachs out of their body to get food.
4. Starfish eat clams.
5. Clams don't like starfish.
6. Starfish can pull clams and mussels shells apart.

How do starfish take out their stomachs?
What do starfish eat besides clams and mussels?

On another day, Steven wrote:

A clam can build his shell bigger on the edges. A shrimp can shed its shell when it gets too small. A shrimp can eat a mussel.

Based on Steven's log entry we discussed the fact that a shrimp is a filter feeder and, in the story, could not have eaten the mussel on Newberry's muffler. Over several readings we discussed fact versus fiction as we posed questions: Are shrimp filter feeders? Do shrimp really eat mussels? The students searched out other sources of information to answer their questions, and we concluded the reading of *Newberry* with a "Clam Facts" bulletin board.

Another book I read to students during science class was Arthur Myers's *Sea Creatures Do Amazing Things*, a collection of short articles about the strange habits of ocean animals. In a three-minute log entry, Sarah recorded the facts she had learned about a fiddler crab.

11/6   11:10

1. Fiddler crabs do burrow in sand.
2. A fiddler crab's biggest claw does look like a violin.
3. A fiddler crab's small claw does look like a bow.

In another note-taking session, children listened to a Random House tape and filmstrip on Newbery Medalist Margaret Henry. In her own words Heather noted what she regarded as the important facts about Margaret Henry's life and the thoroughness of the research that goes into her books for children.

11/23   9:30

Margaret Henry is a Newbery Award winner. She loves horses. She wrote lots of books. She hated doing maps. She wrote mostly animal stories. She likes animals a lot. She traveled a lot. She likes children a lot. She went to horse ranges. She went to the Grand Canyon. She went to Italy three times in a year. She gets a lot of letters. When she was ten, she sold a piece for twelve dollars.

In each of these log entries, students took notes without being tempted to copy: to read and write at the same time. I gave them practice in listening to build up their skill and confidence as note-takers and to build up to taking notes from print resources. Then I turned to *Zoobook*, a monthly magazine published by Wildlife Education Ltd., and they had their first experience taking notes from their own reading.

Each student chose one back issue of *Zoobook* but was not permitted to open it. I asked them to look at the front cover and generate questions they thought they might find answers to in the magazine. Andrea's questions about the wolf set the stage for her active participation as a reader of her particular *Zoobook*.

12/6   2:00

1. What do wolves eat?
2. How do they live? (What is their house made of?)
3. How many years old can it grow up to?
4. Can they eat anything?
5. How many miles per hour do you think they can run?
6. Can they climb trees?
7. Would they eat another wolf?
8. Would they eat a dog that looks like them?

After they recorded their questions, I sent the students away from their desks, their lists of questions, and their pencils, to read for ten minutes. When the time was up they returned to their desks, this time leaving the *Zoobooks* behind. In their logs they wrote any answers they had found to their questions and added any new information they recalled. Students were beginning to take notes without copying. For many, this was difficult; they wanted to retrieve the magazines and copy the relevant information, something that I did not allow. A couple more sessions of writing without reading showed my third graders that they could read and then take their notes.

Through such activities as these, I teach my students how to listen to, read for, and respond to information. They learn how to recognize important facts, use more than one resource to verify information, take meaningful notes, and record facts quickly and easily. Instead of copying someone else's words, they are beginning to see themselves as researchers who take notes. The chances are good that they will not become victims of the plagiarism syndrome.

At the same time that the children practiced note-taking, we continued our ocean study with slide shows, a visit from a speaker from the Department of Marine Resources (complete with live specimens), a field trip to Reid State Park, charts listing ocean life forms, and numerous read-alouds and discussions of fiction and nonfiction books as well as poetry. Eventually, the students were prepared to choose a sea creature to research and report on.

The students began their independent research by using resources from both our classroom and the school library. Each student set up a research notebook, a three-ring binder that allowed easy access to information. The first page was a title page; the second page was a list of questions about their creature; and the third was reserved for listing resources by title, author, and page number. Students recorded notes on the remaining four or five pages. It was a simple, specific format for collecting, organizing, and keeping track of new information.

During the research process, Alice Fossett, our school librarian, helped students become familiar with resources within the library. She planned activities to map library resources and to use the card catalogue as well as the *National Geographic* index to locate magazine articles on chosen topics. Students kept running notes in their three-ring binders.

1/11   1:50

NOTES

Bony meat.
Large eye.
14 inches long.
6–10 inches.
½–1 pound.
Bait on bluefish.
Sweet tasting.
Schooling fish.
Found Penobscot River.
60,000–100,000 eggs.
Goes to fresh water to spawn.
Lives in salt water.
1 ft.
Lobster bait.
Grayish-green.
3 years.
Silver belly.
Related shad.

Gearry's log entry shows how he used the ten minutes that I gave my students, after reading in the library, to record information that he recalled from his reading. His notes had changed since the beginning of the year. Now he used his time to capture many brief pieces of specific information, rather than wasting time composing long sentences. He was also selective, deciding which facts were worth keeping. In a minilesson, Gearry discussed his notes with the rest of the class via an overhead transparency, explaining why he wrote only concise phrases and how this technique helped him to get more information down.

After two weeks of researching and sharing their notes, the students wrote up their facts in the form of acrostic poems. I had read about a high school teacher's use of acrostics, or biopoems (Johnston 1985), and felt that this would be a simpler genre for third graders to control than the complex format of a traditional research report. An acrostic uses the letters of the word that is its subject as the beginning letter of each line. I added one rule: each line must be a fact about the poet's creature.

LOBSTERS

Lays up to 5,000 eggs
One claw is to crush their prey
Bait is what they use to catch lobster with
Sometimes if you hold one it might pinch
Turns red when it's cooked
Eats pogies, mackerel, bluefish, and redfish
Return females with eggs to the ocean
Scavengers!

Betsy wrote lots of facts in her acrostic and showed what she had learned. Wendy, a classmate, listened to another student's draft of his acrostic in a group share meeting and declared that one line— "Clams are neat"—was an opinion, not a fact. From that day on I had many keen observers of the differences between facts and opinions.

I also taught the children interviewing techniques. I began by modeling an interview in a minilesson. I had prepared a list of questions about a marine creature that one of my students was studying, and I interviewed her about it, with her permission, in front of the class. Then the other students, working in pairs, wrote interview questions about their marine animals as log entries and practiced interviewing each other. Afterward, volunteers shared reactions to their interviews with the class, and we noted their strengths and weaknesses on a chart.

My students decided that good interviews featured lots of questions, were prepared ahead of time, and included an interviewer's explanation of why the question was being asked. Then I arranged for them to interview fifth graders who were also studying marine creatures. Because the older kids' topics were also self-selected, the range was so great that we had few matching topics, so each student chose a fifth grader's topic and prepared a good list of marine-related questions. The interviews worked well, showing my nervous students that they could question older children; they also served to generate questions that could be used in their own research. (Some third graders discovered that they knew as much as some fifth graders about a particular subject.) A drawback was that the third graders had no personal need for the information they were gathering.

FIGURE 1–1 ● LOG ENTRY IN PREPARATION FOR AN INTERVIEW

2/5

11:30

Hi! My name is Rae Barter. I live in Boothbay Harbor Maine. I am in third grade and I go to the Boothbay Region Elemantary School.
You see, my class is interviewing people and I chose to interview you.
I only have one question to ask you.
Here it goes.
What are your dreams for schools around the United States.
My dream is for somebody to come in to school and to teach any language we want to know.

Interviewing techniques flowed over into social studies class, where I was reading aloud *Marching to Freedom: The Story of Martin Luther King, Jr.* by Joyce Milton. The children had already discussed their dreams, including dreams for the Boothbay school, so I asked them to brainstorm questions they might ask parents, teachers, school board members, our principal, or some other adult about their dreams for schools. Each student wrote a log entry setting up an interview (Figure 1–1). Then, as a class, they discussed the discoveries they had made: how they needed to explain who they were and why they were calling when approaching people they didn't know, how a good friend was approached differently from a stranger.

Again, they role-played interviews in log entries, and we charted whom they might contact. We also charted how they might contact particular individuals and listed questions they might ask. Students generated their own final guidelines for interviews and listed these on a separate chart:

Tell or Ask:

- Your name
- Where you're from
- Your grade
- What the project is
- Questions to ask
- Follow-up questions
- Thank you

The interviewing techniques I modeled and discussed and the actual interviews they conducted gave my third graders valuable insights into another avenue for research. They needed to look to primary sources—to people—as well as to good literature. The various interview activities helped them overcome their nervousness and take more control of their search for information.

Another research practice I initiated early in the year was keeping logs of observations. Such logs show students how researchers set up and record information, help them to discover the differences between observations and predictions, and allow them to see themselves as resources in their own research.

In the fall, I asked each student to choose a tree in our playground to observe throughout the four seasons. The students recorded observations of their adopted trees and the surrounding environment at the beginning of each month and noted seasonal changes from September to June. This is Wendy's entry for March:

3/12   2:00

1. My tree's trunk has gotten smaller.
2. My tree has a lot of moss on it.
3. My tree has a lot of snow near it.
4. My tree's branches are very bare.
5. My tree has a lot of twigs near it.

In response to Wendy's observation, we had a lengthy class discussion about how she knew that her tree's trunk was smaller. She explained that she could tell by looking. Other students pointed out that that could be inaccurate, and she decided to measure the trunk next time.

A comparison of Dixie's October and March entries shows how she captured the changing of the seasons.

10/4   2:00

Now the tree has more of a greyish color on it. It has three woodpecker holes. Also the tree looked a little bit bigger.

3/12   3:00

1. It changed color.
2. It does not have any leaves left.
3. My tag fell off.
4. My tree got a lot, lot bigger.
5. I have lichen on my tree.

We also kept a caterpillar diary in which we recorded observations of a monarch caterpillar that we kept in the classroom as it formed a chrysalis and hatched into a butterfly. I initiated the activity by reading aloud *The Caterpillar Diary* by David Drew, an excellent example of a diary of observations. The following day I read *A New Friend for Morganfield* by Ann Hobart, and we guessed what might happen to our chrysalis in response to Hobart's prediction of a fourteen-day incubation period. As a class, we discussed the difference between observations and predictions. Then I set up a class diary and students took turns writing an entry each day.

DAY 1

The caterpillar has made his chrysalis. It is green and it is shiny. It has little gold dots on the chrysalis. In a while it will turn into a monarch butterfly.   JUSTIN

Next year I plan to have everyone keep his or her own diary, with daily sharing of individuals' observations to provide more opportunities to practice keeping track of observations.

We also kept a log of daily weather observations throughout the year, noting which data we could observe with our eyes and which we needed to measure. Observing, record-keeping, and categorizing are all important procedures that researchers frequently use.

This variety of methods—note-taking without copying, research notebooks, acrostics, interviews, and logs of observation—assisted third graders as they began to learn what researchers do. A combination of hands-on approaches and writing activities proved much more accessible to eight- and nine-year-olds than formal report writing.

Simple Projects

As the year progressed, I allowed students more choice in formats for final products, now that they had some experience as researchers. As a class, they brainstormed a list of potential formats; they came up with seven, and I added other alternatives that I thought were appropriate for beginning researchers from the list in Appendix A. Individual students then chose the formats that allowed them to share their knowledge of their sea creatures. These five were their favorites.

DIORAMAS

The diorama was one of the most popular formats because it involved painting. (Next year, the boxes will be painted during art class, since they took three or four class sessions to complete.) Each diorama included a written description of the sea creature portrayed. We had dioramas on penguins, the octopus, and killer whales.

PUBLISHED BOOKS

Other students wanted to write up their research as a story to publish in a book, complete with covers made from cardboard and contact paper, with pages bound on a sewing machine. For this project my colleague, Jo Haney, developed an improvised galley sheet: a mimeographed form with six or eight lines at the bottom that helped students divide the drafts of their stories into separate pages to be typed and illustrated. Figure 1–2 shows how Mark used a galley sheet to set up one page of his book about whales and to organize his information.

BULLETIN BOARDS

Dixie organized her research on sand dollars as a bulletin board display with a picture of a giant sand dollar in the middle and relevant facts arranged on cards around it. She planned her bulletin board in her learning log by drafting a web to help her make decisions about her topic and organize her information (Figure 1–3).

GAMES

Two members of my class developed games from their research. One board game was on the narwhal and took players on a trip around the Arctic, posing questions to be answered along the way. Alewives was the subject of another board game and involved a

FIGURE 1–2 ● ONE OF MARK'S GALLEY SHEETS FOR HIS BOOK

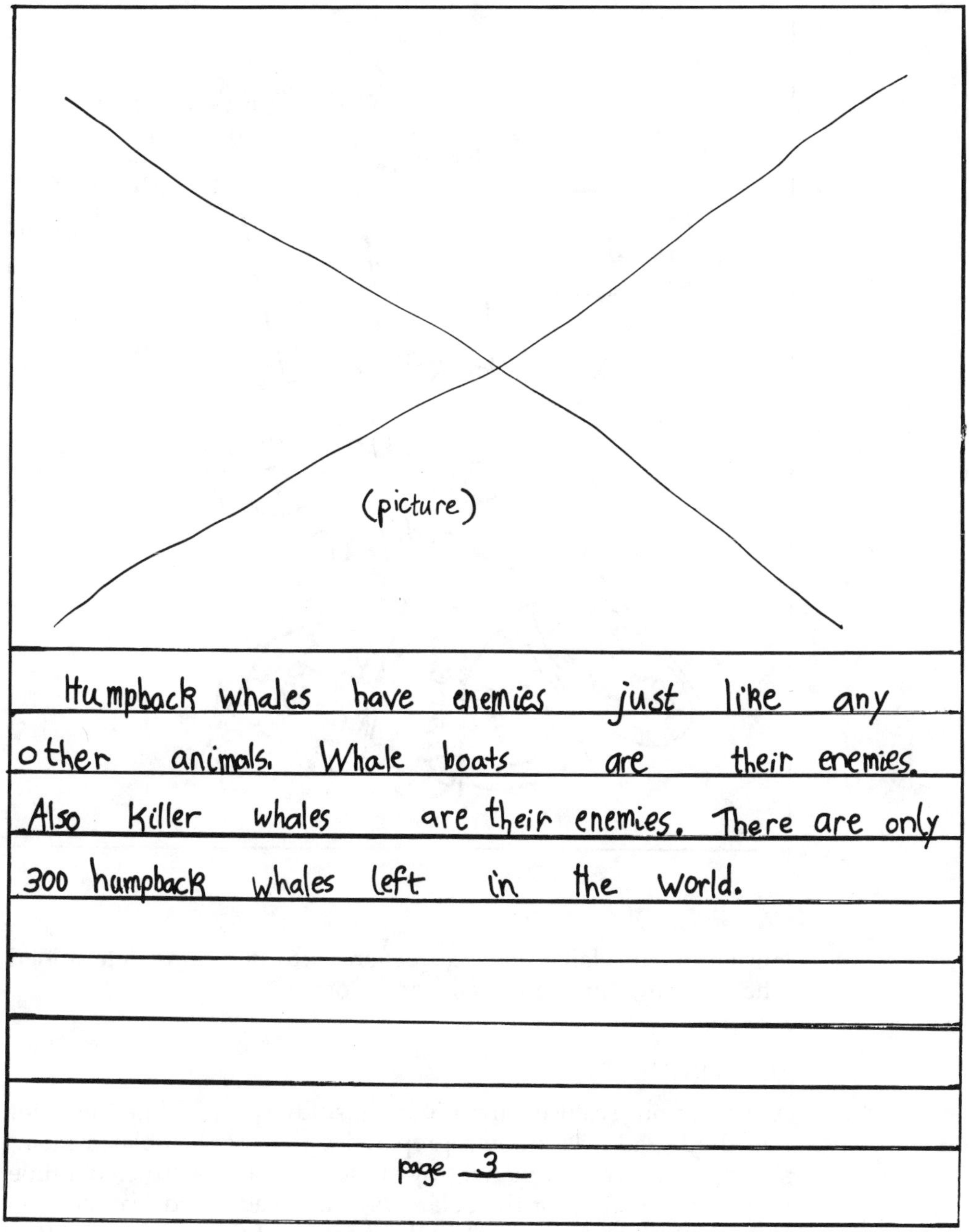

(picture)

Humpback whales have enemies just like any other animals. Whale boats are their enemies. Also killer whales are their enemies. There are only 300 humpback whales left in the world.

page 3

FIGURE 1–3 ● DIXIE'S WEB: PREPARATION FOR HER BULLETIN BOARD

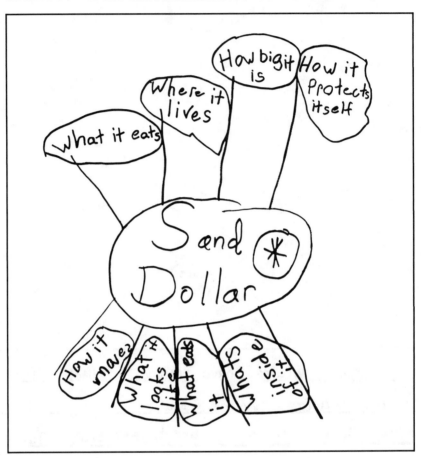

journey up the falls; players' responses to questions determined whether they climbed the alewife ladder.

TIME LINES

As part of our science curriculum we study space. While the other two third-grade classrooms prepared a tour of the solar system, sharing facts on each planet, my students and I constructed a time line of the creation of the solar system. I read aloud *Life Story* by Virginia Burton, an account of the creation of the universe written as a play, and showed several examples of time lines, one on U. S. presidents and another on inventions. Each student selected one era that he or she would take responsibility for in creating our time line. They researched their eras, then drew pictures portraying what they had discovered about each period. Then they drafted descriptions of what was happening in their pictures. The following excerpts show the very beginning of the time line.

> Today scientists think that 4.5 billion years ago, our solar system used to be dust and gases. All of a sudden a star exploded and then our solar system was a large, spinning disk.   MIKE

> Two to one billion years ago the crust of our earth started to form. The earth started to wrinkle. High mountains and low valleys started to form. There were deep ocean basins. Metamorphic rock started to form. The metamorphic rock formed by heat and pressure. There were thick clouds that blocked the sun from shining on earth.   RAE

> About thirty to forty million years ago the climate started getting cooler. Mammals started developing. Plants started blooming. Volcanoes began to erupt, and mountains started to rise.   MEGGAN

We practiced reading the time line aloud and then presented all twenty-six feet of it during an assembly for grades four to six. The idea for this particular project began with a read-aloud, was researched through independent reading, and developed first as an illustration and then as a written description.

After our presentation I discovered a book called *Earth Story* by Eric Maddern, a poem about the creation of the earth. As I began reading it to my class Mike commented, "That's just like what Herbie did in his picture," and as I continued reading, eyes lit up around the room. The children recognized "their" information and were proud of what they had accomplished. When I closed the book, Heather wondered why the poem had not included the creation of life, as our own time line had. Joey's hand shot up. "Maybe he can write another poem to show that!"

My students shared their projects with pride and confidence. During the preparation of final projects I highlighted many techniques in conferences and minilessons: galleys, the use of pen or marker (as opposed to pencil) on bulletin boards, diorama construction, and techniques for making books. When the projects were completed I asked the students to evaluate themselves and to write advice they might offer to next year's class. Because they had taken responsibility for their own learning, they could reflect on and assess what was helpful to them as beginning researchers, and what was not.

Throughout the third-grade year I plan activities that help students explore, investigate, experiment, and record—not in isolation but in cooperation with a teacher and classmates who offer encouragement and questions. I provide as many opportunities and as much time as I can for students to try the procedures I demonstrate.

When Nancy Nash talked with me that afternoon about her students' research, she was affirming our hard work of the year before. As a teacher, I can do something that no commercial program can ever accomplish: allow students' individual interests to become a catalyst for their involvement in their own learning. I can teach research principles and procedures in the context of classroom discussions, activities, and resources. I can expose third graders to rich print resources as well as films, tapes, and local experts, and provide opportunities for them to draw on these resources in investigating self-selected topics. I can make sure that their first research projects do not become an overwhelming task, but rather one approached with confidence and genuine curiosity as they investigate, organize, and share new information in a variety of formats. And I can act as their guide: not expecting students to possess the skills of researchers as if by magic but planning activities, demonstrating techniques, and gathering resources that will help them to take their first steps as beginning researchers.

REFERENCES

Burton, Virginia Lee. 1963. *Life Story*. Boston: Houghton Mifflin.

Dethier, Vincent. 1981. *Newberry: Life and Times of a Maine Clam*. Camden, ME: Down East Books.

Drew, David. 1987. *Caterpillar Diary*. Crystal Lake, IL: Rigby Education.

Hobart, Ann. 1985. *A New Friend for Morganfield*. Portland, ME: Gannett Books.

Johnston, Patricia. 1985. "Writing to Learn Science." In *Roots in the Sawdust*, ed. Anne Gere. Urbana, IL: National Council of Teachers of English.

Maddern, Eric. 1988. *Earth Story*. New York: Barron's.

Milton, Joyce. 1987. *Marching to Freedom: The Story of Martin Luther King, Jr.* New York: Dell.

Myers, Arthur. 1981. *Sea Creatures Do Amazing Things*. New York: Random House.

Zoobooks. Wildlife Education, Ltd., Box 28870, San Diego, California 92128–9848.

2

Bridging the Gap

PATRICIA J. COLLINS

In seventeen years of teaching various grade levels I had tried end-less approaches to report writing—that dreaded assignment we middle grade teachers feel is our sacred responsibility—preparing kids for "some day" when they will have to write a research paper for some other teacher. Over the past year I have realized that writing can be used as a tool to enhance the learning process, and that this is an important goal in and of itself. When I stopped worrying about the next year and the year after that, learning im-proved. My students produced some of the best reports ever. And, perhaps most surprising, I enjoyed the process, found the reports were fun to read, and learned from my students' work. Ironically, I also believe I better prepared them for that future day when they will have to write a research paper for another teacher.

I did not need to be convinced that writing workshop methods worked. In my language arts classes, students had produced some outstanding writing using the workshop model (Graves 1983). I had long since stopped using book report forms, assigning topics, and reading story starters to motivate writing. Instead, I allowed my students to select their own topics and genres, confer, draft, revise, edit, and go public with their pieces. However, in the areas of social studies and science, I was still assigning broad topics, along with a list of the specific content I expected to be covered.

Eventually, I wondered if the approach I was using in my En-glish classes could work in the content areas as well. After reading an article by fifth-grade teacher Jack Wilde (1988), I decided to try. In the process, I hoped to stretch students beyond personal-expe-rience narrative and enable them to apply what they knew to new formats and situations. I wanted them to explore topics other than their own experiences, yet still keep the writing personal and meaningful. Within the context of a sixth-grade social studies class, I wanted students to use the techniques that real authors use to produce research-based writing. By experiencing the process for themselves, students could become not only researchers but also knowledgeable analysts of others' research.

With new resolve, I began planning and working. I firmly believed that the writing process my students would use was as important as the end product. Because I wanted to observe their learning throughout the process, the entire research project was carried out in class, where I could respond to and monitor the progress of the sixty-one students in our sixth grade. Again, the results were better than I could have hoped.

At the end of the school year I asked my students to tell me how our writing workshop approach helped them with their research papers. Their answers fell into four broad categories: planning, class time, teacher response, and student responsibility.

Planning

"You tell us about three weeks ahead of time so we can think about our topics."

"You have lots of books we can use."

"You help us find topics that have a lot of information."

"You pick out books that we can understand."

"You put up posters so we can get an idea of what to write about."

A cornerstone of the writing workshop philosophy is that students write best about what they know. We cannot expect them to write well until they have some knowledge of their topics. Thus, planning ways for them to gain this expertise is essential to the process.

Our particular content area was the Middle Ages. About a month before the project was to begin I gathered materials—books, posters, filmstrips, videos, charts, and anything I could find that related to the Middle Ages. I organized these materials as a research center in our classroom. I told my classes that in approximately three weeks they would choose topics about the Middle Ages on which they would write research papers. I heard some typical groans, a few "Oh goods" from students who were having difficulty coming up with topics in writer's workshop, and got a number of panicky looks from those who had no idea what to do next. I discussed the amount of reading involved in such a project and the importance of selecting topics they would enjoy spending a large block of time studying. I asked that they find time to look over the materials in the research center and be ready with a topic choice at the end of the three weeks. During this time period, I reminded students to go to the center during study periods or whenever they had free time.

I believe this was an important experience for my students. Without pressure from me to make an immediate decision, they were able to browse through the materials, reject topics for which there was limited information available, and become comfortable with the idea of research. This lead time also enabled me to map out the particular strategies I and they would be using once they began working on their projects. I assured students who were apprehensive that everything would be done in class and that the whole assignment was a learning process; I would be there to help whenever they needed me.

In the meantime, I began teaching lessons on the Middle Ages. I addressed a wide variety of topics during my scheduled social studies time: the development and eventual elimination of the feudal system, castle life, the rise of towns, religion, Romanesque and Gothic architecture, fashion, food, crusades, and the Black Plague. I found that students almost always chose their topics from the areas we discussed in class. The more topics I introduced in class, the broader their general knowledge and the greater the variety of topics they selected.

Teachers have been criticized for the project approach to teaching a unit, which assigns each child a different topic and gives the appearance that the whole class has covered the area of study when in fact each student is exposed to only one topic. I wanted to avoid this pitfall. So in my lessons I honored what I believed to be a well thought out curriculum, and then provided individual students with the opportunity for in-depth study. This detailed background information is what real researchers provide for their readers. As Justin said in evaluating his research paper:

> I started to think about what method I was going to use. I thought I would do a book or a story. It was hard to write a story about the Middle Ages. As I started writing I noticed I was missing something. You need general information about the time period, so I took some more notes. With more information I could write better. I added things like setting, time, food. It was very different than writing an essay. Further into my story I noticed I needed to include a siege in order to have a good ending. When I was done writing I noticed there was more to my story than just castle defense. I had life in a castle, food, etc. I really enjoyed writing my story. I do have some advice for other sixth grade researchers. If you are going to write a story about something, you need to include specific information to make it more enjoyable.

I found filmstrips and videos that provided wonderful information. I showed Macaulay's videos *Castles* and *Cathedral* to the whole class. Other useful videos were *Newscast from the Past: A Global*

History Series (programs 1–4). These were brief, fifteen-minute sce-
narios presented in a nightly news format on topics such as the
plague, the Children's Crusade, and the signing of the Magna Carta;
on-the-spot interviews with Joan of Arc and other personalities were
also popular with my students.

Books written on a variety of reading levels became the core of
our research center. *Medieval Days and Ways* (Hartman 1937), *Young
People's Story of Our Heritage: The Medieval World* (Hillyer & Huey
1966), *Datelines of World History* (Arnold 1983), and *Kings, Queens,
Knights, and Jesters: Making Medieval Costumes* (Schnurnberger 1978)
are just a few of the titles that we found. Donna Maxim's bibliography, Appendix C, includes a more complete listing of the fiction
and nonfiction trade books on which we drew.

I also sponsored some firsthand experiences. In order to get a
sense of religious life during the Middle Ages, we donned old choir
robes that I purchased from a local church. Students wore hooded
sweatshirts underneath their robes and (a teacher's dream) took a
vow of silence—except for the abbott, of course. In acting out a day
in the life of a Medieval monk, we ate salted fish and dark bread
and drank only water.

The point of all this activity was to be able to work together
from a shared foundation as a community of learners. Our common
grounding allowed students' individual projects to fit into the whole,
and their own writing was enriched because they could see relationships among aspects of the total Medieval culture.

Class Time

"Class time is organized every day."
"We have lots of books we can use."
"There are books we can understand."
"You let me watch filmstrips on my own."

By February, when we began the unit, the class was used to
the organization of the writing workshop. Now it was time to apply
this predictable structure to content-area writing. (Mary Ellen Giacobbe's 1986 article about Carolyn Currier's classroom was very
helpful to me in this regard.)

I gave each student a research folder in which to keep all notes
and drafts, and we stored these in a drop file, arranged alphabet-
ically. All research folders were kept in the classroom; I did not
want students to lose precious time hunting for their folders or
running back to their homerooms. I established our research center
in the room, rather than the school library, as another way to make
more efficient use of class time.

Students began their research by gathering information related to their specific topics. They read, viewed filmstrips or videos, studied charts, and listened to tapes. Since I had three classes using the same materials, I set up a system for reserving books and materials. Each class had bookmarks of a single color, and one student from each class could reserve any book by putting a bookmark with his or her name on it in the desired material. A student could see at a glance if a resource was available; if the class color was blue, and there was no blue bookmark in the material, the student was free to reserve it. Since all research was done in class, up to three students (one from each class) could use any given resource.

For me, one of the most interesting aspects of this project was how well students took responsibility for their own learning. I did not tell them what they were supposed to know. They realized that they would be unable to write unless they knew what they are talking about, and since they had chosen their own topics, they were interested in what they were reading. The atmosphere in the room was quiet and intense as the students learned. I was amazed at their sustained interest in their work, the maturity they showed, and the respect they demonstrated for the systems I had set up. Each day they came into my room, grabbed their research folders, found their reserved materials, and settled into their work.

Students read or viewed materials for half the class period. Then I would ask them to come to a good stopping place, close their books, and spend the rest of the class time writing about what they had learned that day. During this second half of the period, they might look back at their material to check a spelling or fact, but, in order to avoid plagiarism, they could not read and write at the same time. They kept records of where their information had come from on note sheets that I provided. Figure 2–1 shows notes that Tyler made after reading pages in *The Vikings* (Gibson 1976). Already, his voice is evident in his writing.

Students spent two to three weeks researching and recording information, until they felt they had a sufficient amount of data from which to begin writing. They could also stop and conduct additional research at any time during the project. Most did.

Many students found it helpful to begin by writing up their notes in a simple essay form, in order to get a sense of what they had. This proved a good time for a minilesson on outlining, as the students could see the relevance of a tool to categorize their information.

Because students took notes in their own words, their own voices were evident when they began drafting. I was determined to avoid reports filled with prose beyond my students' abilities as writers, writing merely copied from reference books. I wanted students to be able to talk about the information in their reports. My new approach accomplished these goals. It is Leah's voice I hear in Adam the Monk's letter to King Henry concerning the dreaded Black Death.

FIGURE 2–1 ● TYLER'S NOTES (EXCERPT)

Gibson, Michael
(AUTHOR)
Macdonald Educational
(PUBLISHER)

The Vikings
(TITLE)
1976
(DATE)

London
(CITY)

14-15   Viking Farms

On the farms there wasn't very good soil but they still got what they needed They had vegetable gardens, nut and fruit trees and grew barley, oats and a little rye. The cattle were very important. Just as important as having corn. The cattle gave them beef and milk. Out of the milk they made cheese and butter.

10-11 The Vikings homeland was Scandinavia which later was Sweden, Denmark, Norway.

12-13 To find out if someone was lying or telling the truth in court the person would be wounded. Then the wound would be bandged. Later the bandadge would be taken off If the wound was clean the person was telling the truth if the wound wasn't healed or clean The person would be punished

16-19

Not a lot of Vikings lived on farms. The usual house was made out of turf and timber. The houses started out with only one room but later on the houses were built with moore rooms. A tipicle Viking meal was thick, bread and butter a roast or baked   fruit or vegetables. They drank milk, buttermilk, beer whey and a strong drink made with honey   (over)

Church Lane
St. Ablins Manor
July 5, 1358

Your Grace, King Henry,

I would like to thank you, sir, for choosing me to be on your com-
mission to gather information about the sickness that has struck our
great country. I have traveled for many months. I hope you will be
pleased, although the news will disturb you.

I believe the disease is transmitted by fleas on the black rat, but no
one believes me. This rat was brought from the east. Not to sound
snobby, but the poor health conditions of our time helped spread this
sickness. People should wash themselves and their clothes to be rid
of the fleas. Of course, some think differently. I heard many say that
stinking clouds over our towns and manors cause the sickness. Others
think that God is punishing them for sins, but now some monks are
dying. Others think clouds and gas from the heavens cause it. Balls
of fire are said to be seen falling from the sky. One woman said when
she pulled fresh bread from the oven, blood was dripping from it.
Many also think the Jews are the reason that the plague is here. The
poor Jews are being killed by the hundreds.

Some of the obvious symptoms are the people get nausea, fevers,
chills, and headaches. Lumps form in armpits and groins. Later, black
spots form on arms and thighs. Some who are fine one day are dead
the next.

Cures and doctoring are still not helpful, but we are working on it.
Magic is used a lot. The few doctors who know anything about this
disease only help the high nobles, kings, and queens. Magic brews
and herbs are the most common cures. A plant called the mandrack
is used the most.

Last week I saw a woman having a dog pull up some wild mandrack
and I asked why. The woman said because when being pulled up,
the plant screams and whatever is pulling it up goes deaf. I stayed to
watch, but of course not a sound was heard. Garlic is also thought to
cure and prevent the sickness. Men and women eat garlic along with
hanging it around the house. One man was said to escape the disease
by covering his house with the herb.

Doctors tell their noble patients to leave the towns and go to the
mountains or hills. After escaping to the hills, the rich lead a life of
dancing and singing.

One common cure, which is not effective, is bleeding someone. The
doctor would place a leech or cut a person to release the evil spirit.
This also makes the person weak. The word "Abracadabra" is written
on a piece of paper and hung on the victim's neck. It looks like this:

```
A B R A C A D A B R A
 A B R A C A D A B R
  A B R A C A D A B
   A B R A C A D A
    A B R A C A D
     A B R A C A
      A B R A C
       A B R A
        A B R
         A B
          A
```

I am very sorry to say that the burials of the thousands who have already died seem to get shorter and shorter. Yesterday I went to the funeral of one of my friends, Jacob the Monk. During the procession we were all surprised to see the funeral was not only for Jacob, but also for many others. Jacob and the others' bodies were thrown in a large pit in the yard, which smelled awful. Some corpses are thrown in rivers. Many are left where they died, until the smell is unbearable.

Many of our nobles and lords have died, so no one is around to enforce the laws. Recently, the daughter of the lord of our manor, St. Ablins, died. She was buried with her late family in the noble cemetery, but I've heard even that is getting too crowded.

Well, I studied the plague for many months now, and this is what I came up with for you. I hope you will now be better informed.

Your loyal servant,
Adam the Monk

Teacher Response

"You give us silence so we can do our work."

"You help us find topics that have a lot of information."

"You confer with us and give us ideas for revising."

"If we don't know what book to find information, you help us."

My role during the first weeks of research was to circulate among my students and work with individuals. I might stop and ask a student to read a bit to me or talk to me about what he or she was reading. These conferences were very short, one or two minutes. I didn't want to disturb my students' reading and note-taking, but did want to make sure that they were making the most of their time. I helped wandering students get back on task, suggested specific books or materials to students who were having trouble, and read with students who received resource room aid or remediation in reading.

Once students began drafting, I continued to confer with students as needed. A student might request a conference, or I might stop at a desk for a moment and ask how it was going (Calkins 1986) or tell the student to select a small segment to read to me. I listened to what they said and had written and asked questions to stimulate more thinking about their topics. As students conferred with each other and me, they were able to see areas of their work that needed clarification or expansion, or material that was irrelevant, and ways to polish their writing. We talked about their work writer to writer, researcher to researcher.

In this conference with Jessica, about an apparent contradiction in information from two different sources, I helped her plan a strategy that got her moving again.

PAT: How's it going?

JESSICA: I don't know which book is correct. This book says Joan of
           Arc was sixteen when she had her vision, and the book I
           read the other day said she was fourteen.

PAT: Do you feel that her age is important to your piece?

JESSICA: Yes. She was really young.

PAT: What could you do to find out?

JESSICA: I could try to find it in another book.

PAT: Then you could say, "Most of the books I read said . . ."
           Or if the exact age isn't important, you could say she was
           a teenager, since most of the sources do say that she was
           in her teens.

JESSICA: Good idea. That's what I think I'll do.

I planned my minilessons for the remaining weeks around students' needs as they became evident in class. As I mentioned before, when students were struggling with organizing their information, I did a minilesson on making an outline. As students began writing rough drafts, I presented a minilesson on the importance of a good lead. I made overheads of the leads of some of their favorite books and talked about the variety of ways in which they could begin their pieces. I also did procedural minilessons on how to set up a bibliography and table of contents.

In order for me to keep track of what each student was doing I conducted a daily status of the class conference (Atwell 1987). Figure 2–2 shows what a week looked like. Each day, each writer made a verbal contact with me concerning his or her work. I was able to keep on top of what they were doing, yet responsibility for choices about their work lay with them. They anticipated that I would be polling them at the beginning of class, so they came prepared to work.

After students had written a first draft, they conferred with another student about the content of their work. I might emphasize again the value of all students having general background knowledge. Because the entire sixth grade was aware of information included in individual topics, they were able to give each other a serious response, offering suggestions for sources of additional data and even finding errors in information. Sometimes I suggested that a student confer with a particular peer whose topic could help the writer with related information. Students revised their pieces until they were satisfied with the results.

When students decided their content was set, they carefully edited, I edited, and they were ready for final copy. They composed bibliographies using the citations on their note sheets. Students went public with their research in such forums as a sixth-grade Medieval fair and special group share sessions in class.

Working through the research project with my students, rather

FIGURE 2–2 ● STATUS OF THE CLASS RECORD

	MONDAY	TUESDAY	WEDNESDAY	THURSDAY	FRIDAY
David B.	D-1 Leisure: annotated cal.	D-1 Leisure	D-1	D-1	NO CLASS on FRIDAY
Scott E.	Ab	D-1 Bldg A castle story	Conf (Charl) D-1	D-1	
Charles G.	Play. D-1 Becoming Knight	D-1	Conf (Scott) Revise	Revise	
Warren H.	Writing up notes - Vikings	D-1 Vikings auto-bio	D-1	D-1	
Tyler K.	Ab	Org. notes Plaque	Add'l Research	Organizing notes	
Eric X.	D-1 Monks	D-1 Monk's story	Add'l Research	D-1 Story	
Chris L.	D-1 Story Castle Seige	D-1 Castle Seige Lead	D-1 Story Castle Seige	D-1	
Clint L.	Research Plaque	Research Plaque	Organize. Notes Plaque	Organize Notes	
Colin M.	Research Weapons	D-1 Catalogue Weapons	D-1	Self-conf. Revise	
Derek V.	Research Weapons	D-1 Weapons story	D-1	Add'l Research	
Chad W.	Revise Weapons Self-Conf	Writing an Introduction Revising	Revising Castles	Revise	
Angela B.	Org. notes Cathedrals	Organizing notes Cathedrals	Conf (Shan) Writing notes	Add'l Research	
Shannon G.	Ab	Ab	Conf (angela) Revise	Revise	
Karen G.	T. Conf Peasants	D-1 Script Peasants	D-1	D-1	
Haili K.	Ab	Conf (Jenna) Story Re-copy	Recopy for TE	TC	
Melanie L.	Organizing notes Pilgrimages	D-1 fiction story	Conf (Sara) D-1	D-1	
Sarah M.	D-1 Pilgrimages Letter	D-1 Letter	Conf (Melanie) Revise	SE	
Tina R.	Organizing notes Clothing	Notes	Notes	RD Letter	
Summer W.	Organizing notes Clothing	Conf (Haili) Revise	Notes	RD Catalogue	↓

D-1: First Draft
D-2: Second Draft /   ED Con REWRITE   EDITING Conf it Tch. Then writing final copy   SE - Self-Editing   Conf - ◯ name of person who WILL conf.

than simply assigning a report and evaluating it at the end, bene-fitted me as well as my students. As they worked, I was able to help individual students find materials, understand what they read, write in their own words, edit, set up a bibliography, or address whatever part of the process was difficult for them. They benefitted by getting immediate feedback from me or their peers. We worked, corrected, reworked, and created in collaboration.

Student Responsibility

"I found a topic I liked to write about."
"We got to choose how we want to write it."
"We chose what form we wanted to write our reports in."

Assigning specific topics, requiring a minimum or maximum number of words or pages, demanding illustrations to go with a text, as I had done in the past, were no longer my responsibility. Now, when a student asked me how long his report had to be, I replied that I didn't know how many pages it would take him to tell me what he knew. When a student asked me what to write about, I asked her, "What are you interested in?" When a student wondered, "What do I do next?" I responded, "What do you think?"

It was a relief not to have to come up with sixty different topics for sixty students. Duplication of topic choice no longer concerned me, since each student handled the material in his or her own way. Students took responsibility for their work because it belonged to them. If I expected students to think of themselves as researchers and authors, I had to give them the responsibilities of researchers and authors. My students responded positively and productively.

Selecting a genre to present their material was also the students' responsibility. They knew that at the end of the research process they were to go public with what they knew. During one minilesson, I talked to my classes about the options available to them for their final products. From the choices listed in Appendix A, I selected a range that I felt appropriate for sixth-grade researchers and writers:

1. Books: informational, historical fiction, children's book, alpha-bet, autobiography, and how-to.
2. Letters: a correspondence between real or imagined historical personages.
3. Journals: recollections of a person of the time.
4. Scripts: play, slides, filmstrip, puppet show, video.
5. Newspapers: articles covering events, ads, recipes, etc., of the time period.

6. Annotated coloring books.
7. Annotated calendars with drawings.
8. Poems about the topic.
9. Essays.
10. Games or puzzles that demonstrate knowledge of the topic.
11. Catalogs.

I asked my students to decide for themselves the most interesting ways for them both to share what they knew and show their work to its best advantage. For some students, this added depth to their work and generated new enthusiasm for what they were doing. In a conference about her genre choice, Erinn said, "I was getting a little bored with my topic. A lot of the books say the same thing. Then I had a great idea—I'd write a play!"

The typed script of Erinn's play about the plague, titled *The Will of God*, was twenty pages long. It included a cast of fifteen characters and a prologue that explained the genesis of the plague:

> The plague is carried by a rat flea which has a plague germ in its system. The flea rides on the rats, then jumps on another animal or human and bites it. The germ mixes into the bloodstream of the human, and he or she becomes the proud owner of the famed black death.

One of Erinn's characters is a talking parrot that functions as a kind of chorus as it comments on the action and warns the unheeding passengers of a cargo ship of the vermin onboard:

FIRST MATE: Captain! Some of the crew are very sick. They're getting nauseous!
CAPTAIN: Must be the sea. It happens to the best of us. Now please, I'm very busy.
FIRST MATE: But Captain, they're very ill!
CAPTAIN: Leave my quarters now!
[*The First Mate leaves and the Captain goes back to his log.*]
BALLADEER: Meanwhile, the poor First Mate is very busy with the sick.
FIRST MATE: How could the Captain be so ignorant? I just don't understand him.
PARROT: Don't understand, don't understand.
FIRST MATE: You are lucky you're a bird. When things get tight, you fly away.
PARROT: Lucky bird, lucky bird.
[*Finally, the Captain comes up on deck.*]
FIRST MATE: Ahh, Captain . . .
CAPTAIN: What's all this about illness?
FIRST MATE: Well . . .
PARROT: Look at the rats. Look at the rats.

Robbie chose to report his research on the medieval minstrel in first-person voice, as an autobiography of one "Robert the Minstrel," which was typed as a book for the classroom library. His book's author blurb notes that Robbie "is a member of the swim team and plays baseball in Little League. He enjoys skateboarding, guitar playing, motorcycle riding, and all kinds of sports." And for six weeks one spring, he became Robert the Minstrel.

> Come gather around people of
> All ages.
> Come hear of Robert the Minstrel from the
> Middle Ages.
> Come hear how he lived in inn and
> In hall.
> Come listen to tales, come one,
> Come all.

> I am Robert the Minstrel. I am on my way to Lord Den's castle. I am hoping to get a full time job in the castle.
> Being a minstrel is really the only thing I'd ever want to do. I'm always welcome at inns, courts, and taverns. People love my stories and are hungry for the news and gossip I bring from the next town. Not too many people read, so they all love to sit down and listen to my tales and songs. Usually, in exchange for some tales and songs, I receive a meal and a place to sleep in the tavern. In a palace I might receive some leftovers from the dinners and a place to sleep in the great hall, and if it were a special occasion or the lord was generous I might receive a few coppers . . .

The short story proved to be the most popular genre choice among my sixth graders and, in my opinion, one of the more challenging, because it requires students to personalize the information they have gathered. This excerpt from Eric's short story shows how a twentieth-century boy might react to the tedium of monastic life.

> Pierri followed the silent chain of monks down the night stairs to the church. They sang the mass and heard a short sermon. Pierri saw another monk come down the stairs. It was his job to make sure nobody slept through the service. For the next hour or so he prayed. Every once in a while, a monk would walk down the aisle looking for sleepers. After a while, it was time to sing Lauds. When Lauds was over, he climbed back up the night stairs and crawled into bed. "It is good to have a service right after midnight to greet the new day," he thought, reassuring himself for the thousandth time.

Students who elected to write in an essay format said that they did so because it was the easiest mode. Tyler chose to write about Vikings as a traditional essay and included a formal outline. But his essay is still a crafted piece of writing. His lead is a question, and he tells the reader in his opening paragraph exactly what information he will provide.

Did you know that the Vikings were the first people to land on America? The Vikings were fierce warriors from Sweden, Denmark, and Norway. In my essay I will tell you about the Vikings' boats, homes, raids, rules, and things that they used in battle.

The Vikings' longships were canoe-like warships. They were one of the finest ships ever built. The ships were made out of oak planks and iron nails. The longships were one hundred feet long and had up to eighty oars to be rowed. They were used to travel from place to place and also to fight sea battles . . .

As did each of the reports, no matter what the genre, Tyler's essay concluded with a list of the resources he had tapped in his research:

What fierce people! The Viking Age is one thing I'm glad I was never involved in. I say that because in this day and age, people have it easy. I'll bet that back in the Middle Ages people would have wanted to be Vikings. Do you think you would have wanted to be a Viking?

BIBLIOGRAPHY

Cairns, Trevor. *The Middle Ages*. Minneapolis: Cambridge University Press, 1972.

Gibson, Michael. *The Vikings*. London: Macdonald Educational, 1976.

Marvin, Mariah. *The Human Adventure*. California: Addison-Wesley Publishing Company, 1976.

Pluckrose, Henry. *Vikings*. New York: Gloucester Press, 1976.

In the past, evaluating finished research papers had been an arduous task. This time around I wanted an evaluation system that would reflect the entire process through which students worked, and one that would be manageable as well as time effective. What follows is a list of criteria I generated to grade each student—guidelines I shared at the beginning of the project so that students would be fully aware of what I expected. Each category was awarded a ten-point value.

EVALUATION CRITERIA

1. Research questions were carefully thought out.
2. Used class time well.
3. Took careful notes.
4. Showed a willingness to revise and improve drafts.
5. Edited the piece carefully before submitting it to me for editing.
6. Submitted all work to me with the final draft.
7. Showed creativity and careful thought.
8. Correctly completed bibliography.
9. Completed work on time.
10. Project format enhanced the research.

In addition to these ten criteria, I offered a bonus to students who put exceptional effort into some part of the project. Mark, for example, made parts of a suit of armor out of metal to go along with his short story, "The Black Knight."

Because I conducted frequent conferences with students throughout the project, observed them closely, and became familiar with their work, the grading sheet was easy to complete. My evaluation was ongoing throughout the project, as was my students' responsibility for their efforts as researchers.

Bridging the gap between the writing workshop and content-area writing is a natural step, but one I had to take thoughtfully. I could not expect that my students would apply the techniques they were using in writer's workshop to other areas of the curriculum unless I showed them how. Thus, I planned each step of the research project to correlate with the familiar components of writing workshop so that my students might build on their strengths as writers.

As a middle-school teacher, I wanted to know what my students could do with topics of a broader scope than the personal experiences they were accustomed to writing about. My challenge to them was a genuine one: Tell me what you know about your topic in a way that you find interesting. The dreaded assignment is dreaded no longer. I enjoyed reading their research because my students' responses were real. They told me what they knew in a fashion all their own.

REFERENCES

Arnold, Guy. 1983. *Datelines of World History*. New York: Warwick Press.

Atwell, Nancie. 1987. *In the Middle: Writing, Reading, and Learning with Adolescents*. Portsmouth, NH: Boynton/Cook.

Calkins, Lucy. 1986. *The Art of Teaching Writing*. Portsmouth, NH: Heinemann.

Giacobbe, Mary Ellen. 1986. "Learning to Write and Writing to Learn in the Elementary School." In *The Teaching of Writing: Eighty-Fifth Yearbook of the National Society for the Study of Education*, ed. Anthony R. Petrosky and David Bartholomae. Chicago: University of Chicago Press.

Gibson, Michael. 1976. *The Vikings*. London: Macdonald Educational.

Graves, Donald H. 1983. *Writing: Teachers and Children at Work*. Portsmouth, NH: Heinemann.

Hartman, Gertrude. 1937. *Medieval Days and Ways*. New York: Macmillan.

Hillyer, V. M., and E. G. Huey. 1966. *Young People's Story of Our Heritage: The Medieval World*. New York: Meredity Press.

Schnurnberger, Lynn Edelman. 1978. *Kings, Queens, Knights, and Jesters: Making Medieval Costumes*. New York: Harper & Row.

Wilde, Jack. 1988. "The Written Report: Old Wine in New Bottles." In *Understanding Writing: Ways of Observing, Learning, and Teaching*, 2nd ed., ed. Thomas Newkirk and Nancie Atwell. Portsmouth, NH: Heinemann.

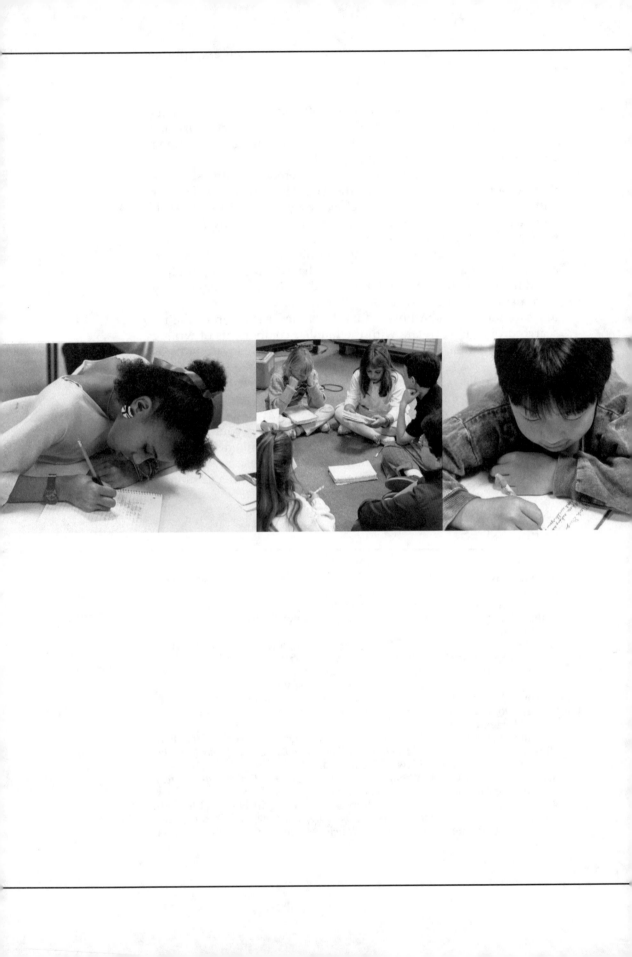

The Power of Learning Logs

3

Thinking and Writing in Learning Logs

ANNE THOMPSON

In June I asked my third graders to write a final entry in their learning logs. I told them to think and write about what it was like to keep logs throughout the school year. Some telling excerpts:

> I like writing. It helps you learn about things. ALYSSA

> I think a logwrite is to be abel to remebere things you nomaly wouldent. ISAAC

> It makes you think a little harder when you do the logwrite. JESSE

> When you write in your learning log it don't have to be perfect. RATHA

These kids already know some things that I only learned this year. They know the power of informal writing to help thinking.

Alyssa knows that writing helps her learn. She used her log to discover what she knew and thought. Writing and thinking helped her make meaning out of her experiences.

Isaac knows that if he writes his thoughts down, he has them forever, captured in his own handwriting within the pages of his log. During the year he frequently reread his log entries, reflecting on *how* he had learned as well as *what*.

Jesse knows that he stretches when writing a log entry. Writing is thinking. It is hard work.

And Ratha knows that what he writes in his log is for him. He is the audience, and, indeed, it doesn't have to be perfect. His learning log is a place where he can experiment, and in this context

35

messiness is a sign of thinking. There are no rights, no wrongs. He is free to write without censure or correction.

When critical thinking skills became the buzzword in our school system, I read texts and journal articles, attended workshops and in-service sessions, signed up for extensive training, and piloted a thinking skills-drills program in my third-grade classroom. But where was the context for all of the exercises? How did the program fit with my teaching and my students' learning? Dissatisfied, I abandoned thinking skills and drills but continued to search for something better for me and my students.

When I began to use learning logs with my third graders, I naturally looked carefully at what they wrote. Almost immediately I noted the thinking evident in the logs. Here was a natural vehicle for thinking critically about teaching and learning, in the context of our everyday classroom activity. I began to photocopy favorite entries and to name the kinds of thinking I found. Eventually, I categorized and filed my students' log writing under seven headings: focusing, gathering, remembering, organizing, predicting and elaborating, integrating, and evaluating. My collection grew and grew.

At the end of the school year my students reluctantly loaned me their learning logs for the summer, with dire threats of what would happen to me if they should not get them back the first day of fourth grade. Within the pages of their logs I found so much evidence of thinking going on, so many critical thinking skills learned and applied in context, so convincing a case for using learning logs across the curriculum to promote student thoughtfulness.

Focusing

For appropriate units in science and social studies, my third graders conducted formal, sustained research projects on topics of their own choosing. Focusing skills—defining problems and setting goals—came into play when my students struggled first to narrow their topics and then to expand them as they established direction and purpose for their research. Most of this happened in the pages of their logs.

I usually teach ocean studies as the first science unit of the school year because of our proximity to the Atlantic Ocean: a busy working harbor is just a few minutes' walk from the school. We spent September learning about plants and animals of the open ocean, rocky intertidal zone, salt marsh, and beach. The kids brought in their beach treasures—driftwood, shells, sea glass, beach pebbles, and sand—and I read aloud picture books, short stories, a chapter book, poems, and pertinent newspaper articles. Students read and shared books brought from home and borrowed from the school and public libraries. I also brought in live marine plants and animals for hands-on investigation, and we visited an aquarium, a rocky beach, and the waterfront.

In early October we brainstormed a list of all the topics we could think of under the broad title *Ocean Studies*. I recorded my students' suggestions on chart paper as a group log entry:

sunken ships sharks whales dolphins seals lobster stingray plankton eel seahorse starfish tiger sharks barracuda porpoise horseshoe crab redfish jellyfish tuna dogfish catfish butterfly fish weeds swordfish bugs octopus hermit crab crabs barnacles mussels clams sand dollar porcupine fish squid puffers dragonfish periwinkles shells sand sea glass rocks sponges plants birds turtles lighthouses boats ships buoys lobstering jobs pollution food from the sea

The next day I told the kids that they would be choosing marine topics to write about, and I asked them to name their choices in their learning logs. During a group sharing of individuals' choices, Jesse and Kelsey found that both had selected whales. They decided to collaborate on their research. Because I've learned that it is important for students to establish what they already know about a topic, Jesse and Kelsey began note-taking in their logs with this prompt and response:

10/6   1:40

WHAT I ALREADY KNOW ABOUT WHALES

1. That they are mammles.
2. That they are very very very very large.
3. The biggest whale is the blue whale.

Once they had narrowed their focus from all of marine life to whales, they could begin to expand the focus and to brainstorm what they knew about this specific topic.

The next step in the process was for them to begin to set goals. What was it that they really wanted to know? From my prompt "These are things I want to know about my topic," Kelsey and Jesse compiled a list of questions in their logs:

10/7   10:12

1. How far do whales jump?
2. Why do whales mate?
3. When whales are born why do they come tail first?
4. How big are newborn whales?
5. Does the father whale help get the baby whale out when it's due?
6. Do mother whales talk to their young?
7. Do father whales stay with his family all the time?

8. What do whales eat?
9. Why do people kill whales?
10. How many different kinds of whales are there?
11. Where do whales live?
12. How long can a whale hold its breath?
13. How long are whales?
14. Do whales like sharks?

Their focus had expanded broadly to include all the information they wanted to gather about whales. The list pushed their thinking and allowed them to collaborate and to piggyback ideas.

As a class we discussed how to find information about topics, both general and specific, and we brainstormed a long list of possible resources. Using the prompt "Some things I might do to learn about my topic," Jesse and Kelsey made another list, this one of things they might do to learn the answers to their questions.

10/8   11:00

1. Call a whale watcher.
2. Go on a whale watch.
3. Go to the Boston Aquarium.
4. Talk to people on fishing boats.
5. Go to the library.

Taking responsibility for their learning became Jesse and Kelsey's new focus. They began their research, filling many pages of their logs with notes. They met regularly to discuss what they had learned from their sources. They went back frequently to the October 7 entry, checking their list of questions, clarifying, redefining, and refocusing their research tasks. When they concluded that they had enough information, they discussed options for publishing their findings. Kelsey decided to make a poster, Jesse would make a papier-mâché whale, and they would write a collaborative story. I prompted their next log entry by asking them to write "What I'm going to do next," again trying to help them focus their efforts.

10/26   2:20

WHAT I'M GOING TO DO

1. Make a paper mashey model.
2. Do the paper mashey.
3. Make a poster.
   Decide what to draw with.
   What to draw.
   Draw with a pencil.
   Coler it.
4. Read notes and write a story.

5. Make the final copy.
6. We think the story will be two pages long.
7. Take the final copy to the typest.
8. Bring everything in.
9. Get a grade, get a very good grade!

Jesse and Kelsey began their study of whales by concentrating on what they already knew, then deciding what they wanted to know, and, ultimately, taking action. They used log entries to narrow and expand their focus, to define their tasks, set direction and purpose for their study, select and record information, and establish next steps. Learning logs were the means by which Jesse and Kelsey made their first research project a manageable undertaking. Their log writing helped them to define and demarcate their knowledge about whales and to make it their own.

Gathering

The basis of all thinking is observation: gathering information through listening, smelling, seeing, tasting, and touching. My third graders learned firsthand by participating in a variety of hands-on activities, field trips, and interviews. They also used books, magazines, newspaper articles, audiovisual materials, and role-plays to gather information. Students recorded their observations of all of these activities in their learning logs, and in the process created a kind of living textbook of their knowledge.

In October, as part of our ocean studies unit, we role-played the effect of the tides on plant and animal life in the salt marsh. In preparation I read "Estuary" from *Will Curtis, and This Is the Nature of Things*, Warren's "Salt Marsh," which had been published the previous year in our school literary magazine, and a newspaper article about the Scarborough Marsh Nature Center. Then I gave out prompt cards, each featuring a picture and description of a plant or animal, to students who wanted to be plants and animals in the salt marsh. The others, who were to be the ocean, took sheets of blue paper. We went to the school amphitheater and positioned ourselves. The ocean moved from low tide in the amphitheater's pit to high tide on the top steps, and the plants and animals acted out what they would do in a salt marsh. For example, the fiddler crab crouched down low to hide in its burrow, and the killifish swam into the marsh with the tide. When we returned to the classroom, I asked the kids to write in their logs about their experiences. Together we brainstormed prompts and I wrote them on the blackboard: Who were you? What did you do? What happened as the tide came in and left the marsh? Ratha responded:

10/1   11:13

I'm a mussel. The great blue heron and the crabs tride to have me for
lunch. I eat tiny plants. I pump water through my body. If I sea any
insect that trys to eat me, I close up my shell. If the tide goes down,
I close up my shell and I hold my breath until the tide comes back.

Ratha internalized how the salt marsh works through his role as a
mussel. He discovered the relationships among plants and animals
in that habitat and the effects of the tides on their lives. His log
entry allowed him to record and reflect on his learning.

During a visit to the Maine Aquarium, also in early October, I
made a brief entry in my own journal: "Bringing our learning logs
was a *great* idea. They are really using them!" My students had
been reluctant to take their logs to the aquarium: they claimed the
logs were too heavy and awkward to lug around and that there
was so much to do and see that they wouldn't get to use them. But
use them they did. With no prompting from me, they took notes
during presentations by the aquarium staff. They sketched. They
made lists of exhibit creatures. They described favorite exhibits and
animals. They recorded what they heard, smelled, saw, and touched.
On the way home on the bus, many of them summarized the day's
trip in their logs. Already it was second nature for them to write
in order to capture experiences.

In early November I brought in collections of living marine
plants and animals and set up stations with a variety of specimens,
hand lenses, measuring tools, and reference materials to aid in
identification. Each station was assigned to a group of four students,
and I asked the groups to record their observations in words and
pictures, then to write about what they had learned by looking at
live sea creatures.

Ratha used adjacent pages in his learning log to set up a double-
entry journal (Berthoff 1981), recording his firsthand observations
on the left-hand page and his reflections on what he had learned
on the right (Figure 3–1). Ratha first listed all the marine plants and
animals that he could identify. He sketched what he saw. And then
he recorded what he had done and learned. Information that might
have been lost at the end of the experiment was preserved for
Ratha's future reference in the pages of his log.

As part of the social studies curriculum, third graders in Portland study their city. We are fortunate that our school is located in
an historic section of the city, with many buildings of architectural
and historical significance a short walk away. Isaac chose to study
the Victoria Mansion in detail and in his learning log made a drawing to accompany his research notes (Figure 3–2). Isaac's learning
log allowed him to capture the essence of the historical home and
the significant architectural details of the Italianate style. The log
often served as a way for students to store information through
visual representations that enhanced their writing.

FIGURE 3–1 ● RATHA'S DOUBLE-ENTRY JOURNAL

11/4   9:30
Starfish, sea earchent, eggs,
live ocean animals
barnickles, sea anemone,
mussel, sea letess, hermit crab
green crab, anemone, limpit, sea weed
rok.

10:18

What I lernded by looking
at live sea creaders.

I drew alot of pictures of the
sea creaders. We thought that
the stearfomes were eggs. The
starfish blew his stomach out to
eat the hermit crab. There was
a green crab. There was a
tinny sea worm stiking to the
starfish. The sea archent didn't do
any thing. We had fun. the crab
bit Ms. Tompson. The water
was dark. The sea anemeney opind
it solf.

Writing questions was another way that students focused attention on and generated information. During our study of weather, third graders brainstormed lists of questions that might be used in a weather opinion poll. From Amy's log:

2/23   10:25 a.m.

Do you think more people like hot weather than cold?
Do you like the climate in your state?
Do you enjoy snow?
Have you ever been in a hurricane?
                              tornado?
                              flood?
Are you scared during thunderstorms?

In group share I recorded students' questions on the blackboard. The kids selected what they felt were the sixteen best, and I put these on a ditto and gave copies to everyone. They polled family

FIGURE 3–2 ● ISAAC'S VICTORIAN MANSION

and friends, compiled and charted the data they collected, shared the results on a large poster, and wrote an article for the school newsletter about their findings. The initial, individual log entries helped the whole group to focus on the way people feel about weather and spurred the formalization of the weather opinion poll. When my students observe, document, and question, they become actively involved as learners, recording what they know, what they need to find out, and what they want to remember.

Remembering

I begin most new units of study with a log entry to find out what my students already know about the topic. For example:

11/17   9:15

> WHAT I ALREADY KNOW ABOUT THE MOON
>
> It has craters.
> No gravity.
> It is smoller then the sun.
> It lights up the erth a little bit at night.
> The moon has no grass.
> The moon is all difint shaps
> When it looks like a half moon but it isn't it is still all there.
>
> FLORENCE

Florence recalled information she had previously learned about the moon, in school and from personal experience and observation. When she and my students write a "what I already know" entry, they connect with prior knowledge. Their logs help bridge the gap between the individual and the curriculum. During a group meeting, kids read aloud their entries, each in turn around the circle, sharing their thinking about the topic at hand.

Brainstorming is a particularly effective strategy for remembering and retrieving information and for quickly getting down on paper a quantity of related ideas. When students brainstorm in their logs they draw on their long-term memory stores in productive and unpredictable ways. Given the prompt "List as many things as you can think of that have seeds," George recorded:

2/29   9:22

SEEDS

apple	pineapple	punken	radse
ornge	peapod	squesh	green bean
tangean	flower	zewcainy	corn
aggeplant	apedracot	graps	watermelen

tomatose	plums	peach	pare
potottow	storberry		

George surprised himself with the breadth of his response. Writing in his log helped him tap buried knowledge that would not have surfaced in an oral response.

Learning logs played a significant role in helping my students remember. Through prompts, I invited students to delve into their memories, to write what they already knew, and to appreciate their prior knowledge. Through sharing written recollections, we discovered differences in what we brought to the task at hand, and we learned from each other.

Organizing

My third-grade students gather information from many sources but must also organize information so that it makes sense to them. Students used their learning logs in a variety of ways to organize the relatively unorganized data they collected, writing to compare, categorize, and classify their information.

All content areas invite comparisons—identifying similarities and differences, looking at how things might be related. My kids make frequent comparisons in the pages of their learning logs. I asked them to write a log entry comparing the moon and the earth. After they had read a selection from a science text, both Jeremy and Selena set up same/different lists.

12/1   Jeremy

SAME	DIFERENT
same rocks	no life on the moon
same age	no water on the moon
same galiksy	no air on the moon

12/1   Selena

SAME

both round
rocks

DIFFERENT

earth has atmaspher/moon doesn't
moon is a satalite
plants
air
gravity

The log prompt helped the kids to graphically represent differences and similarities, to juxtapose and consider earth and moon, and to organize their distinct features.

Classifying is also an aid in organizing information. Christopher developed this chart in his log to classify information he learned from a filmstrip about marine life:

PLANKTON   THINGS THAT FLOAT WITH THE CURRENT

Jellyfish
Diatoms
Copepods
Radiolarians
Dinoflagellates

NEKTON   THINGS THAT SWIM FREELY

squid   swordfish
butterfly fish
cusk
sunfish
bluefish
cunner
grubby
pollock

BENTHOS   THINGS THAT LIVE ON THE OCEAN FLOOR

sea star

Christopher grouped items into three categories on the basis of like attributes. He also organized the information graphically: plankton at the top because they float, benthos at the bottom because those creatures live on the ocean floor, and the nekton swimmers in the middle. Again, the log was a means for making this knowledge his own.

Becky predicted what she might see on a field trip to the beach at Kettle Cove. She grouped her guesses into categories, then made a tally sheet in her learning log (Figure 3–3). Using the tally sheet as a framework to guide her observations, Becky easily captured what she saw during the beach walk. Through writing in her log she is learning how to anticipate, structure, and systematize experience, a thinking skill no one ever learned from a worksheet.

Predicting and Elaborating

Predicting and elaborating are constructive thinking skills that students use to connect new ideas to prior knowledge. They are skills central to taking the posture of active learner.

FIGURE 3–3 ● BECKY'S TALLY SHEET

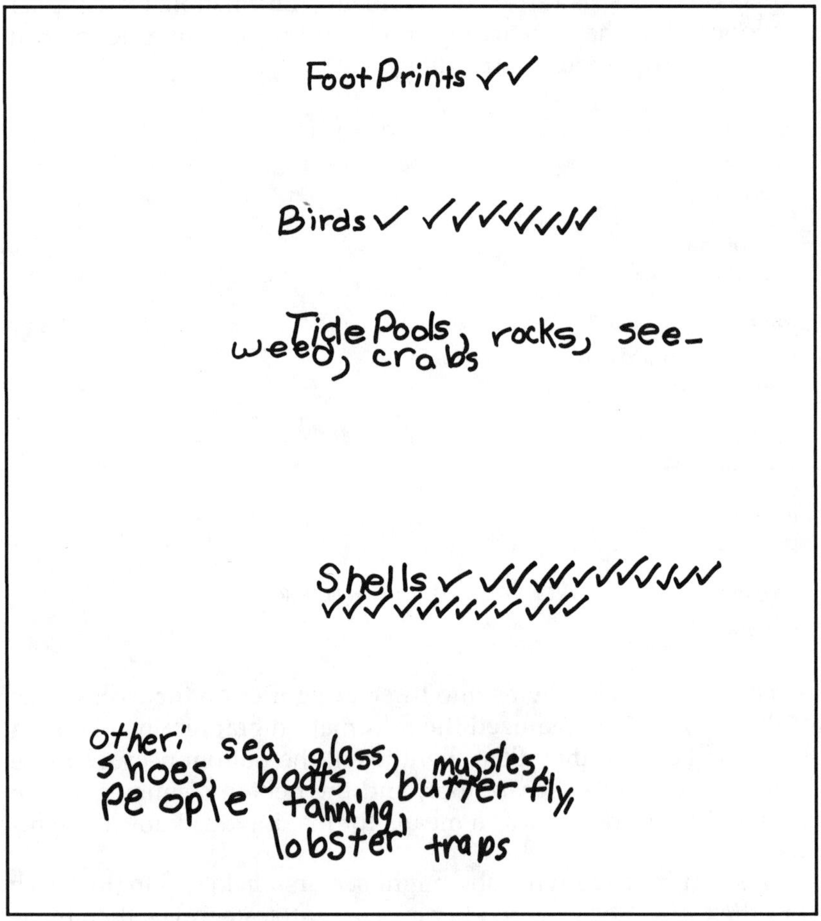

FootPrints ✓✓

Birds ✓ ✓✓✓✓✓✓

Tide Pools
weed, crabs rocks, see-

Shells ✓ ✓✓✓✓✓✓✓✓
✓✓✓✓✓✓✓ ✓✓

other: sea glass,
shoes, boats, mussles,
people tanning, butter fly,
lobster traps

I often ask third graders "What will happen next?" in reading, science, math, and social studies. We also write predictions in our learning logs before experiments and field trips. Prior to a trip to the historic boyhood home of poet Henry Wadsworth Longfellow, I asked, "What do you think you will see when we visit the Longfellow House for Christmas at Henry's?" Melissa's adjacent learning log pages (Figure 3–4) show her predictions on the left and her reflections on them, after the visit, on the right. Melissa tapped what she knew about Longfellow as well as recollections about other historic homes to write her predictions, which gave the experience of the field trip more meaning. Melissa was *looking for* information—for confirmations or contradictions—when she walked into Longfellow's house.

Rebecca went on the same field trip. She used the skill of elab-

FIGURE 3–4 ● MELISSA'S PREDICTIONS AND REFLECTIONS

Christmas at Henry's

12\15 12:08
⁰There might be a place
were there are books to read
like a libary.
② Maybe a lot of
clocks in the house.
③ Maybe a window that goes
to the floor and old
curtins that go on the
windows too.
④ There has to
be some bedrooms in the
house insteda of sleeping on
the floor. I think there
⑤ might be a lot of other things.

12\17 9:23
① There was a place
where you can read
but there was not much
books to read at all
②. There were three clocks
in the house and they
were very old too. ③There
was no window that
goes to the bottom of the
floor in the house. But
there was some nice
curtins on the windows.
④ there was some bed rooms
in the house very old
bed rooms too. ⑤ yes there
were alot of other things too
like
a nice little kicen
too. And A pretty christmas
tree with lots of popcorn
strings and little bells.

oration to put herself into the Longfellow House in the late eighteenth century. In response to the prompt "Pretend that you lived here as a member of the family," she wrote:

12/17 9:23

My mother had to cook. I helped her. My brother and father had to chop down a Christmas tree and chop down firewood for the fireplaces. It was a lot of wood when they came home. We were the only people in the neighborhood. We had to put in a bedwarmer at night. We had candles. We had to make our own candles. We went to a nearby school.

Rebecca added details and relevant prior knowledge to information she gathered during the field trip. In the pages of her log she internalized life in another time and place. Through predicting and elaborating in their logs, both girls gained an improved understanding of early Portland.

Integrating

Whereas analyzing involves taking things apart, integrating involves the putting together of relevant parts, the building of meaningful connections between new information and prior knowledge. Summarizing is one way that children assimilate data and make it their own. When writers summarize, they combine information, condense it, select what's important, and discard what is not. Because shorter summaries for oneself are easier to write and potentially more useful than longer ones written for others, I often urge my students to write brief summaries in their learning logs.

After I read aloud *Squirrels* by Brian Wildsmith, students summarized the facts embedded in the text. From Becky's log:

1/6   10:12

Squirrel nests are called dreys. Squirrels tails are used for leaps, a parachute, change directions, swim, balance, blanket. Sometimes squirrels steal eggs.

In this brief entry Becky recalled what she felt were the most important facts in the text. She later used this summary, written in her own words, as part of her report on squirrels as urban wild animals.

From pages of unorganized notes in his log, Warren wrote this summary of life in the salt marsh:

3/16

THE SALT MARSH

A lot of salt marsh animals live in the salt marsh area: the blue crab, the fiddler crab, the killifish, the mussel, the clam worm too. When the tide is high the blue crab feeds. When the tide is low, the blue crab buries itself in the mud. The blue crab can get eaten by a raccoon. A raccoon feeds on the killifish, the blue crab, and the clam worm. There is a food chain with the salt marsh animals, where one animal eats another. The blue crab and the fiddler crab are king of the salt marsh. They can eat almost anything. The tide can affect the salt marsh animals' lives. It can change the salt marsh animals' natural habitat.

In this final log entry on the marsh, Warren condensed all the information collected in his log notes, selected what was important for him to include in this summary, and discarded what he deemed unimportant. He made connections between new information and prior knowledge—for example, applying what he already knew about food chains to salt marsh animals. He used his log to combine relevant aspects of life in the salt marsh into a meaningful whole.

Just before a lesson on Maine's bald eagles, Kim wrote in her log what she already knew about the topic:

10:57   sharp claws
              eats fish
              eagles are not mamals

Then she participated in a variety of activities designed to help kids learn more about eagles. After the lesson, she again summarized what she knew:

11:55

eagles are not mamals. eagel eggs are thin. in the winter they fly to south. When winter is over they come back to there own nest. When they come their nest is horrible. latar they took time to fix it. eagles eat fish, birds, field mice and snakes. Some insects are poison for eagles to eat. working men spray poison in the whole forest. it kilt moskidos and other bugs. eagles have very sharp claws and beeks.

In her second log entry, Kim integrated what she had known before with what she had just learned, incorporating the first entry into the second. This writing allowed her to be her own teacher and to build her own set of constructs, rather than trying to assimilate someone else's information handed to her from on high.

Selena showed her understanding of weather symbols by integrating them into a story about weather (Figure 3–5). Not only did she use a variety of symbols, but within the ten minutes I set aside for log writing she created a cohesive narrative, one in which the weather symbols fit the context beautifully. The narrative form of the log entry allowed her to imagine a relevant situation in her own life. When students draw on familiar forms, prior knowledge, and personal experience, including their own previous writing, their mental models are that much richer and that much more likely to result in genuine learning.

Evaluating

I give my students time to reflect on their experiences and to record their thoughts in learning logs because I feel it is important for kids to assess what makes sense and why—to take responsibility for thinking critically about what we do as a class. They evaluate field trips, class activities, guest speakers, audiovisual presentations, my

FIGURE 3–5 ● SELENA'S WEATHER STORY

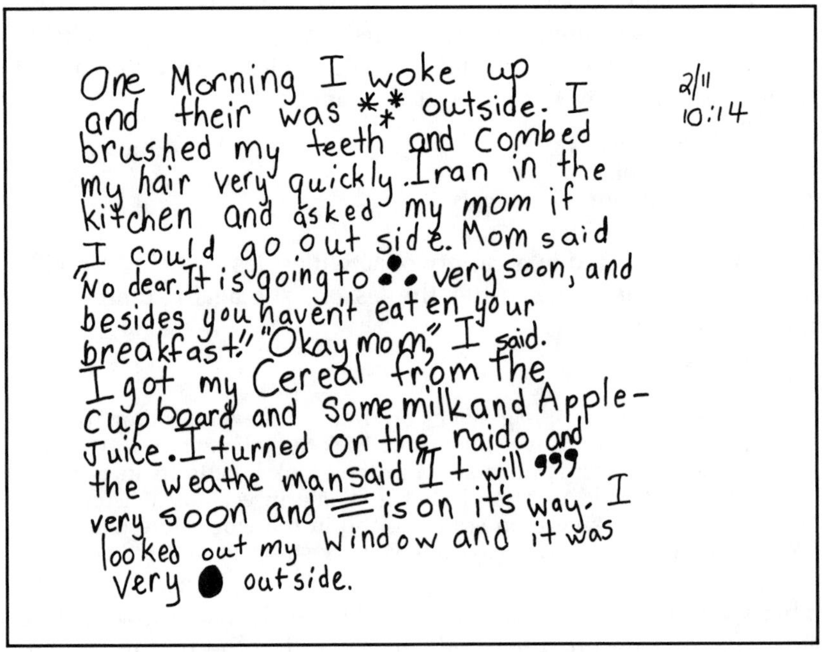

One Morning I woke up and their was *** outside. I brushed my teeth and Combed my hair very quickly. I ran in the kitchen and asked my mom if I could go out side. Mom said "No dear. It is going to ●●● very soon, and besides you haven't eaten your breakfast!" "Okay mom," I said. I got my Cereal from the Cupboard and Some milk and Apple-Juice. I turned on the raido and the weathe man said "I+ will 999 very soon and ≡ is on it's way. I looked out my Window and it was Very ● outside.

2/11
10:14

teaching, their work. Their evaluations are important to me as I plan. They also take me inside students' thoughts and feelings.

10/24   10:12

I like math but today I didn't. I hate speed tests because I get all tense and hiper. Then I get all screwed up. I like division but I'm not that great in it. I mean I don't know it real quick if somebody asked me it.   JULIE

11/16   1:44

what it was like at our science exhibit today I felt proud to be showing something of mine to someone else. Not many people came to my desk but I still liked it. People mostly looked at my book. Nobody knew what was inside my shoebox. I had to tell all of the people.
KELSEY

3/11   10:00

I found out how to do those two didget multiplying problems! They are so easy now.   JOHN

6/6   9:58

In my learning log I have lots of notes. It helps me whenever I need to write down information about what I'm studying on, or when I half to write a log write, I just open my log to my empty page and start to write. At the end of the year I will get a chance to take my learning log home. and do some studying in it. My Learning Log Helps Me Alot! CARRIE

When I talk with my kids and ask for their opinions about something we've done in class, they are likely to give one-word responses: "Good." "Stupid." "Boring." But when I give them time to reflect in the pages of their logs, they respond with depth and feeling. They give criteria for why they feel as they do and critically examine their own work. They also tell me how effective my teaching is and show me steps I can take to improve its quality.

Mary Ellen Giacobbe (1986) has written:

> A productive classroom in any subject should provide opportunities for the student to wonder, to pose questions, to pursue possible answers, to discuss with others, to come to some conclusions—all in writing and all in an attempt to come to a greater understanding of what they are trying to learn. (147)

I saw this model for a productive classroom become a reality as my students and I discovered the power of informal writing to help thinking. When kids are asked to write regularly in a variety of ways for many purposes, critical thinking becomes the normal activity of the classroom. Learning logs are an ideal vehicle for thinking, for making meaning out of experience. Logs became a place for my students to wonder, pose questions, pursue possible answers, discuss with others, and come to conclusions, all within the context of their everyday experiences as third graders.

REFERENCES

Berthoff, Ann E. 1981. "A Curious Triangle and the Double-Entry Notebook: or, How Theory Can Help Us Teach Reading and Writing." In *The Making of Meaning: Metaphors, Models, and Maxims for Writing Teachers*. Portsmouth, NH: Boynton/Cook.

Curtis, Will. 1984. "Estuary." In *Will Curtis, and This Is the Nature of Things*. Woodstock, VT: The Countryman Press.

Giacobbe, Mary Ellen. 1986. "Learning to Write and Writing to Learn in the Elementary School." In *The Teaching of Writing: Eighty-Fifth Yearbook of the National Society for the Study of Education*, ed. Anthony R. Petrosky and David Bartholomae. Chicago: University of Chicago Press.

Wildsmith, Brian. 1984. *Squirrels*. Oxford: Oxford University Press.

4

Learning Logs in the Upper Elementary Grades

MARCIA BLAKE

Grade four is a year of change, a year when children begin to assume many new responsibilities. On the most basic level, we expect them to come to school each day with all the necessary equipment—pencils, erasers, books, and sneakers—and we begin to try to wean children away from excuses, like the mother who doesn't pack phys. ed. gear or who throws homework away.

Fourth grade is the year of real, honest-to-goodness homework. We lead the children slowly and carefully into the world of independent study until it becomes a part of their daily routine.

Fourth grade is the year when content-area study becomes both broader and more concentrated. The curriculum demands that students delve deeper than hands-on activities and short readings. The approach becomes more academic as we introduce specialized vocabulary, critical thinking, multi-leveled questions, and daily discussions. There is a new emphasis on remembering facts and concepts and finding systems of logic among them. Report writing becomes more scholarly through the use of such references as atlases and almanacs. Perhaps most important, this is the year when we begin to make big intellectual demands of children and expect them to become serious students.

The learning log is a unique method for collecting and identifying material that can help upper elementary learners focus on, compare, and classify information. In this chapter I will show a variety of techniques that I have used with a class of fourth graders to help them create systems and patterns among information presented in class, which in turn helps them respond to the challenges of the upper elementary grades. These techniques—mapping, webbing, predicting, listing, tapping prior knowledge, and brain-storming—help students both to generate information and to capture it on paper where they can see and respond to it. They also allow a writer to make connections to other academic areas. Logs can be used in any subject—science, social studies, reading, writing, or math. I will concentrate here on the use of logs in science and social studies.

My students used one log for both subjects, as the subjects were so closely related. The kids kept their logs in a basket on a shelf so the desks wouldn't eat them and so they would not be taken home by mistake. I assigned learning log prompts at three points during a course of study: before I taught a concept, while I was teaching it, and at the completion of the lesson or unit.

My students liked to be able to tell what they already knew about a subject because they felt their answers would not be challenged and that every answer was correct. A prompt that taps prior knowledge serves as a good introduction to a new unit. I'd ask, "What do you already know about . . . ?" and give students ten minutes to respond. At the start of a unit about mountains of the world, Tyler had a chance to formalize what he knew.

4/5   11:20

THINGS I KNOW ABOUT MOUNTAINS. . . .

1. they are covered with snow and ice year round at the top.
2. some you can't find a foot hole because they go straight up.
3. some are made of volcanoes or earthquakes.
4. some are pointed at the top.
5. some have weather stations.
6. some are in a long line.
7. some have to be climbed by ropes.
8. they can reach great hights.
9. most of them have clouds near the top.
10. they can have cliffes.
11. you can get blistered by the sun and snow if you don't protect.

Then, I recorded individuals' responses on big pieces of light-colored construction paper during a whole-class sharing session. These lists were on display for the duration of the unit so that students could compare and contrast their answers with those on the chart. We also liked to refer to the responses during class discussions. Another way I used the lists in conjunction with logs was to ask at the end of a unit, "What have you learned that you didn't already know?" It was always interesting to compare the pre- and post-unit information.

A prompt that I used to introduce a topic was "What would you like to learn in this unit?" This worked especially well in map reading and map making. After the children wrote in their logs and shared their responses, I recorded these as a group list and incorporated my students' questions into my plans. Their queries included:

- Why do they call a legend a legend?
- Who made the first map? How did he know where the places were and what they were called?
- How many rivers are there in the world?
- Do all maps always have to be political, physical, or both? Do all maps have a key?
- How many different types of maps are there?

As I taught an item or students found an answer, they checked off the question on the posted list. At the end of this particular unit, students used their logs to draw their own maps with legends, to capture and show their knowledge.

Listing was another way that students showed what they had learned. The class brainstormed differences and similarities between two groups of islands in the Pacific Ocean and entered them into their logs, as Wyatt has done below.

12/14

IFALIK		HAWAII
	Differences	
coral made		volcanic made
	Income	
copra		pineapple
		sugar cane
		tourists
		cattle
	Clothing	
little or no clothing		muumuus
		ordinary
	Houses	
woven		wood
thatched huts		
	Population	
few		many
	Similarities	
	have people	
	both islands	
	tropical	
	need outside world	

On the next page of their logs they drew webs of the lists, to show the major topics as well as the details. Gearry shows one style of webbing in Figure 4–1. Notice how he separates the two island groups in terms of their differences and then draws the similarities in the middle. He has made the same connections through webbing that Wyatt did through listing.

During our study of the Polar regions, fourth graders drew webs in their logs using specific colors to show similar subjects so they could relate major topics better. John's web (Figure 4–2) shows how he made connections between the two Polar regions through brainstorming their features. He could then compare their similarities and contrast the differences.

The kids concluded that webbing was both a fun activity and an effective way to learn and retain facts. Webbing can follow listing, or it can be done first, and lists or outlines can be created from the details drawn on the web. It is also a marvelous tool for reviewing information. I often assigned a web prompt before testing students' knowledge at the conclusion of a unit.

We also put logs to good use when it came time to conduct

FIGURE 4–1 ● GEARRY'S WEB

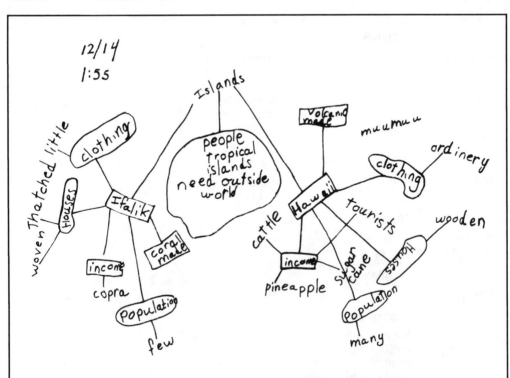

FIGURE 4–2 ● JOHN'S WEB

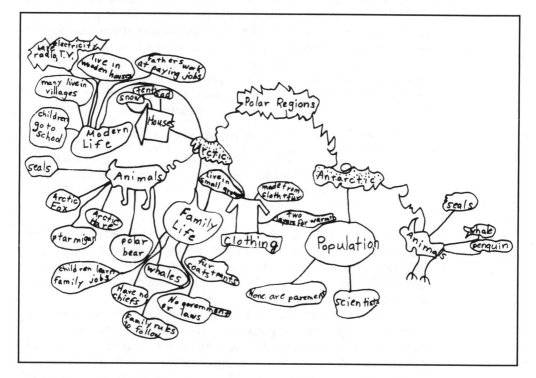

science experiments. I asked children to predict outcomes of certain experiments in their logs and then record the results. They got a chance to compare their thinking and many times found that the initial prediction and final result were very close, sometimes identical.

For one experiment, I built up beach sand against one end of an oblong glass dish. One of my students carefully poured water into the empty end until the dish was half full. I began to make "waves" toward the "beach" and asked students to predict in their logs what would happen to the sand in the dish. When the experiment was over I asked, "What happened?" Gearry had predicted that the water would cause erosion and the sand would wash away. His second entry read: "It was the same as I thought!" Wendy had predicted that the water "will make a crest and a trough." Afterward she wrote: "No, it took some of the sand out." Log writing served as a private way for students to risk predictions and learn from experience.

One of my favorite ways to use the logs was as a place for students to brainstorm. Brainstorming allows learners to write down whatever comes to mind, to generate a lot of data quickly, and to bounce ideas back and forth among them. Small group brainstorming worked well all year, and I encouraged each member of the group to participate in the discussion. The small-group approach made it easier for shy students to respond and share their knowledge, whereas a large group setting sometimes proved intimidating.

After completing a combined science and social studies unit that dealt with water and geographical locations, I challenged my students to solve a survival problem as a small-group activity. I stated the problem to them in this fashion:

> Your sailboat has capsized and you are in a small rubber craft. There are four of you. The raft is five hundred miles from land and shipping lanes, in tropical water. Because your sailboat sank quickly, you have only the clothes on your back and what might be found in your pockets. You have no maps, food, or fresh water with you. How do you hope to survive?

The children sat in their small groups and looked at each other, and then a buzz of noise broke the silence. They were busy trying to come up with an instant answer—with no luck. I spent some time with each group and listened in on their conversations; one seemed to be heading in a good direction.

"We have a survival knife, string, matches, hooks, and a compass. We might have a piece of lead in our pockets, to put on a string and let down to use as a minianchor," Brian observed. He continued, "We could use our sneakers for something."

Jason chimed in. "We could catch rainwater in our sneakers!"

I knew this group was on its way, so I left them to listen in on another. I overheard Areth telling his group, "I know a way to make fresh water from salt water. You take a plastic bag, put salt water under it, and the water evaporates up to the top of the bag and drips into the bailer." Another boy was figuring out how to take Gretchen's braces off so they could be used as a hook, when tied to a shoelace, for fishing. They were going to make sails out of oars and shirts.

The other groups were listing similar items that might be found in their pockets and deciding how to use them. This is Gearry's list from his log:

> A bailer, braces, paper clip, glasses, shoelaces, bracelet, earings, shels, scout knife, headband, buttons, yo-yo, watch, neclace, pen, Emegency raincoat, remmingto shaver, Make up

John's entry, which he organized with headings, was more detailed (Figure 4–3). Each student invented his or her own method for recording and organizing the information generated in the groups.

This session lasted about forty-five minutes. When the groups had finished and returned their logs to the basket, I asked the kids

FIGURE 4–3 ● JOHN'S LIST

Raft

12/3 We are more than 500 miles from land
and any shipping lanes.
Our clothing is on our backs.
We have no maps, food, our water.
Our raft is in tropical water.
This is how we hope to survive.

Pockets
Survival-Knife
Peanuts 2
2 little juice-boxes
cantines
Money
Sunglasses
Hard-line
Bonnuckulors

Find
Coconut
Wood
Seaweed
useful-Junk
Pinapple
Orange

Cloths
t-shirts
Rain-coat
Snikers
Shorts
belt
hat

Use-survival-knife-to-carv
any-wood-we-find-into-oars
Use-shirts-to-strain-water
into-basin-made-out-of-junk
our-wood. If-no-junk-our
wood-use-rain-coats-our
empty-juice-boxes.

Notes
John-Brian-push-raft
Amy-cook
Jason-helper-diver
Use-survival-knife-to-cut
open-coconuts. Pour-coconut
milk-into-empty-juice-boxes.

Wether
Hot !!!
Water
Warm !!!!

to continue thinking and to bring any new ideas to the next session, which would be in several days. I also told them that they would be in their rafts for a total of fourteen days.

After eight days of perfect weather, a rainstorm passed over each raft so the passengers could have fresh water. Each group got back together and madly tried to find a way to catch and keep the water. They used sneakers, the bailer, clothing, and the innards of a small flashlight.

On the fourteenth day a lone shark was spotted circling the boat. The groups met one last time to see if they could survive this menace. As I walked around the classroom, I heard Lindsay and Betsy suggest that the oar be used to knock the shark out. Adam and Andy had decided to stab it with their pocketknife. Only one group remained cool and calm and decided to leave the shark alone.

When all the groups had finished and shared their answers with the class, I discussed each solution. The children who decided to leave the shark alone "survived" the adventure. This group knew enough about sharks to realize that blood, even shark blood, would attract others.

The raft problem called on all group members to write, record, and share ideas, and it allowed everyone to join in the conversation. It also required students to make a major decision about a situation related to real life. At the beginning of the exercise I had placed a pin on a world map, just south of the equator and west of South America: the site of our shipwreck. I left it there all year and frequently heard students ask, when using the world map, "Remember how we tried to survive?"

Learning logs have proven very valuable resources, for both my students and me. The children wrote a lot, learned a lot, and had a record of their accomplishments in the spiral notebooks at the end of the school year; I discovered how and what fourth graders learn through academic journals. Learning logs are great sources of information in all grades for any subject, but I am especially convinced of their usefulness in the upper elementary grades.

I saw my students make giant leaps during our year together. Through the new responsibilities they assumed, I saw students emerge as serious learners and writers. I watched them grow socially, emotionally, and academically. And logs were one agent for that growth. Logs helped my students focus on information, record it, and retrieve it when they discovered they needed it. Logs brought them together as a learning community and nudged them to take an active stance as learners. Grade four is a year of many changes, and logs can play a positive role in helping students grow.

5

How Learning Logs Change Teaching

NANCY CHARD

Like most teachers, every year on the first day of school I sit down with my class and talk with them about the coming year. I explain the rules of the room, its procedures and routines.

This September I wanted to know what my students had understood after my annual two-hour explanation, so I passed out their learning logs and assigned the first prompt of the school year: "List what you learned about this classroom today." Every child recorded the procedure for signing up to go to the bathroom. Next September I'll dispense with the two-hour lecture. Instead I'll just explain bathroom procedures and begin teaching.

I am a fourth-grade teacher in a team situation. My responsibilities include two periods of social studies each day. In this chapter, I'll explain how I use learning logs to help me determine what I teach, gain my students' cooperation, fine-tune methods, and develop new ways of teaching. I use learning logs as a part of every one of my social studies lessons. At the beginning of a unit, I want to find out what the kids already know so I can better teach the material. Do I need more background information? Can I skip some information? During the unit, logs help me to find out how well the children are understanding a topic. Do I need to reteach some concepts? After a unit, logs help me to evaluate the effectiveness of the activities, resources, readings, and discussions that comprised the unit. How did the children understand what I was trying to teach?

Learning What to Teach

When I begin a unit, I ask a general question of my kids to determine what background they already have in the area we are about to study. My teaching plan will reflect the information I gain from their log entries.

One of my first log prompts each fall is "What is social studies?" Their answers tell me right away what my students know. When Angela wrote, "It's a book you can study with at school. Sometimes you have to use it if you need it or not," I knew that her definition was limited.

Susan, who had a deeper understanding, stated, "It teaches you a lot about space, what we live on. It teaches the solar system, map, and globe. It shows where we live, about what people do, and different kinds of people."

And Kelly wrote, "Social studies is things that you learn about: history, the future, animals, people, and the world. It's where you learn about the states. And about your country and a lot of other things. You learn about people."

Clearly some kids, like Kelly, knew exactly what our subject encompassed, while others had only a vague idea. We formed a circle, and each child read his or her log entry. The process took about twelve minutes. It was a simple way for me to find out what kids knew and to provide them with needed information. At the same time, kids learned from each other's definitions.

The first unit in social studies is glossary map terms. The unit is based on a list of sixty-five words that we use for the rest of the year. It includes terms such as *continents, oceans, rivers, mountains, zones,* and so on. In one of my first lessons I teach latitude and longitude. To find out what the kids already knew about this topic, I assigned the log prompt "What do latitude and longitude mean?" Every member of the class wrote, "I don't know." I knew immediately that I would have to teach the topic in depth. We spent the rest of the period discussing latitude and longitude and using them to help locate places on a map.

The next day's class began with the same log prompt: "What do latitude and longitude mean?" This time the responses were very different. Jeff wrote, "Latitude and longitude lines pinpoint where you are. They are on a map and a globe."

Lisa responded, "Longitude and latitude lines are lines that help separate the world; for example, say you were on an island and you were 40°N. 20°E. People would be able to find you. We have them so we can look things up on a globe or map or locate places."

Even my special education student, who is mainstreamed for social studies, wrote, "Latitude and longitude mean it is on a globe or map and helps to find places."

After listening to all the responses, I knew that everyone had understood yesterday's lesson and we could move on to the next topic. If a majority of kids still had not grasped the meanings of latitude and longitude, I would have stopped and approached the concept again from another angle.

In January, when we began our study of Martin Luther King, Jr., I asked, "Who is Martin Luther King?" Their log entries demonstrated that a majority of children in each class already had a good idea. Ian wrote, "MLK is a civil rights leader. He wanted to bring black men and white men together." And Katie logged, "MLK was a black man who wanted black people to have the same freedom as whites, for them to be equal. He stands for freedom." Since the class already had a good understanding of who King was, I could immediately start a discussion of segregation, sit-ins, and civil rights. The kids were ready to go deeper because they had a foundation, as I had learned through their logs.

One night after school, when I was reading a new set of log entries, I noticed how many children knew nothing at all about Antarctica—did not even know that it was a continent, let alone where it was. I knew exactly what my lesson would be for the next day: I would read aloud the book *Antarctica* by Lynn M. Stone.

After I read to them, I asked my students to list in their logs facts they knew about Antarctica. We formed a circle and read around it, adding new facts until no one had any more. Their responses included: "It's very cold," "It's located in the southern part of the world," "No one owns it," "Only scientists live there," and "Scientists do research there." Kelly commented, "I don't know how anyone could stand the cold!" It was a good way to introduce Antarctica. With their help I'd accomplished my goal, and we'd done it in one period. And, once again, learning log entries had allowed my students to teach each other.

Helping Students Cooperate

Over the past two years I have completely changed my way of teaching social studies. Instead of lecturing, assigning pages from the social studies book, passing out worksheets, and testing, I act now as a facilitator and a resource person. I have adopted students' research and writing as my methods for teaching social studies. This new approach was a challenge both to me and to my fourth graders. As they would now be working in groups throughout the year, it was very important for me to establish a working relationship among the members of each class. Through logs, I discovered how to foster a cooperative atmosphere.

During the unit on map terms, I broke the class into four groups and gave each group the list of terms. They worked together to research and write the meaning of each term. To define their words, the children used dictionaries, encyclopedias, filmstrips, atlases, and a variety of other resource books. The groups worked well for the first few days, then started to fall apart. There was a lot of talking (not about map terms), and kids were fooling around.

I stopped the class and called them together at the board. I asked them to write in their logs in response to the prompt "How's it going? Make two columns. Label one column 'What's working' and label the other column 'What needs more work.' " Each child wrote for as long as was needed, which took until the end of the period.

The next day, the groups met and members shared with each other what they had written in their logs about the workings of their group. I circulated around the room and observed. Ian's group was doing exactly as I had asked. Katie's group, two boys and two girls, had a real split; there was lots of giggling, the boys weren't even facing the girls, and they were blaming each other for their failure. Colby's group was more concerned with who would lead the discussion than with answering the question, and Todd's group was on task. I evaluated the situation and knew it was not going well. Half of the groups were on task, but the other half were still fooling around.

I called the whole class together again, and, using an overhead transparency, we listed what was working and what needed more work, based on their log entries.

WHAT IS WORKING	WHAT NEEDS MORE WORK
• dictionary is helpful	• talking too much
• whispering only	• arguing a lot
• writing is okay	• need more time to work
• we are studying	• throwing things
• reading well	• name calling
• good attitudes	• looking up "bad" words
• it's fun	• talking too loud
• finding interesting words	• not paying attention
• getting work done on time	• feeling left out
• taking time to do a good job	• hitting each other
	• stealing
	• need to work faster
	• need to share
	• only one group member working

When we finished, we had ten areas where their progress was satisfactory and fourteen that needed attention. As a teacher, I became aware of things that were happening that I had not known about: stealing, name calling, hitting, looking up "bad" words. I was then able to talk individually to the students who were having these problems.

Making our list took half an hour. I asked the class if they wanted to continue working in groups or if they preferred to work individually. The looks on their faces said it all—they definitely wanted to continue in groups. I had a strong argument to stop: more things were not working than were. The students knew it. They also realized the seriousness of the problem.

Once again I turned to log writing. I asked each child to answer the question "What can I do as an individual to improve the working of my group?" Donna wrote, "I am going to work harder so it won't take so long to do it." Billy offered to pay attention to the other children and to work together with them. Todd agreed to stop laughing and fooling around. Katie suggested that she might only talk when she was sharing. Colby wanted to try to accomplish more, to use the time to work instead of talk. The children had committed themselves to improving the group situation.

By writing about the problem, discussing it, and taking responsibility for it, the children determined to improve the situation. This was all done through log writing. It took us two periods to resolve the problem, but it was a valuable lesson because the groups worked well from then on, and a tone was set for the rest of the year.

When the unit was completed and each child had made an alphabet book of glossary map terms, I asked them to take out their logs and respond to the prompt "What have you learned from this unit?"

Micah really liked working in groups because it was fun. He liked to do hard work and to look up things. Michelle learned about words she never had heard of—*plateau*, *tributary*, and *canyon*. Todd had learned how to use a dictionary better. He had enjoyed working in groups, and wrote, "I liked the ABC book a lot. I think I will enjoy social studies in the future!" And Donna summed up her experience well: "I have learned about lots of words, like quay—a landing place for ships. Or port—a place where boats anchor. I like learning new things in social studies. Some day you might be needing this stuff when you are an adult."

By reading their log entries—an easy way to check on student progress—I knew that my kids had enjoyed the unit and at the same time learned the content. My goal was accomplished. But perhaps most importantly, I knew I had laid the foundation for a year's worth of productive small-group work.

Fine-Tuning Methods

By teaching the same subject to two classes each day, I am able to fine-tune my methods. If something does not go well in the first class, I can change my strategy for the second class. Learning logs help me to adjust my teaching: they tell me specifically what worked and what didn't.

One day, during our Maine unit, we were discussing occupations unique to Maine people. The children wrote in their logs at the beginning of the class, listing as many occupations as they could think of. In the first class everyone listed at least one occupation, while two children listed two jobs, and two others came up with three. The class then watched a filmstrip that described over thirty-five occupations unique to Maine. Afterward, I asked the class to add to the lists in their logs. On average they added eight jobs.

I was concerned with this result, believing that they could have generated more data. So in the second class I started with the same log prompt, occupations of Maine people, but when I showed the filmstrip I highlighted the various occupations by stopping and discussing the filmstrip at appropriate times. I asked the children where a job might take place, what it would feel like to work at a particular job, if they had relatives or friends who held a certain job. This process took longer, but the results of the second log prompt showed a difference: an average of twelve occupations were added to the lists in their logs. Through discussion, they had absorbed more than the children who had just watched the film. I had learned another simple, effective teaching technique through the logs, and I continued to use this method throughout the year whenever I showed a filmstrip.

Logs also helped me to change my approach to reading aloud. I read *Deserts* by Elsa Posell, which is divided into five sections. In the first class, before I read each of the sections, I told the children what log prompts they would later be responding to. The kids were so concerned about what they would write that they had a hard time listening to the story. In the second class, I changed my strategy and told the kids that eventually they would be writing in their logs, but for now they should just sit back and listen to the story. This group was able to write many more facts about deserts in their logs than the first class.

After working for several weeks in small groups gathering all kinds of information on deserts, I assigned each group the task of coming up with captions for a big book on deserts. The four categories were deserts, desert animals, desert plants, and desert people. Once again I learned from their log entries and changed my lesson. In the first class, I asked each group to write three captions under each category. The groups had a difficult time doing this, and their captions were broad and general—a disappointing result after all the weeks they had spent on research. So in the next class, I asked each of the four groups to write as many captions as possible for just one category. The results were much richer and more detailed.

In our study of tropical forests, I again began the unit with a definition prompt: "What is a tropical forest?" In the first class of twelve children, eight kids knew and four did not. But in the second class of sixteen children, twelve kids did not know, while four did. Clearly, one class had a strong background in the subject, while the other would need more information. Their logs had shown me that I needed to teach them differently. With the first group I started the unit by discussing locations and reasons for tropical forests, but in the other class we needed to determine what made forests tropical and to explore their characteristics.

Because my students write regularly and informally in logs, I know when to present information differently or reteach a particular concept. Their immediate responses help me to determine the effectiveness of my lessons and give me insights into individual students' understandings, and misunderstandings, of social studies concepts.

Developing New Methods

Logs also help me to develop new ways of teaching and give me a chance to enhance my students' ways of learning. In the spring I read aloud *The Desert Is Theirs* by Byrd Baylor, a book written in poetry form about the relationship between the desert and its people. I wondered if the children would gather any information about deserts from this kind of book. They did. In their logs children wrote that the desert is a sharing place where people and animals are brothers who respect each other's ways. I had been doubtful about the knowledge they would gain from such an untraditional resource, but I thought I'd let the kids determine the book's usefulness. I learned to overcome my prejudices about the material and let my students benefit.

Last winter I was fortunate to have a British exchange student, Nicky Manning, help in my class once a week over a five-week period. Before Nicky came I wanted the children to be prepared with questions to ask her about herself, life in England, and the British Isles. In their logs the kids brainstormed individually and then in groups, writing down as many questions as they could think of. When Nicky arrived the children were ready to greet her. Michelle wanted to know if England had the same credit cards as the

United States. Sara asked what foods Nicky missed the most from home. Micah wanted to know about the queen, while Lucia was more interested in Diana and Charles. It proved to be a very interesting lesson. Instead of the awkward silence I could have expected in other years, we had more questions than she had time to answer. Best of all, the questions were sincere. Brainstorming questions also proved a good method to use prior to a field trip, as well as a visitor or guest speaker.

The learning log has become an integral part of my teaching. It is a simple technique that helps me to evaluate my teaching and my students' learning. Their logs tell me when to adjust strategies and when to totally change a lesson. Logs help me to figure out if a lesson has been successful, or if it has bombed. Logs provide me with the motivation to change, and they keep my enthusiasm for teaching high.

When school starts again in September, I will happily pass out a new set of spiral notebooks. I will also forgo the two-hour lecture, fill my kids in about how to sign up for the bathroom, and get on with the business of teaching and learning.

REFERENCES

Baylor, Byrd. 1975. *The Desert Is Theirs*. New York: Aladdin Books, Macmillan.
Posell, Elsa. 1982. *Deserts*. Chicago: Children's Press.
Stone, Lynn M. 1985. *Antarctica*. Chicago: Children's Press.

6

Knitting Writing:
The Double-Entry Journal

CHARLENE LOUGHLIN VAUGHAN

Teach me how to knit and I can, with time and practice, make a sweater. Teach a student how to hold a hammer, pound a nail, measure, and saw wood, and with time and practice the child can make a book rack or napkin holder. The double-entry journal, called DEJ here for short, serves as knitting needles or nails to help children connect new strands of learning to what they already know. Children go back and forth between the pages of the DEJ and make new meaning from its contents.

During the first week of school, I asked my students to set up double-entry journals for science and social studies from single subject spiral notebooks of approximately seventy to ninety pages. Drawing on Ann Berthoff (1981), I gave instructions that the page to the left of the wire binder was for drawings, notes, diagrams, observations, word clusters, mapping, and metaphors, while the adjacent page was reserved for "cooking" those ideas.

I assigned prompts, rather than asking students to develop their own subjects, because I wanted children to focus quickly on a narrowed topic. My questions for writers not only saved time but also allowed quick mental rehearsals. As the year progressed, third graders challenged my prompts: "Can I write about how I felt instead?" or "I'd rather tell it a different way." They became confident enough as writers to find their own focus for the right-hand page.

I tracked several of my students' science and social studies journals through the school year as they tested hypotheses, set goals, extended concepts to their own experiences, and applied and evaluated new information. I observed how my third graders benefited from a planning page as they used the left-hand side of the

DEJ as a place to culture ideas, draw, doodle, map, web, or outline. I found that they were better able to pay attention since their work-place was right in front of them: a fresh page to think alongside a page for data. I also noted how the DEJ often served as a basis for longer pieces that evolved in our class writing workshop.

In deciding what my third graders would react to in their DEJs, I considered Berthoff's premise: "Thinking begins with perception: all knowledge is mediated" (1987, p. 11). Often the double-entry journal's left-hand page provided a place to collect raw data follow-ing a minilesson, with the right-hand side reserved for reactions to the data. After I read aloud Jean Fritz's *Can't You Make Them Behave, King George?* during a unit on colonial life, children wrote down on the left-hand page what they remembered about the tyranny of King George III. On the adjacent page, following a minilesson on what constitutes a good book review, they used their notes to review Fritz's novel. I wrote with the children during the ten-minute re-action time, and then the group shared. Emily's review highlighted the detail "When George was little, he blushed a lot and his toes faced the wrong way." Jolieke thought Fritz portrayed George as an ogre: "King George was *mean*." Tina wrote, "He was a stubborn old king. He thought he ruled the world. When he gave them taxes on tea, they thought it had gone too far." I discovered that in their DEJ writing third graders were very casual in their use of pronouns, and that often a pronoun's antecedent was vague (or nonexistent). They wrote in a kind of shorthand, since the writing was directed toward the writer.

Bruner's belief that when people articulate connections, they learn and understand information better (1966) is exemplified by the writing found in DEJs. For a science lesson, my students drew leaves—simple or compound, alternate or opposite, smooth, toothed, or needlelike—in their DEJs on the data side. Then they lugged their DEJs outside on clipboards and adopted playground trees of their choice. They described and drew specific attributes of their trees on the right side of the journal. Maple, pine, oak, and birch were easily identified, but the ash tree sent the whole class to trade books, and finally to the tree identification books that I had found at an Audubon bookstore. Drawing trees in their DEJs was a chal-lenge to young artists, but some of the children quickly figured out how to do leaf and bark rubbings and willingly taught others in their groups, so that these techniques quickly spread from DEJ to DEJ. Figure 6–1 shows how Tina took notes in the form of captioned line drawings on the left-hand page and then applied these data to the tree she chose to learn more about.

In October, two visiting teachers from the University of South-ern Maine used the DEJ to facilitate an electricity unit with my class. The double-entry journal quickly showed them what the students had or had not learned. On an easel, Ms. Morse and Ms. Cox set

FIGURE 6–1 ● TINA'S NOTES ON TREES

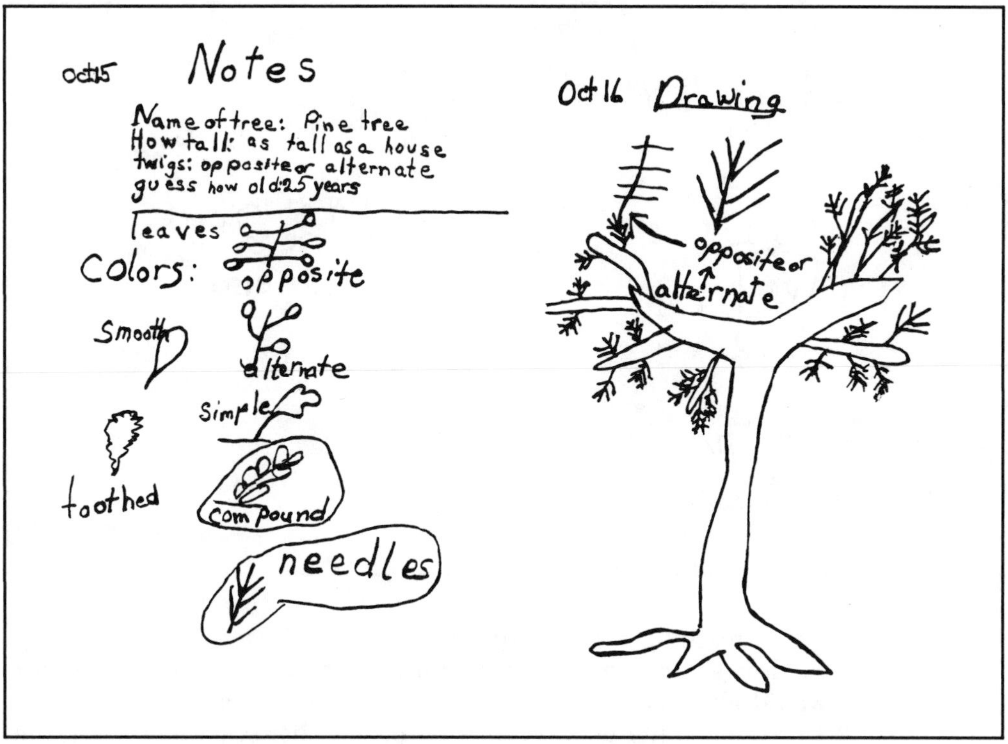

up a language experience chart book as a huge, spiral-bound DEJ and demonstrated how to use the left side for battery drawings and the right side for "What I learned." The children experimented with batteries, bulbs, wires, and various conductors and drew their observations whenever they discovered a circuit that lit up. They noted other students' discoveries of parallel circuits and included these in their DEJs as well. On the adjacent page they reacted to what they had learned (Figure 6–2). Then they tested hypotheses about conductors and insulators and tried to determine the actual path of electrical circuits. The electricity unit combined short lessons, hands-on participation, and DEJs to record and react to data. It resulted in high involvement, peer teaching, and new, lasting understanding.

I also used double-entry journals to make sure that my students knew how and when to use a particular research procedure. When I asked third graders, in a survey at the beginning of the year, if they were researchers, they responded with blank looks. Skills that they learned in conjunction with DEJs enabled my students, at the end of the year, to say yes, of course they were researchers.

FIGURE 6–2 ● EXPERIMENTS WITH BATTERIES

In teaching a science unit on animals, I used the DEJ to help children set their own research goals, form questions to which they would like answers, and take notes in answer to their questions. Tina defined her goals on the left page of her science DEJ. On the right page, she generated the questions that she was most interested in pursuing and that made her animal study a more personal inquiry.

GOALS	QUESTIONS
I will look up a mink. These are the things I will find out about my mammal:	1. What do you do in winter?
1. description	2. How do you live if you've been hurt?
2. habitat	
3. what it eats	
4. family	
5. enemies	
6. relatives	
7. other facts	

Then she read, absorbed my lessons about habitats, predators, and prey, and set out to find answers to her questions. She and other students also composed birth announcements for the animals that they had studied by using the facts they had gathered in their double-entry journals.

In conducting research in social studies, I taught the children how to interview people as sources of information. This skill carried over into their DEJs in a letter-writing project. On the left-hand page, third graders formulated questions to ask in letters to children in a school in England. On the right side they generated information to share about our school, city, and state. A visiting student teacher from King Alfred's College hand delivered the letters to England and brought us the responses when she visited us again during her spring break. Emily made these notes in preparing to correspond with her British pen pal, Elise:

QUESTIONS	FACTS ABOUT PORTLAND
1. Why do you wear uniforms?	1. Portland is close to the ocean.
2. Is a holiday like a vacation?	2. We are famous for blueberries.
3. Do you have a big room?	3. Portland is a fishing port.
4. Do you have a playground?	4. Our state bird is the chickadee.
5. Do you have a state bird?	5. Our state flower is the pine cone.

FACTS ABOUT REICHE

1. It is an open school.
2. It has a swimming pool.
3. We have a computer lab.

The double-entry journal was also a forum for learning how to play a locally marketed Bicentennial game that familiarized youngsters with a map of Portland and taught them how to compute prices and pay off IOUs. Noting Portland's boundaries on the left page and game rules on the right page helped the children learn both Portland geography and the game more quickly. Their writing showed the children what they didn't yet understand about the game and helped them clarify its rules in their own words. The DEJ also prompted a spin-off activity. The class made a slide show, in which each child illustrated one rule, to teach next year's class how to play the game. In fact, the DEJ often provided a launching pad for classroom activities.

Double-entry journals also served as holding tanks for data to use during the writing workshop. Children took information from their journal entries and created formal pieces of writing, a phenomenon that Ann Berthoff (1987) affirms: "Inventing topics, recognizing points of departure, choosing perspectives—all of that flows from learning to question" (16). For example, in one DEJ entry the class brainstormed a list of home fire hazards on a left-hand page. I gave a prompt for the right page: "Choose a fire hazard you know a lot about and briefly tell about it." Steven wrote about a stove fire. Then, during writing workshop, he made a "crankie," a TV-like scroll story in which he recounted, caption by caption, a story about the burns his little brother had suffered from scalding water. Steven connected his journal writing with a real experience and reported it. In contrast, Emily turned to fiction and became luncheon pals with Smokey the Bear during writing workshop. Starting with a list, both children carried concepts far beyond my narrow prompt.

At the end of a health unit on the human body, children wrote individual books as a way to evaluate the information they had learned. Throughout the unit, the DEJ had helped as a place to think about and understand course material. Referring to concepts developed in her DEJ (Figure 6–3), Jessica wrote a play, *The Complaining Feet*, in which she expounded on the patella, tibia, fibula, and phalanges, all specific vocabulary from her DEJ. Jolieke created a dialogue between different bones in a book called *The Bone Retirement Party*. At the beginning of her story, secretary Ms. Elise Cliff is the stage for a debate between her fingers, feet, back, and ear over whose bones have the hardest job: " 'Mine do,' said the fingers. 'I have to do typing all day.' 'I do,' said the back. 'I have to sit all day.' "

Coreena, who captured her new knowledge about bones in a

FIGURE 6–3   •   JESSICA'S BONE STORY

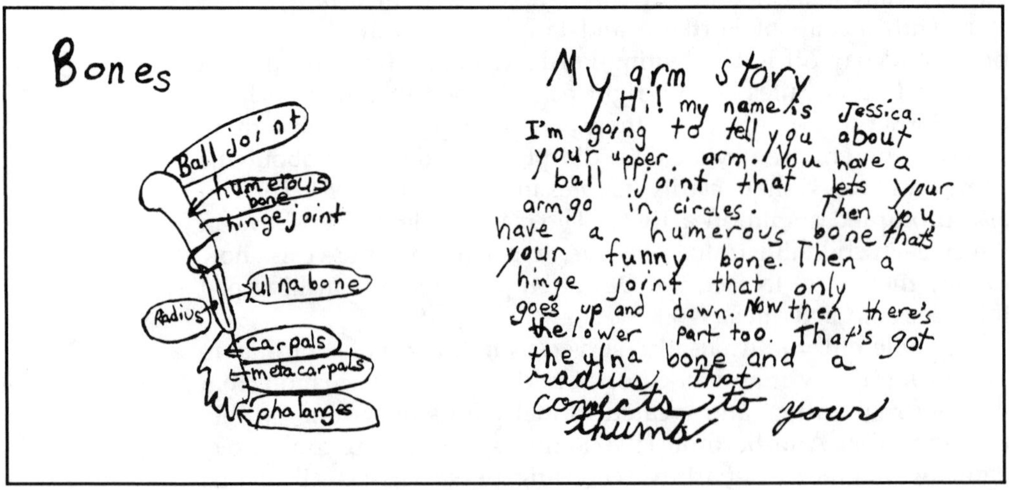

story about a teacher who taught bone facts to her students, frequently referred to her DEJ and pulled out information she wanted to use in her story. It amazed me how oblivious third graders were to the self-doubts that plague older writers. They wrote as experts on their subjects, and the seeds of their expertise germinated in double-entry journals.

Ultimately, double-entry journals are like the first stitches novices knit on large needles. In their DEJs, children knit new information and different perceptions. If they see a skipped stitch, they can retrace their steps and make a new pattern. And they can connect thought strands and weave words to construct their own meanings.

REFERENCES

Berthoff, Ann E. 1981. "A Curious Triangle and the Double-Entry Notebook: or, How Theory Can Help Us Teach Reading and Writing." In *The Making of Meaning: Metaphors, Models, and Maxims for Writing Teachers*. Portsmouth, NH: Boynton/Cook.

———. 1987. "Dialectical Notebooks and the Audit of Meaning." In *The Journal Book*, ed. Toby Fulwiler. Portsmouth, NH: Boynton/Cook.

Bruner, J.S. 1966. *Towards a Theory of Instruction*. Cambridge, MA: Belknap Press of Harvard University. Quoted in Toby Fulwiler, ed. 1987. *The Journal Book*. Portsmouth, NH: Boynton/Cook.

Fritz, Jean. 1977. *Can't You Make Them Behave, King George?* New York: Coward McCann.

7

In the Schema of Things

LAURA FARNSWORTH

The third-, fourth-, and fifth-grade students assigned to my special education program are in serious trouble academically. Even with modified curricula, tutorials, and pull-out programs, these children continue to be at risk in the regular classroom setting and have fallen two or more years behind their peers in all subjects. They enter my classroom discouraged and unhappy with themselves but still hoping for the magic cure for their learning problems. Of course, there is no magic cure—just hard work. My job is to make sure that the hard work makes sense.

From the first week of school, my special education students write. They write to find out what they know, to learn more, and to anchor concepts in tangible and memorable ways. In the beginning, they struggle even to respond to my prompts in their learning logs. Their thinking processes are so runaway and tangled, they find it difficult to think and write at the same time. They have difficulty supplying the names of common objects because they lack vocabulary, experience, or efficient ways to retrieve memories. Most have difficulty relating new information to old and selecting important details over unimportant ones. The connections between sound, symbol, and meaning in reading and writing elude them. It's as if they were being asked to think and communicate in a second language—except that they haven't learned their first.

My students need to be immersed in language—the language of instruction and literature as well as the give and take of conversation. They need to write, not only because our society demands literacy as a survival skill but also to help them think better. I have learned to make writing tasks an integral component of every part of the special education curriculum and to model my own thinking, language, and writing processes at every opportunity. With my help my students develop charts, diagrams, time lines, maps, topic posters, and quote books: modes of writing that allow them to collaborate with me and with each other instead of struggling in isolation. More importantly, these writing activities capture and focus my students' attention so that they can begin to process information efficiently and take a giant step toward solving their own problems as learners.

Mapping Schema

Rigidity of thinking is one of my students' areas of difficulty as learners. When I introduce a new topic for study, I start with a brainstorming session. Like an athletic warm-up, brainstorming seems to increase mental flexibility; it also involves my students in creating their own vocabulary for a particular topic.

To begin a unit about weather and other natural phenomena, my students brainstormed a list of weather words: *thunder*, *lightning*, *hail*, *rain*, *snow*, *sleet*, and *wind*. This list represented every single thing that my students, working together, could categorize as weather. To them, *weather* was synonymous with *storms*.

I wrote the word *weather* in the middle of a huge piece of paper on which our map diagram would be constructed. More than an outline, a map is a graphic representation of simple and complex relationships among subtopics. When lines are drawn to indicate relationships, the diagram resembles a road map. I inserted the heading *storms* and above it listed the vocabulary the children had brainstormed as subtopics. In successive lessons, three more categories—atmosphere, astronomical events, and geology—joined storms on the map (Figure 7–1).

I changed the color of my marker for each session. As children brainstormed vocabulary related to each category, they also decided where I should place elements, and why. When some members of the class were able to establish relationships between major and minor topics, other children began to see them, too.

After our initial session, I left the map on display so students could see it and suggest additional strands over the next days. At the conclusion of our unit, I asked the children if they had any questions about weather that they could use research to answer, and I listed their questions below the map:

- Why isn't it hotter up high than it is down below?
- Why does heat rise inside the house and when you're outside, it doesn't rise?
- Why is it hot in the house and when you go out it's cold?

FIGURE 7–1 • A MAP OF WEATHER AND NATURAL PHENOMENA

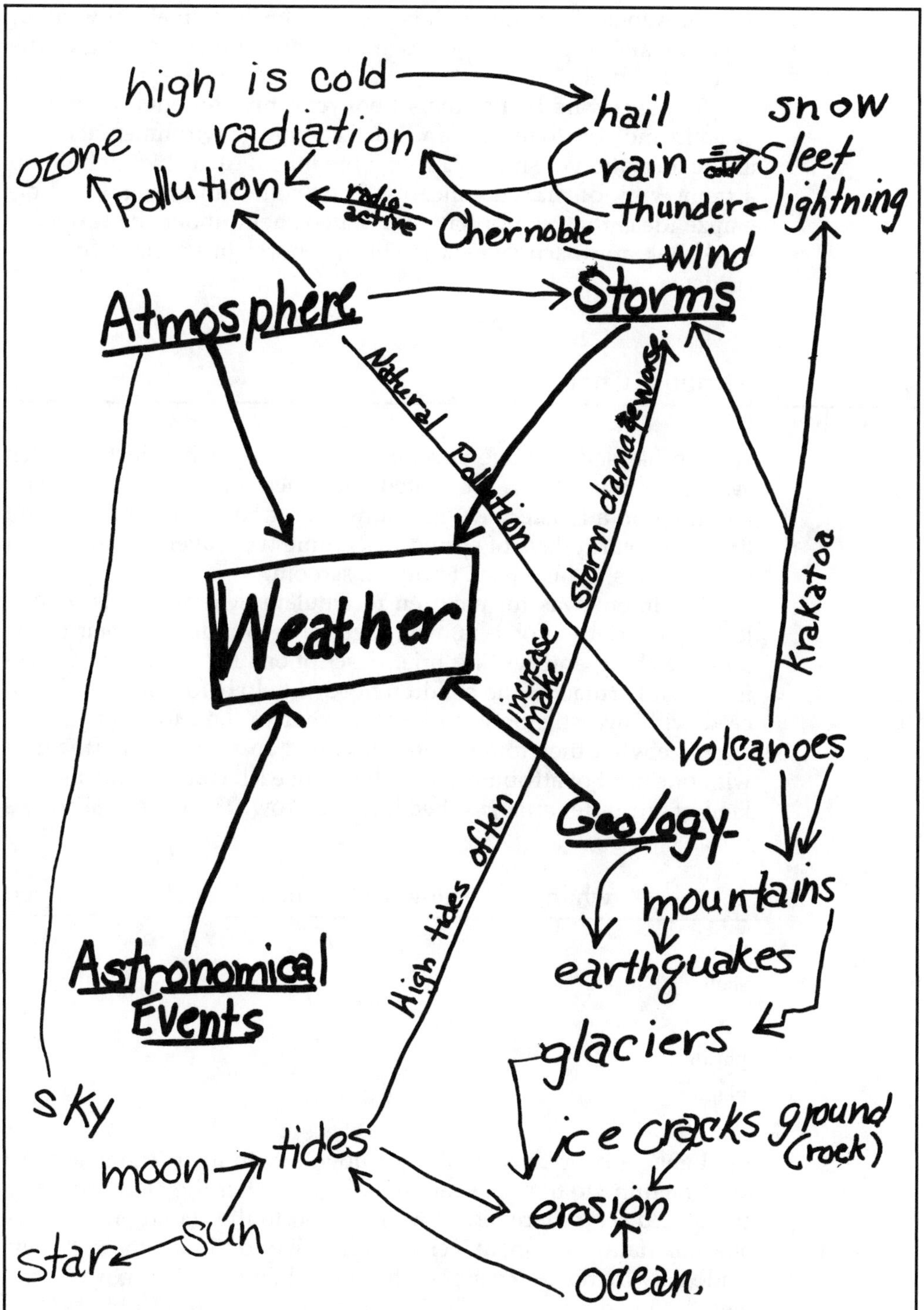

The questions showed students' new sophistication about weather concepts and kept the topic open after my formal teaching of the unit had ended.

By the second half of the school year, my students were interested in and able to understand such complex environmental issues as the formation of smog. Through the maps, each student built up a framework of related concepts. They could understand and organize ideas that would have frustrated them under the textbook/workbook approach, which is still the norm in special education curricula.

Attribute Charts

We are blessed to have several interesting beaches just minutes away from our school. We visited one beach three times: in the late fall, then on a blustery day in midwinter, and again on one of the first truly warm days of spring. Each time we scavenged the beach for materials to take back to our classroom.

My intent was for children to emulate field scientists by collecting a variety of objects, using references to identify their finds, and sketching and writing brief descriptions for a catalog of specimens and artifacts. The children needed help before we could proceed with investigations—to know what to look for and how to organize what they found—so I designed an attribute chart, a grid with one kind of attribute, *colors*, heading each column and another kind of attribute, *materials*, heading each row. The chart looked like this:

	white	yellow	orange	blue	green
rock					
shell					
glass					
plastic					
plant					

I gave a copy to each of my students with instructions to look for something to fit each space on the grid. After they had recorded and sorted their discoveries, we returned to the classroom to compile our data on a giant version of their individual charts. They made tally marks to register each find. When the tallying was completed, they discussed their collections, referred to the objects they had found by name, wrote descriptive statements, and raised questions:

- Did the periwinkle go out that little hole?
- How come there's so much plastic stuff at the beach?
- How did all that net get way up at the top of the beach?
- Why did the sea moss get white when it got dry?

Some queries were answered by children as soon as classmates posed them, and the others were left open for interested individuals to pursue before our next field trip to the beach.

Time Lines

I made our classroom time line nearly five feet long and vertical to fit a specific space. Most dates pertinent to my curriculum fall within the nineteenth and twentieth centuries, so I fixed the time line at between 1800 and 2000 A.D., printing the dates down the strip of paper in five-year increments. Throughout the year, whenever I read a reference that mentioned a date, my students were eager to stop me. I kept a supply of self-sticking note paper handy for student interruptions, and they gradually gained prowess at placing the notes at just the right point. Subsequent readings peppered our time line with yellow sheets. I also planned some lessons with the time line as the focus, to provide practice in time perspective. Here is a portion of our time line:

1880 Flatboatmen were the "truck drivers" of the Mississippi

Island of Krakatoa in Indian Ocean exploded 1883

1885 Susan B. Anthony was born

1890

1895 Last USA whooping crane nest 1896

1900 First sea mammal protection law—New Zealand

Pelorus Jack—1904

Knowledge of specific dates was not nearly so important to me or my students as the ability to sequence events. In addition to acquiring a perspective on history through the time line, my students read year notations, practiced focused listening, compared and contrasted, and learned such concepts as numerical progression, estimation, and interval. There wasn't a great deal of writing on the yellow slips, yet the time line provided significant evidence of children's thinking and learning.

Geographic Maps

Two big maps shared a bulletin board space in my classroom—one of the United States, the other a map of the world. On the world map we marked Maine to understand where we were and Jamaica to show Paul's place of birth, and we linked Cambodia, Thailand, and the Phillipines to show the migration of Jeffrey's family from the terror of Pol Pot's regime. We also marked locations relevant to our year-long study of conservation at every opportunity, in the same manner in which we had annotated our time line throughout the school year.

Kids cut up note paper to resemble sperm whales and stuck them to Japan and the Soviet Union to symbolize continued participation in a useless and barbaric industry. Other notes showed places where wetlands were being conserved, where the red wolf found sanctuary, and where tropical rain forests provided a unique habitat for endangered flora and fauna. A red-yarn equator stretched across South America, Africa, and Malaysia. Clear sheets of plastic in amoeboid shapes crowned the northern hemisphere to show how the ice caps once dominated these oceans and continents.

About once a month, I focused on one of the maps as a means of review. By the year's end the maps were adorned with diverse symbols, and my class had made astonishing gains in their knowledge of geography. They learned about places in the context of events and ideas, and I believe that this brief, frequent, contextual writing served them better than formal reports or textbook geography lessons ever could.

Topic Posters

I invented topic posters to help children when it came time to narrow topics for reports, stories, and projects in science and social studies, and I certainly encouraged my children to use the posters in that way. But as time passed it became apparent that topic posters were also wonderful vehicles for modeling the sort of writing I hoped to see in my students' learning logs.

Over the summer, I had developed thirty-two subtopics related to our major curriculum topic, conservation. I printed each subtopic at the top of a blank piece of paper and mounted the posters on a bulletin board. During the school year, the posters provided space for the children to dictate information that they had gleaned from all of the sources we had gathered relevant to conservation. As the children dictated, I wrote as fast as I could, stopping only to prompt or mediate a discussion. When there was a debate that resulted in addition or deletion, I inserted or crossed out just as if I were writing in my own learning log. I let uncertainties about spelling and misprints stand as written. Here are our contributions to the topic poster labeled *Water*:

1. A new machine to save our water from pollution.   Josh
2. In Cambodia, had lots of water—sun.   Jeffrey
3. There's salt water what fish live in.   Josh
4. In Cambodia, there are houses right in the water and people have to get into a boat before going to the store.   Chris
5. There's only one kind of water and it all connects to each other. Jeffrey
6. There's no different kinds of ocean, only one big one and it doesn't have a name.   Josh
7. In Cambodia you have to go a long way to get water for cleaning and drinking.   Jeffrey
8. There is water in the rainforest.   Sarah
9. Cutting down the rainforest may flood cities on coasts around the world.   Mrs. Farnsworth
10. Rain falls onto the ground, sinks into the ground and trees suck in the water through the roots.   Sarah
11. Water helps rocks grind together.   Josh
12. When rocks are in the water, the water makes the rocks smooth. Sarah
13. Water keeps animals alive so they won't die.   Chris
14. Water makes rocks get smaller and streams they bump up against other rocks and it chip them until they get smaller.   Josh
15. Whales and dolphins get help by water because water holds them up.   Elizabeth

I encouraged my students to borrow the posters, to use the data as a source for their research, and to add entries based on their readings. The posters served as our conservation textbook, but with several special differences: they were immediately accessible to students who had a difficult time using references to find information, and the language was students' own.

Quote Books

Field trips were important to my students' learning because they provided firsthand experience and provoked rich discussion. We took trips into the community, sampled it, and brought its offerings back to the classroom for further study. Then we extended the field trip experience by writing quote books: booklets of word posters, one page for each child in my room. The quotes record each child's strongest impressions of the field trip and reflect the sort of short, thoughtful writing found in guest books at historic sites and village churches.

We visited a Cerebral Palsy Center in our community so that my students could better understand the special needs of severely challenged people. These are excerpts from the quote book they authored to commemorate the visit and consolidate their new knowledge:

You shouldn't stare at handicapped people because it's not nice to stare.   GARY

Over at the Cerebral Palsy Center, there's lots of people in the lunch room eating. The handicapped people need a little help to eat.
                                                                ELIZABETH

Handicapped people have some problems. Some handicapped people can't drive cars, but some can.   JOSH

Some of the handicapped people need help with their manners because they have severe brain damage.   CHRIS

Don't help handicapped people too much because:

1. They might ask too often.
2. They might not learn how themselves.
3. They might think that they are not capable of doing it themselves.
                                                                SARAH

I made photocopies of each quote booklet. We made sure to send a copy of this one to the Center when we wrote and thanked them for letting us visit. I also sent copies to our school administration as a way of saying, "See what we've done with the field trip money you budgeted for our program."

The intrinsic value of quote books is the way that all of the individual impressions come together to create a lasting sense of the knowledge the children gained. Each quote is from the heart and reflects an individual child's depth of understanding and interest.

In Retrospect

Over the school year, my students began to understand the concepts comprising conservation and, through this central topic, increased their general knowledge of the world and their place in it. They began to read in order to learn and to integrate new knowledge with old. They recorded information and retrieved it. They began to question: This is how it is. Is this the way it should be?

In my experience, most self-contained special education curricula only scratch the surface of science and social studies concepts. This means that the students who need the most enrichment receive the least depth. This year, in addition to and because of the modes of writing I've described above, my students kept learning logs and published formal pieces of writing touching on the feeding behavior of moose, rain forest habitat and climate, the life cycle of frogs, and the formation of smog through inversion. They learned through writing, without a single ditto, skill and drill exercise, basal, textbook, or workbook. The challenge to me was to keep abreast of their new ideas and to develop appropriate ways to engage them as writers, not to provide the discipline often associated with special education classes.

In evaluating my students' progress, I found significant evidence of improved thinking, increased literary enjoyment, and more effective communication. I also discovered children who loved to write, viewed themselves as authors, and began to examine ideas and concepts as writers do—manipulating language and playing with genre to give voice to coherent thoughts. The powerful, daily writing experiences in which they engaged, in collaboration with me and others, taught my students what learners do.

8

Letters to a Math Teacher

ANNE THOMPSON

"Write in math class? Are you crazy?"

"You can't write in math! You add, subtract, multiply—stuff like that."

"How can we write about math?"

"What?!—You mean we're gonna keep journals in math, too?"

"What on earth will we write about?"

A chorus of moans and groans began our math class the day my fifth graders discovered the pile of new spiral notebooks in the math center. After the furor died down I began to talk with the students about when and why they write during their school day. They write in writing workshop on topics of their choice, for a range of audiences and in a variety of genres. They correspond about their reading in dialogue journals and keep learning logs in science and social studies, recording their observations, experiences, and the information they gather. They write and publish the findings of the research they conduct. In short, they write often, for a variety of purposes, and to good effect. Why not in math class, too?

On this October morning I asked them to open their new journals to the first page where, as usual, they entered the date and time. Then I directed them: "Think about and list many different, unusual ways that we might write in math." After a few minutes, the excitement of sharing responses began. I drew up a composite list as students read their ideas aloud:

MATH WRITING

Addition, subtraction, multiplication, division
Ways to improve math class

Math tricks and shortcuts
Rules for math games
Sorting activities
Word problems/story problems/problem books
Money problems
Talk to the teacher through letters
How I'm doing in math
Difficulties I'm having/what I can or can't do
How to solve problems
How I got the answer
Things I like and don't like in math
Multiplication table books
Some fun ideas to help people who are having trouble
Ways to teach math to other kids, to help them learn it
Mystery stories using problem solving clues

Their initial skepticism about math writing was swept away as the kids offered suggestions, affirmed each other's ideas, and spontaneously added to the list.

When I looked through the math journals that night, I found frequent variations on a request to "talk to the teacher through letters." The kids were already corresponding with me about their reading, so writing to me about their math and receiving my responses was a natural, comfortable option for math journals.

I decided that at least once a week I would provide ten minutes or so during math class when students might write a math letter to me in their journals. My only condition was that they must write about math and themselves as mathematicians, just as the topic of our reading correspondence revolved around books, authors, reading, and writing (Atwell 1987). Six weeks later I was overwhelmed by the diversity of content in the letters I had received.

My students have written wish lists, telling me what they want for materials in the math center and what they would like to do in class:

Dear Ms. Thompson,

I wish that we could use some more geoboards, play more games, and throw the books away. Have math first thing in the morning.

Ian

Dear Ms. Thompson,

I would like to work a lot with some other ways to do math problems and other ways to do math. I would also like to do some more with tangrams and beans and cups (tiles too) . . .

From,
Annika

Dear Ms. Thompson,

I like playing math games but I'd rather write in my journal on Fridays.

Your friend,
Chris

My students tell me candidly what they like about math and what they don't like. They look critically at the text, materials, and methods we use, and they let off steam.

Dear Ms. Thompson,

I wonder what kind of jerk prints these math books. They could at least make it easier to follow. I kept losing my place on the test.

Sincerely,
John

Dear Ms. Thompson,

I like geometry, but it's really a challenge. It's hard to do it right. Using math journals is a lot different than anything I've ever done in math before. I like it.
Some days I get really sick of math.

Your friend,
Chris R.

Dear Ms. Thompson,

I've been learning neat ways to multiply, add, and subtract. I'm not having any trouble in math at all. I think that the tangram and the sixteen piece triangles were a great idea, fun too. We didn't have a real sophisticated math teacher before. This is a real change.

Julie

Dear Ms. Thompson,

. . . I think we're going too fast on math all of a sudden. We're doing problems that are like 125×82. It's very confusing. I wouldn't be surprised if I got it wrong.

Chris L.

They tell me when they are confused or frustrated and ask for help when they need it. I wonder how many of their questions would have been lost in the hurly-burly of math class, if not for the opportunity to raise issues in their logs.

Dear Ms. Thompson,

I really don't understand math problems like 862×24. . . .

Dear Ms. Thompson,

Math is frustrating me. I hate it and get so frustrated because they take so long. I take five minutes on each question. . . .

Dear Ms. Thompson,

I need help with the three digits. I can't hold it in my mind that long. I have an auditory processing problem. It runs in the family. My sister has it, and my brother. So I need some help from you a lot.

Dear Ms. Thompson,

Geometry is confusing, especially if you're one number off. . . . Protractors are weird because I don't know which sets of numbers to use. Help!

Dear Ms. Thompson,

I am having a hard time figuring out how to use the protractor. I want you to help me be a little bit better on them so I won't be so confused, okay?

> Thanks,
> Annika

P.S. Because I was not here the first day they learned how to use one.

My students tell me their concerns about entering middle school next year—that they won't be ready, that I'm not assigning enough math homework. When I know what they're worried about, I can assuage their fears.

Dear Ms. Thompson,

. . . I also wish that you would give us more homework because next year we're not going to be ready with all the homework they'll give us. That is all.

> From,
> Chris B.

Dear Ms. Thompson,

What new things are we going to learn how to do this year? I like math and I think it is fun. My parents don't think we are really doing math. They are going to make me bring my math book home every day. I don't want to do math after school. What should I do?

> Your friend,
> Christopher R.

And in my favorite letters, fifth-grade mathematicians tell me, better than any score on any test, how they are doing in math. They chronicle their breakthroughs, mastery of new concepts, discoveries of tricks of the math trade, personal satisfaction and accomplishments, and genuine pleasure in mathematics.

Dear Ms. Thompson,

I never knew how fun and exiting geometry could be! I really like using a protractor. At first I was a little mixed up, but after some practice and you and my parents helping me, I was amazed at all the things you can do in geometry. I liked the spider web activity we did. I think it's fun to be able to use segments, rays, and angles and actually be able to make a spider web.

Emily

P. S. I miss division.
P. P. S. I don't like having to be so precise when I use a protractor. Oh, well.

Dear Ms. Thompson,

The dividing by two digit numbers is easier than two digit multiplication!

Sincerely,
John

Dear Ms. Thompson,

I was having trouble in long division but I think it's kind of easy now, and I had a little problem in geometry and using the protractor, but there's a secret and that is the 90° angle.

Stephen

Dear Ms. Thompson,

. . . Last year I had a lot of trouble with long division. But this year it seems clear as a bell.

Chris R.

Dear Ms. Thompson,

I *love* using protractors. Every night I look at the shadows on the wall or ceiling and think ". . . Is that above ninety or below? Yeah, that's below." I really *like* and *understand* using them.

I'm enjoying math this year. It's made me understand things real clearly, and if I don't understand I will go home and ask my mom or her boyfriend (who is a carpenter).

Well, I really don't have anything else to say.

Your math student,
Julie

When my students first began writing their weekly letters to me, I took the journals home that night and wrote brief words of encouragement in each journal in response. I also made notes of particular concerns that surfaced in the letters and addressed these in minilessons and in one-to-one conferences in which I answered specific questions and provided the advice and extra help that students had requested.

I think it is important to have a twenty-four-hour turnaround on dialogue journals, so that the kids will see that I am serious and take our correspondence seriously. But after a few Fridays' letters, I realized that I had too many journals coming to me at the same time. It was taking much longer than the hour or so I had set aside to answer the letters, and I knew I wasn't responding with enough detail or depth. So I took my concerns back to the kids.

"I know how you feel about writing all those letters," Marty commiserated. Chris B. and Karen suggested that they could stagger the dialogue journal entries. David thought each student should be assigned to write on a certain day, but John said they should be able to write whenever they wanted. After more discussion, group consensus was reached. I would require a minimum of one letter per week, which they could write whenever they needed or wanted to. This created another problem: how to provide time each day for those who wished to write. We decided to arrange our math class time so that during a ten-minute period each day kids could choose among a variety of math activities, including journal writing.

Since implementing these revisions, I usually have three or four math journals to respond to each night. My students have taken their responsibility seriously, writing out of their needs as mathematicians rather than because it is the assigned day and time to write a math letter to me. And I write what I feel are better letters. I have moved beyond neutral responses to correspondence in which I share my thoughts, feelings, and experiences. In my letters I reassure, teach, reteach, suggest, nudge, and question.

When Julie recently queried, "What's your favorite kind of math?" I wrote back:

> . . . The kind of math I practice most is subtraction. From one pay day to the next I subtract from the balance in my checkbook and the cash in my wallet each time I buy groceries or gas or pay a bill. It's not my *favorite* kind of math, however. I really love long division problems with two-digit divisors. In long division I practice a lot of math skills—division, multiplication, subtraction. I have to know about place value and make sure I keep my numbers lined up correctly. I like the way long division looks on the paper. I like to check my work by multiplying the quotient (my answer) times the divisor, adding in the remainder if there is one, to see if I get the larger number I started with. . . .

To Chris B., who wrote two sentences, one of which was an admission that he was hurrying to write something—*anything*—I responded:

> . . . Before you write to me again, think about math. Think about what we've been doing in math class. Think about other kinds of math you do. What's on your mind? What have you discovered or mastered? What's bugging you? Do you need anything explained? Do you want some extra help or practice? . . .

When Chris R. suggested that he wanted some new math games, I answered:

. . . If you have some good suggestions, I'd be willing to buy or make some. You might conduct a class poll to see what the kids would like, using this journal to record, tally, and report your findings. Could I get some ideas from you by Friday?

To Marty, who had been having a lot of difficulty with fractions, I wrote:

Dear Marty,

Today when I sat beside you in math class, I noticed you were having trouble following what we were doing with fractions. Let me try to re-explain.

Equivalent fractions name the same number:

$$\tfrac{1}{2} = \tfrac{2}{4} = \tfrac{3}{6} = \tfrac{4}{8} = \tfrac{5}{10} = \tfrac{6}{12} = \tfrac{7}{14}, \text{ etc.}$$

To make an equivalent fraction, multiply both the numerator (top number) and the denominator (bottom number) by the same number.

To reduce fractions to lower terms, divide both the numerator and the denominator by the same number:

$$\tfrac{3}{9} = \tfrac{1}{3} \; (\div \text{ by 3}).$$

Sometimes you will find that you can divide again:

$$\tfrac{12}{18} = \tfrac{6}{9} = \tfrac{2}{3} \; (\div \text{ by 2, then divide by 3}).$$

We'll spend some more time with this in class on Monday and throughout next week. I'll check in with you. If it still isn't making sense, let me know. Perhaps we can take some after-school time to work with manipulatives.

I know the importance of writing to develop thinking across the disciplines. We have just begun using math journals, and already I can see how they help my students to formulate questions and theories. In their letters students extend so-called critical thinking skills *in context* as they analyze, synthesize, and describe their reasoning. They explore, criticize, clarify, confirm, and question. And as their math teacher, I have a front row seat. I know what is on their minds because they make their thinking explicit in the pages of their logs. I become a wiser, better teacher.

I know that I want my kids to write in math class. Letter writing in our journals was a way to start. I have begun to use prompted log entries too, some of which are included in Appendix B. I see many possibilities for writing—and reading—in math: creating fiction and nonfiction books to tutor primary grade children, reading children's literature that illustrates math concepts, and having children write their own math literature in many genres.

I can't wait to see what they will do.

REFERENCE

Atwell, Nancie. 1987. *In the Middle: Writing, Reading, and Learning with Adolescents.* Portsmouth, NH: Boynton/Cook.

Reading
and
Writing

9

Writing Informally About Reading

JANINE PIERPONT

September 21

Dear Mrs. Pierpont,

I am reading a book called *The Iceberg Hermit*. It's about a man who lived on an iceberg. It's a good book.

from,
Marc

September 22

Dear Marc,

I'm glad you found a book you like. Who's the author? I'm curious—why do you like that book? Does it have lots of adventure?

Mrs. Pierpont

Dear Mrs. Pierpont,

The author is Arthur Roth. It's about a guy on a whaling ship that crashes into an iceberg and he lives on the iceberg. I don't know why I liked it. I just did.

from,
Marc

Marc's letters are typical of many that I received from fifth-grade readers at the beginning of the school year. Nancie Atwell's *In the Middle* (1987) was my inspiration to try dialogue journals with my students. Simply put, my students and I wrote letters back and forth to each other about the books we were reading. They used spiral-bound notebooks, wrote every week, and followed certain guidelines that I established the first week of school.

I decided to try dialogue journals, instead of assigning the traditional book report, because I wanted to hear my students' reactions to and feelings about the books they were reading, not read countless plot summaries. I encouraged them to be open and informal when they wrote to me in their journals. Then, instead of getting back a book report with a grade inscribed at the top, each student received a letter from me. When I wrote to them, I hoped that the interest I expressed in what they were reading would encourage them to want to read more.

My decision to assign dialogue journals also stemmed from a curiosity about how upper elementary students might write about literature. What would they have to say about books they were reading if they felt free to express themselves informally, without the constraints of book reports or other graded assignments? And what could I learn about how my fifth graders read and thought about literature from reading their letters?

In the beginning, I established a time when everyone would write in his or her journal, but as the weeks went by, more and more students began to take the initiative and write to me on their own. When the first few letters were brief and hardly did more than tell me title and author, I was not surprised. I expected that it would take my students some time to get to know and trust me. (Later in the year, two students told me that they kept expecting me to correct their letters for spelling and grammar.) Students who obviously loved to read soon began to write longer letters, but they still never ventured far from summarizing plot. A pattern began to appear in most of the dialogue journals. The letters that follow, from Wayne, Josh, and Tony, illustrate the pattern.

September 25

Dear Mrs. Pierpont,

I've been reading a book called *The Mystery of the Talking Skull*. It's by Robert Authur. I think it is a pretty good book. The three investigators are trying to find some hidden money.

Your student,
Wayne

October 10

Dear Mrs. Pierpont,

I'm reading *The Runaway's Diary*. It is about a girl who runs away. Her name is Cat Toven, and she has a dog named Mike with her. The book is what she is writing in her diary. I think it is a good book.

Yours truly,
Josh

October 20

Dear Mrs. Pierpont,

I'm just about to read *How to Eat Fried Worms.* The person who wrote the book is Thomas Rockwell. I didn't read it yet but it might be a good book.

Sincerely,
Tony

These boys certainly agreed on one thing. The "it's a really good book" refrain was one I heard over and over again that fall. When I wrote back to ask, "Why is it a good book?" their replies were similar to Marc's letter at the beginning of this chapter: "I don't know why I liked it. I just did."

I suspected that my students *did* understand why they enjoyed certain books. But they did not have much experience articulating their reactions to literature, other than providing answers to questions in their basal readers or writing book reports. They needed practice in talking and writing about literature, and they needed to gain confidence in themselves—to learn that their ideas and opinions mattered and were important. I decided I could help to instill that self-confidence in three ways. One was to respond to their letters in a positive, nonthreatening way, to encourage them to think and tell about what they thought—and to be patient. (I knew from Nancie Atwell that teachers who introduce dialogue journals to their reading students often expect letters of the caliber of those in *In the Middle* right from the start.) Secondly, I tried to create an atmosphere in my classroom that invited literary talk. To do that we needed some common ground. So my third idea was to add a new dimension to the dialogue journals by establishing, in addition, student literature logs, a technique I had read about in *The Journal Book* (Fulwiler 1987).

Literature Logs

The literature logs were separate, spiral-bound notebooks. In November, I began to assign open-ended prompts for my students to think and write about, questions that pertained to literature and reading. (Appendix B of this book lists many of the questions I set.) The prompts gave my students something specific to focus on and write about, as opposed to their letters, and usually evolved naturally from the five- to ten-minute minilesson that I taught at the beginning of each reading class. After I had assigned a prompt and students had had time to respond in their logs, we often gathered together for a share time to discuss their ideas.

For example, in one day's minilesson we discussed different

ways that authors end their stories. At the time, I was reading aloud *Where the Red Fern Grows* by Wilson Rawls. When I finished the minilesson on conclusions, I sent my students back to their seats with this prompt: "How do you think the story will end?" (We had only a few chapters left to read.) I was interested to see how they would predict the ending. Jon chose a happy ending. He wrote in his literature log:

> I hope the ending will be like they catch the ghost coon and they would get into catching bigger animals and they would win more cups and Billy would get more pups and Little Ann and Old Dan would teach the pups how to hunt and the four dogs would all go hunting, and the pups names would be Old Dan 2 and Little Ann 2.
>
> P.S. I didn't like it when the boy cut down the tree. It took too long.

Khatera was a bit more pragmatic, but still couldn't resist hoping for a happier ending.

> I think at the end the dogs will have to die sometime. If that is what happens, I wish I could change it to "and the dogs lived happily ever after."

Josh had finished the book on his own and knew how it ended. He wrote anyway, because he disagreed with Rawls's conclusion.

> The ending was really sad. I only read the end once. I think the dogs shouldn't have died. I don't think the end was good at all.

One of the most thought-provoking prompts turned out to be one I assigned the day I finished reading aloud *A Bridge to Terabithia* by Katherine Paterson. I asked students to write how they felt when one of the main characters, Leslie, died. This is Anna's response.

> Well, I knew she was going to die because a friend told me. But while I was reading it I thought of one of my friends dying. After you read the part about Leslie's death, I had to stop and think. I thought, what if I were Leslie's friend, how would I react? Then I wished that nothing like that would ever happen to me so I wouldn't have all that pain.

André never had much to say during our share times and kept his feelings to himself, so his entry was a strong expression of emotion for him.

> I knew Leslie was going to die. But when you read it I wasn't ready for you to say it. Then you said it and I felt a kind of weird feeling inside me. It stunned me when you said it because you said it fast. I felt sad.

I also assigned prompts that any reader could relate to in response to his or her self-selected book. After a minilesson about main characters I asked, "Who is the main character in your book? What does he/she discover? What is he/she like?" Heather wrote:

January 5

The main character in my book *Superfudge*, by Judy Blume, is Fudge. He's the main character because he is little and he doesn't know much and his mom is having a baby and he's really jealous. He discovers it's OK to have a baby.

Adam identified closely with the main character in his book:

The main character in my book, *Mostly Michael*, is Michael. He's just like me doing stupid things. I like him. I think he discovers that growing up isn't easy. I think he's right!

Angela wrote:

The main character in *Trumpet of the Swan* is Sam. He discovers a pair of Trumpeter swans and a female was in her nest laying eggs. Every night he writes in his diary and this time he wrote about the pair of swans. I think Sam was really lucky. I've never seen a swan.

Adam and Angela's letters are examples of how many students began, on their own, to make connections between books they were reading and their own experiences. The whole class was ready for the prompt "Can you make any connections between the book you are reading and your life?" Danny was painfully honest when he responded:

I'm reading *Runaway Ralph* by Beverly Cleary. Garf in *Runaway Ralph* is lonely, too.

Heather also could identify closely with what was happening in her book.

I read a book called *My Brother Stevie* and it's about a boy who is eight and a girl who is twelve. And she has to watch her brother, make sure he doesn't get in trouble, and my brother is eight and I am eleven and I have to watch over my brother. And make sure he doesn't get in trouble!

After I had assigned different kinds of prompts, I asked my students if they could generate their own. Although many of their questions were spin-offs of mine, none sounded like a basal reader question, and a few were original and interesting. Heather came up with this idea: "What do you think about the problems taking place in your book? How could they solve them?" Then she responded to her own question.

Well, when Harvey's dad ran over him he wasn't sure if the car was in reverse. The hospital thought that he was drunk. If he was, maybe he could get some help from a doctor and try and understand Harvey better.

Billy is a movie buff. He asked, "Do you think the book you are reading could be made into a movie? Explain." And he did.

I like the book *Where the Red Fern Grows* because it is exciting and funny, also because it has a good story and Rawls told it in a great way! I think the end is perfect for a movie because of the way the dogs die—Big Dan because he was helping Billy, and then Little Ann for love for the other dog, Big Dan.

A favorite prompt of mine, and one that the children used frequently when I asked them to come up with one on their own, was "Why did you choose the book you are reading?" Their answers generated some exciting discussions during our reading share time. Elena described why she chose her book, *Otherwise Known as Sheila the Great*:

The author of this story, Judy Blume, writes such interesting books, and this one is about a girl named Sheila and she hates a boy named Peter. Peter has a dog named Turtle and Sheila hates him too. She says that Turtle smells bad!

Then Elena dared to tell what she didn't like about the book:

This is a good book except for one thing. Sheila tells the story. I guess that's called the first person. When she talks about Sheila she doesn't say Sheila, she says "I". That's what I don't like. But I would recommend this book to you.

Anna chose her book, *Runaway to Freedom*, because

I like the adventure and the little tricks the slaves pull to lead the bloodhounds off track. I like the way everyone in the family cares for each other. They seem like a happy family. I like the way the author describes them and the people they meet. It sounds so real. Julilly seems like a really kind person. And I think she would be nice to hang around with.

Changes in the Dialogue Journals

As the year went on, the benefits of keeping literature logs extended into students' dialogue journals. We had continued to write letters back and forth, at the same time that students were responding in literature logs, and by midyear I began to receive letters in the dialogue journals that went beyond the familiar "it's a really good book" refrain. My hunch proved right. The combination of positive, supportive responses from me, the literary atmosphere created by my read-alouds and students' self-selected trade books, and the common ground we found in the pages of the literature logs gradually helped readers to initiate their own responses to literature. In the pages of their dialogue journals, students began to delve deeper into their thoughts and feelings as they read.

I think that the experience of responding to literary prompts in their logs played an important role in giving kids the perspective and vocabulary to go beyond plot and articulate a personal response to literature. The open-ended questions I asked suggested ways that they might respond on their own in their letters. Niki's letter, below, exemplifies the change. For months her correspondence with me had merely reiterated the plot of whatever book she was reading. Then, her letters began to show that she had internalized a new stance toward literature.

February 24

Dear Mrs. Pierpont,

I think the ending of *Where the Red Fern Grows* stinks because Old Dan risked his life for Billy and Old Dan dies but the worst part is Little Ann. I felt the same way as Billy. They have been together for so long that Little Ann dies of loneliness. It reminds me of my two pups I had. One is Coco and the male was Buddy. They always stuck together. One day we were going for a walk when they saw another dog and ran and a car tried to stop but it was too late. My best friends were gone. That is why I feel sorry for Billy in *Red Fern*.

Love,
Niki

Niki learned how to share her feelings about a book that she loved, and she was able to verbalize how closely she related to the main character, Billy.

Every one of my students showed this kind of growth. Jocelyn's letter to me about a book she was reading for social studies is another example of my fifth graders' new thoughtfulness as readers.

January 8

Dear Mrs. Pierpont,

I'm reading *Freedom Train* by Dorothy Sterling. It's sad in some parts, scary in some parts. It's scary that once *people* had *slaves*. I really like this book, I guess because it has feelings.

Your student,
Jocelyn

This letter from Karen is much more specific than those she had written earlier in the year; now, Karen responds to the author and the writing first, and plot second.

March 15

Dear Mrs. Pierpont,

My story is a Judy Blume book, *Superfudge*. I really love her books. I have almost all of them. The story is about a family and two boys —Peter is older and Fudge is the young boy. Peter hates Fudge! When he hears that his mother's having another baby he gets mad. He doesn't want his mom to have another baby because he thinks it's going to be another one like Fudge. I really like this book and all of Judy Blume's books because it's like she really knows all the types of writing that kids love. I like *Superfudge* a lot because it's so funny. It really seems like two children fighting. Judy Blume makes it real. It is a great book and I'll never get sick of it!

Sincerely yours,
Karen

Partners in Learning

After a few months of exchanging letters in dialogue journals and reading and discussing responses to prompts in literature logs, I realized that I was learning as much as my students. I began to get glimpses of how they read, why they chose particular books, why they favored some authors, and who or what influenced them in their selection of books.

For example, I found out that I had a great deal of influence over what they read. They loved the books that I read to them, and many would buy the book to read along with me or to read again on their own. Karen wrote, "Sometimes when I start a book it's boring. But then when you read stuff to us in class you make it interesting and I want to read it again." Susan wrote, "The teacher said the poems in *Ride a Purple Pelican* were really good so I read the book. The poems were weird but funny." During our reading workshops many students were curious to find out what I was reading, and invariably two or three would say, "Can I borrow that when you're done?"

I also learned that students read different books for different reasons, sometimes simultaneously. Wayne's letter is a case in point.

Dear Mrs. Pierpont,

I have been reading a book about skiing because I want to improve on my skiing. I have been reading *The Indian in the Cupboard* for fun.

It surprised me how many students were juggling two or three books at the same time. Most kids had a book that they reserved for in-school pleasure reading and another that they read for enjoyment at home. Some had even a third book, usually one that related to a school assignment.

Some teacher friends of mine expressed dismay at the thought of keeping track of twenty-four students' individualized reading, not to mention reading and responding to twenty-four literature logs and dialogue journals each week. I discovered that using journals in a reading program was neither complicated nor time-consuming. I began each reading workshop with a speedy status of the class conference (Atwell 1987) during which I ran down my class list, called each student's name, and jotted down titles of books that the kids were reading. After a while it became easy for me to remember who was reading what. Different students passed me their dialogue journals different days of the week, so I only had a few letters to answer each day. I assigned literature log entries at least a couple of times each week, usually at the beginning of the reading workshop and, since the reading workshop was a workshop for me too, I read them during that time, as they were passed in to me. I generally wrote a brief response but set aside for later those logs that needed a more thorough reply. Some days students held on to their literature logs after writing their responses and then shared them in a group meeting at the end of the workshop. I never responded, in either dialogue journals or literature logs, to grammar, spelling, or punctuation. I wanted to know what my students were thinking about books, not how well they could spell.

Informal writing about reading worked. Their dialogue journals became an effective way for my students and me to share our feelings and thoughts about the books we read. They were writing for me but without the constraints of a book report—they had a new kind of teacher audience for their writing. At the same time, literature logs served as a vehicle for kids to learn how to think and write about books, with the prompts suggesting a new stance toward literature. Next fall I will use both dialogue journals and literature logs right from the start. The more opportunities that students have to read and to write about books, the deeper their responses to literature will be, and the likelier the chance that we will become partners in learning.

REFERENCES

Arthur, Robert. 1969. *The Mystery of the Talking Skull.* New York: Random House.
Atwell, Nancie. 1987. *In the Middle: Writing, Reading, and Learning with Adolescents.* Portsmouth, NH: Boynton/Cook.
Banks, Lynne Reid. 1980. *The Indian in the Cupboard.* New York: Avon.
Blume, Judy. 1972. *Otherwise Known as Sheila the Great.* New York: Dell.
———. 1980. *Superfudge.* New York: Dell.
Cleary, Beverly. 1970. *Runaway Ralph.* New York: Morrow.
Clymer, Eleanor. 1967. *My Brother Stevie.* New York: Holt, Rinehart, and Winston.
Fulwiler, Toby, ed. 1987. *The Journal Book.* Portsmouth, NH: Boynton/Cook.
Harris, M. 1983. *The Runaway's Diary.* Archway.
London, Jack. 1905. *White Fang.* New York: Macmillan.
Paterson, Katherine. 1977. *A Bridge to Terabithia.* New York: Crowell.
Prelutsky, Jack. 1986. *Ride a Purple Pelican.* New York: Greenwillow.

Rawls, Wilson. 1961. *Where the Red Fern Grows*. New York: Bantam.

Rockwell, Thomas. 1973. *How to Eat Fried Worms*. New York: Watts.

Roth, Arthur. 1976. *The Iceberg Hermit*. New York: Scholastic.

Smith, Robert. 1987. *Mostly Michael*. New York: Dell.

Smucker, Barbara. 1977. *Runaway to Freedom*. New York: Harper & Row.

Sterling, Dorothy. 1987. *Freedom Train*. New York: Scholastic.

White, E. B. 1970. *The Trumpet of the Swan*. New York: Harper & Row.

10

Whether You Eat the Vegetables or Not

JO ANNE LEE

Literature became a separate subject for our school's fourth graders over sixteen years ago. From its birth the literature program was allowed to grow and change, but finally I found I could no longer stretch it to fit my new theories about how and why readers read. Driving into school on an August morning to begin preparing for the new year, I decided to abandon the literature program. I walked into my reading area, took every book off my shelves, and built a classroom library out of brick and mortar. (Actually I used old cinder blocks, and even older boards dragged from the greenhouse.) I was about to hand over literature to my fourth-grade readers.

Armed with new knowledge about reading workshop approaches (Atwell 1987), I decided to let my students be responsible for their own literature learning—both what and how they would learn—with me there as their guide. Even though I was uncertain about how it would work, I felt happier and more excited about a new school year than at any other time in my teaching.

The Literature Program Reborn

That fall I watched my students, helped them, learned from them, and confided in them. I felt more like a member of my class than its leader. Not teaching? I discovered that teaching is not always standing in front of the class. Teaching is allowing control to lie responsibly with others—even fourth graders.

Planning became both more interesting and less complicated

because the new format did not revolve around me. Most days, my daily planning would depend on what each child needed me for on that particular day. Each day our literature time followed a predictable pattern. Within that pattern, individuality in production, skill, effort, and motivation ran the gamut. But the pattern was clear. Literature was to be listened to, chosen and read, and written.

First, I allowed myself the pleasure of reading to the children. Whether *Tales of a Fourth Grade Nothing* or *The Indian in the Cupboard*, my students loved to listen to stories. For John, this was a time to "rest his brain," to become caught up in the rich goings-on in the lives of fictional characters.

The next feature of the new program was the first big change. Although my old literature program had initially allowed for the free selection of books, the free selection had dwindled to a "free" choice from a select few books to, finally, "Now we're going to read this book." It had seemed easier for me to take control of the choice.

Letting the children choose their books worked. There were always a few who, like David, found the book "awesome" one day and asked, "Can I change my book?" the next. But this was fine with me. I knew now that abandoning books is something that readers sometimes do.

The final change in the program was the most important. Upper elementary teachers traditionally have assigned book reports, and there is some justification for asking a child to account for reading and understanding a book. However, most book reports, similar to the conference sheets we used in our old literature program, do not allow students to write their own feelings in their own styles. Instead, readers parrot what they think the teacher wants. The writing is a test of the reading.

Now, as a teacher who wanted readers to accept responsibility for their own learning, I had the responsibility to show them new ways to develop and present what they were learning: hence, our literature projects. I had assigned projects before, always craft oriented, to be undertaken only after the conference sheets had been correctly filled out. For the children, this must have been like serving them dessert only after they had eaten all their vegetables. I hoped our new approach would more resemble a restaurant meal where dessert comes with the dinner—whether you eat your vegetables or not.

Literature Projects

After reading a book, each fourth grader consulted a list of options for project formats—as great a range of genres as I could come up with. In the beginning, children were hesitant about making choices and figuring out how to proceed once they had chosen. They immediately designated certain projects (calendars and filmstrips) as favorites, but by the second quarter the tide had changed toward other formats. Some options (alphabet books, poems, dioramas, time lines) developed slowly and then were chosen often. A select group of formats (mobiles, interviews, autobiographies, puzzles, newspaper front pages, and coloring books) remained popular throughout the school year.

I encouraged kids not to repeat a particular project within a grading period. Some students were willing to try many different types of genres. Others were careful to watch the different final products as they went public. And others tended to rely on a certain few formats. I was not concerned, since all of the options involved thinking, learning, and writing. I kept a running log of each child's completed projects. If I thought that a particular format would lend itself more appropriately to a book than the student's intended choice, I would confer with the reader and suggest a change. But since the children, as readers and writers, needed to learn how various genres worked, as well as feel a strong sense of personal involvement in the literature projects, I never allowed my suggestions to become assignments.

After completing their drafts of the written portion of their projects, students edited in conference with me as we readied the writing for publication. Depending on the child and the skills not evident in the draft, I would quickly teach a new skill or ask the child to self-edit mistakes. I circled all spelling errors, and students made their own corrections.

I provided as many final copy materials as I thought a child might need. Through our school's publishing center, the class was able to obtain supplies I couldn't offer in the classroom. From the beginning, I displayed all of the completed literature projects. Since our school is an open space and my classroom has only one wall, I showed projects anywhere space allowed—on tables and portable bulletin boards. Students' mobiles were hung from an egg crate configuration on the ceiling. It was important that children be able to find each project as it went up, to read it, acknowledge the writer, and use it as a model for future responses to literature. As it turned out, the open area in which I teach broadened the audience for students' work. All the teachers and children on Reiche's second floor could enjoy and learn from the fourth graders' projects. In addition, our school literary magazine included many of the pieces written in response to literature.

For too long in my classroom, literature, as a school subject, had provided only a slight variation on a typical reading program. It is true that the children and I read literature. However, the emphasis was on record-keeping and evaluation, not on literature—and certainly not on children's responses to literature. In this chapter I'll share examples of the formats for response that allowed my students to think about and engage with the literature they had chosen to read.

ALPHABET BOOKS

Alphabet books became a popular project after the children worked with this format in a social studies project. Through the letters of the alphabet, children showed their knowledge of characters and events in their books. Certain letters of the alphabet provoked a great search through the book to find an appropriate term, character, or event to use. ("X" usually marked the spot.) Through brainstorming, the kids and I arrived at several different formulas to use when writing alphabetical information, demonstrated below.

Megan produced *Andre's ABC's* about Maine's famous seal in the story by Lew Dietz.

A is for Andre the seal.
B is for the boat that Andre napped in.
C is for Carol who is one of the little girls.
D is for Dick, one of the pet squirrel's names.
E is for evenings when Andre curled up and went to sleep.
F is for the fish that Andre used to eat.
G is for gulls who used to stand on the wharf.

Vanessa's project drew on class discussions about the Newbery Medal after she read *The Cat Who Went to Heaven* by Elizabeth Coatsworth.

H is for Housekeeper—The housekeeper is the one who goes out to buy rice and teacakes.
I is for Imagine—Imagine is what the artist does when he paints.
J is for Japan—Japan is the country where the story took place.
K is for Kitchen—The kitchen is where the cat, the housekeeper, and the artist weep for joy.
L is for Lacquer—The artist's hair shone like lacquer when he went to pray.
M is for Master—Master is what the cat called the artist.
N is for Narcissus—Narcissus is the cat shining in the sun.
O is for Old Woman—Old Woman is the housekeeper of the artist.

Ben's alphabet book showed the essence of literature read from one's own interests and experiences. *The Snake That Went to School* may have been below his reading level, but it was fun and I did not tell him he could not read it. The impish smile on his face showed he relished the idea of conferring with a teacher petrified of snakes.

Q is for quiet. The room was very quiet when the snake was missing.

R is for rattlesnake. Hank's mom thought the snake he had was a rattlesnake.

S is for school. The snake was missing in the school.

T is for Timmy. Timmy is Hank's best friend at school.

U is for unusual. The class thought the snake was very unusual.

V is for voice. Hank's mother lost her voice when she saw the snake.

W is for West. West is Hank's teacher.

X is for X. X marks the spot where Hank found his snake.

Y is for yell. The teacher gave a shrieking yell when she saw Puffy.

Z is for zoo. Hank went to the zoo in case they captured his snake.

AUTOBIOGRAPHIES

The autobiography of a fictional character proved difficult at first for many of my students: it was easier said than done to put themselves in the position of a main character and use the pronoun *I*. Often, I would sit with students and ask them to practice talking as the character.

Martin's first draft about *Ramona Quimby, Age 8* was written third person: "Ramona is just starting third grade. She is looking forward to riding the bus." After a conference, Martin became Ramona:

> I am just starting third grade. I can't wait to ride the bus. Now that I'm eight I have to be more responsible. . . .

I found that children did not use this format to respond to biographies. Instead, they seemed to take pleasure in relating fun events first person, and chose this option more often with novels than with nonfiction. One day James and I sat and talked about the main character in *The Indian in the Cupboard*. First orally, and then in written form, Omri's life appeared before me:

> My name is Omri. I live in England with my parents and two brothers, Adiel and Gillon. My best friend's name is Patrick.
>
> I had a big surprise on my last birthday. Gillon gave me an old medicine chest he found in the alley. My mom gave me some keys, and one of them worked. When I locked the plastic Indian that Patrick had given me in the cabinet, I heard noises coming from it. It really scared me.
>
> The plastic Indian came alive in the box. I was even stabbed by him when I opened the door! I found that the Indian wasn't what I thought Indians were like, because I had only seen Indians on T.V. I had my own, real, live Indian. . . .

CALENDARS

We divided the calendar project into thirds. The top third was a drawing connected to the story. The middle third was a written explanation of the picture. The bottom third was the month, with its proper numbering. I was amazed by what many fourth graders did not understand about calendars. The children needed this format to go by.

Initially, students were intrigued by the calendar format. Although they were pleased with the final results, the time needed to complete this project proved a drawback. I think it would, however, be a good project for a class to work on when the curriculum calls for a project, such as on Martin Luther King's birthday in January—class reading, discussions, and a calendar project as a culmination.

DIORAMAS

I quickly realized that most of the children did not know what a diorama was. When it came to choosing formats they seemed to work under the precept "When in doubt . . . don't do it." When Leslie finally decided to construct a diorama, the class watched with anticipation. They followed her each day, checking her progress and asking about each new item that she brought into class. Finally, the completion day arrived, and her diorama went up on the board. The next day, I ventured over to a student studying the diorama.

"Nice project, isn't it."

"Awesome. . . . Can I do one?"

"Sure. Do you have a shoebox?"

"Yup! I'll bring it in tomorrow."

"Why don't you do your writing today?"

"Hunh?"

I pointed out the synopsis that Leslie had displayed beside her diorama. The student looked at the writing, read it, and looked at the diorama again—several times. With relief, I heard, "No sweat . . . I can do that."

FILMSTRIPS

I asked the children to plan a draft with fifteen frames, twelve of which were for retelling the story, with illustrations. The physical set-up of a filmstrip lent itself to recounting major ideas of the story in sequence.

Conor's filmstrip was a delight. His true love for cats came through in words and illustrations after his reading of *Hurray for Christopher! The Story of a Maine Coon Cat* by Virginia Langley. This is the text of his filmstrip.

1. Hurray for Christopher
   by Virginia Langley
   Script and Illustrations
   by Conor

2. Purr Productions   1988

3. Looking out on the bay, Christopher Cat is unhappy. His mother persuades him to go down to his friends.

4. The other kittens tell Christopher about their family stories and origins.

5. They tease Christopher because he doesn't know what kind of cat he is.

6. Unhappily, Christopher trudges home and cries over his milk, making it overflow.

7. Christopher's mother, seeing Christopher so unhappy, understands his problem, and tells him to go to his great-granduncle, Captain Tom.

8. Christopher takes heed of the advice and walks down to the fish pier where Captain Tom is sunning himself on some lobster traps.

9. Christopher is told of Norwegian Skagcats, who had tufted ears like Christopher's. He tells Christopher to come back with his friends.

10. The next day, Captain Tom tells the kittens about Marie Antoinette's Royal French cats that had bushy tails like Christopher's.

11. He goes on to tell of seafaring cats, who sailed around the world and settled down in Maine. They grew more paw fur to keep warm.

12. The kittens are puzzled. Captain Tom keeps answering "Maybe just a little bit" to the question of what kind of cat Christopher is.

13. Finally Captain Tom discloses a secret. Christopher is a Maine Coon cat, "a little of this and that around the world," and the only all-American cat.

14. The kittens cheer him. Christopher is happy.

15. The End.

INTERVIEWS

I set one guideline for interviews: show a story's character through the questions the interviewer asks and the ways the character answers each question. Some children opened themselves up to different types of interviews, one time a T.V. reporter, the next a talk show host. For most, however, the interviewer simply jumped in with a question.

In the best interviews, students added delightful expressions and feelings of their own, while still keeping the plot intact, as in Cindy's interview with Beatrice Quimby of *Henry and Beezus*.

INTERVIEWER: Beatrice, how do you like being in almost all of Beverly Cleary's books?

BEATRICE: You can call me Beezus. I like it fine. I feel honored and proud.

INTERVIEWER: Is it true that Henry hated girls?

BEEZUS: Still does. Except for me. He thinks girls who talk about sweet things like butterflies are nuisances.

INTERVIEWER: Why does he only like you?

BEEZUS: I like worms and icky stuff, like boys, I guess.

In another interview, Megan showed her understanding of Caleb, the main character in Tasha Tudor's *Corgiville Fair*:

INTERVIEWER: So Caleb, how do you feel about being the head of the story?

CALEB: I was honored and shocked because I never thought I would be so good in something.

Angela showed she understood her main character in this excerpt from her interview with Beverly Cleary's Socks:

SOCKS: Mr. and Mrs. Bricker sat down and let me see what it was.

INTERVIEWER: What was it?

SOCKS: A baby boy named Charles William.

INTERVIEWER: How was the house after the baby came?

SOCKS: I had no lap to sit on, the washer and dryer were banging, and lights went on and off in the middle of the night. But I got the baby's milk!

This particular project proved to be a favorite of mine as well as the children's. The format invited children to write in greater detail. During conferences students would sometimes see that an answer naturally developed into another question for the interviewer to pose. They did not become discouraged when I suggested the interview needed more, because they simply drafted the new questions and answers on another piece of paper. After editing, the writer and I would read through and act out the interview. It was a real pleasure when children became their characters.

MOBILES

The separate parts of the mobile made it easier for fourth graders who were not fluent readers or writers to select important parts of the book and then to write about these on one side and illustrate on the other. Damon had read *Just Plain Cat* by Nancy Robinson. Although he found reading difficult, he was able to follow and to show what happened in the story:

1. Chris wanted new clothes for the first day of school.

2. Chris and his mother went to a shop to get a kitten.

3. Chris's father was up all night making photographs.

4. Chris's cat got out of the room and was on the varnish.

5. Chris's cat chewed the film from the commercial.

This project proved to be the most fun to watch kids complete. I did require that the mobile balance when hung. Children used some ingenious methods to obtain that balance. They also enjoyed asking one of my colleagues to hang the mobiles; he didn't mind climbing on tables to reach the ceiling.

POETRY

As in the case of the alphabet books, poems appeared after a unit study in social studies during which children had written acrostics. They still tended to shy away from poetry in general but developed a fascination with the acrostic format. I do not think I convinced them that they were actually writing poetry. January had read *Nothing's Fair in Fifth Grade* by Barthe De Clements and developed what seemed to her to be the important ideas in the book as lines in her poem.

ELSIE EDWARDS
by January

Everybody laughed when she walked in the room.
Laughs it off.
She used to be fat, now skinny.
In fifth grade,
Even Jennifer likes her.

Everybody laughed when her skirt fell down.
Diane invited her to her party.
We had grape juice, Elsie had grapefruit.
At school, she was made fun of.
Remember, she's good in math.
Does most things she's told.
She can see her shoes!

One day Vanessa, who had also read *Socks*, came wandering up to me. "I want to write some poems. *Real* poetry," she clarified.

"Hummm. . . . Have you looked at your poetry file?" I asked. Borrowing an idea from Nancie Atwell (1987) I had asked each reader to keep a poetry file. I provide copies of poems several times a week, and individual readers then choose whether to keep, and file, a particular poem.

"Yeah, I've looked, but I just can't seem to begin," Vanessa responded.

"Okay. . . . Write a paragraph about your main character, about Socks, and I'll see you later."

Vanessa returned five minutes later. "My paragraph's done."

"Now, let's rewrite it as a poem," I suggested.

Vanessa and I sat with her paragraph, dividing it into lines. When she saw what I was doing, she took over. "Is it okay if I change your line breaks?" she asked. "They're not so good."

SOCKS

Socks was named
  for his white paws.
He lives with the Brickers
  in an
  old
  comfortable house.
He's quite an adventurer,
  even in a fight
  with a cat
  who ate *his* food!
                    VANESSA

Conclusions

After the initial confusion of beginning a new approach, I found
very little to be concerned about. I learned that children of this age
do need help judging time effectively, and that some will have to
establish deadlines for their reading and writing. For me, the lack
of class deadlines was an advantage. I could do different things
with different children. Although the conferences took a lot of time,
these one-to-one conversations gave me wonderful teaching and
learning moments with my kids.

Megan was reading *Corgiville Fair* by Tasha Tudor. She happily
showed me her book because I have two Welsh Corgi puppies.
When she finished, I brought out *Drawn from New England*, a book
about Tasha Tudor. I showed Megan the section written about Tasha
Tudor's love for Corgis and we had a great laugh when I read: "In
time Pups and Mr. B produced some beautiful offspring. The pret-
tiest and most winning of them all was Megan."

On another day I knew Christina had not read her book; the
information in her project told me. It was pointless to tell her to
read again a book she had already "read." Instead, I found another
book about the same topic, Daniel Boone, and in between other
children's conferences she read the first few pages with me. I suggested that she make a list of events that transpired in the biography. When I read her list I knew that Christina had read her new
book. In another conference we talked about a time line as an appropriate project. When her special project went up on the board,
there was a rush on biography reading and time lines.

My classroom area was very active during literature time. I
circulated among the children and kept track of each student's progress. Although I did keep written records, I found it easy to remember what each student was reading and working on. I simply
sat alongside a reader and began talking as though we were picking
up a conversation. Often I would see children get up and look
around for me. I was part of this class, not just in charge of it.

The projects became an integral part of fourth graders' literate lives. At the end of the school year, a few children would still consult the master list of project formats. Most often, children would be able to tell me what format they were going to use before finishing a book—the books themselves suggested the appropriate approach.

I observed children as they helped each other plan, edit, draw, and even offer a suggestion or two as to how to balance a mobile. They liked to read their books or projects in the library area—our classroom library that I had set up so many months before. And I liked to listen to children read literature—their own.

REFERENCES

Atwell, Nancie. 1987. *In the Middle: Writing, Reading, and Learning with Adolescents.* Portsmouth, NH: Boynton/Cook.

Banks, Lynne Reid. 1980. *The Indian in the Cupboard.* New York: Avon.

Blume, Judy. 1972. *Tales of a Fourth Grade Nothing.* New York: Dell.

Cleary, Beverly. 1952. *Henry and Beezus.* New York: Dell.

———. 1973. *Socks.* New York: Dell.

———. 1981. *Ramona Quimby, Age 8.* New York: Dell.

Coatsworth, Elizabeth. 1958. *The Cat Who Went to Heaven.* New York: Scholastic.

De Clements, Barthe. 1981. *Nothing's Fair in Fifth Grade.* New York: Scholastic.

Dietz, Lew. 1979. *The Story of André.* Camden, ME: Down East Books.

Langley, Virginia. 1986. *Hurray for Christopher! The Story of a Maine Coon Cat.* Portland, ME: Guy Gannett Publishing.

Moore, Lilian. 1985. *The Snake That Went to School.* New York: Scholastic.

Robinson, Nancy K. 1981. *Just Plain Cat.* New York: Scholastic.

Tudor, Bethany. 1979. *Drawn from New England: Tasha Tudor, A Portrait in Words and Pictures.* New York: Putnam.

Tudor, Tasha. 1971. *Corgiville Fair.* New York: Thomas Y. Crowell.

11

A Love of Books

DONNA MAXIM

"Wow! This room looks just like a library," Jason declared as he entered my classroom for the first time. "This is the best day of my life!" He made his way to the science books and informed me, "I'm going to be a doctor someday, you know."

I've always collected children's books, and since my first year of teaching, a library corner has been an essential part of my classroom. Now, however, that corner has grown to fill my entire room—not only because I have spent the last fourteen years collecting literature but also because my approach to teaching is so changed. The basal reader is long gone. Now, the third graders in my classroom use lots of good literature in every subject area—to read, to research, and to learn.

Each year before the start of school, I carefully choose and display books that will help students identify the different resource centers in my room. Jason had little trouble finding the science books along the large bench in the back of my room. National Geographic books adorned the shelves, and Ruth Heller's *Chickens Aren't the Only Ones*, *Animals Born Alive and Well*, and *Plants That Never Ever Bloom* were lined up underneath the bench. To these I added *The Magic School Bus: Journey to the Center of the Earth* and *At the Waterworks*, both by Joanna Cole, all to tempt my budding scientists.

I created a social studies center in another corner by hanging maps, displaying atlases, and arranging collections of such books as *A More Perfect Union: The Story of Our Constitution* by Betsy and Giulio Maestro, *Ben's Dream* by Chris Van Allsburg, and *Maps and Globes* by Jack Knowlton. *How Much Is a Million?* by David Schwartz and *Anno's Counting Book* identify the math center, and X. J. Kennedy's *Knock at a Star*, Lee Bennett Hopkins's *Click, Rumble, Roar*, and *Talking to the Sun*, edited by Kenneth Koch and Kate Farrell, announce the poetry area. I organize paperbacks as a resource center in two large bookcases in the center of the room. Each book's proper location is indicated by a colored tab on its spine: green for biographies, blue for fiction, red for animal stories, and so on. I also keep collections of books by author, theme, or series scattered about my room in plastic baskets. These are all arranged to tempt readers and encourage them to look inside.

These baskets, collections, and displays change as our curriculum evolves throughout the year. The resource centers remain in the same places, but the resources within change as we investigate new topics and pursue new interests. Resources come from my home library, students' homes, and the school and public libraries. Rae took it upon herself to count the books in my classroom last year, but gave up as she neared two thousand.

In this third-grade classroom, literature is a cornerstone of the entire curriculum. I provide thousands of good books so my students will love reading, but also so they will know, and love, what reading can do for them as students and as individuals. At the start of each school year I read aloud Peter Spier's *People* to teach about the uniqueness of human beings, and along the chalk tray I display books that portray unique characters: *Miss Rumphius* by Barbara Cooney, *Old Henry* by Stephen Gammell, and *Need a House, Call Ms. Mouse* by George Mendoza. Then we talk about our own special qualities as we discuss those of the characters.

When I plan any unit in science and social studies, I begin with children's literature. I cover the surface area of four clustered student desks, first pulling together and spreading out all of my relevant literature, then adding filmstrips, tapes, booklists, and so on. Then I sort through the resources, decide how I'll introduce them to my students, and plan activities for which children will need the materials. For the remainder of this chapter I'll illustrate how my children and I draw on literature to learn about and enjoy the third-grade curriculum.

Literature in Social Studies

When I began planning a study of Native Americans as a social studies unit, I collected all the literature on Native Americans that I could find. I decided to incorporate this theme in reading as well, with a study of myths and legends. I began my social studies class by assigning a focused log entry: "Things I already know about Native Americans." Reading class began with a read-aloud, *The*

Legend of the Bluebonnet by Tomie de Paola. Our discussion centered around Native Americans' belief in more than one god and the sacrifice that the girl made, in de Paola's book, to save her people. I sent the children off to read other myths and legends from our collection in the library corner and asked them to note any elements that we had discussed in *The Legend of the Bluebonnet* or any new aspects of myths and legends that they might discover through reading on their own. Then we shared. Joey said that his character also had to give up something, and two students echoed, "Mine too!" We listed these and other common elements on chart paper. We discovered new aspects as well—for example, a character who had superhuman powers. Then the students went off to read silently from books of their own choosing. I watched as five children took myths and legends with them.

That afternoon we again referred to *The Legend of the Bluebonnet* in investigating how the Native American culture was different from our own but shared similar basic needs: food, water, shelter, clothing. I had written across a large piece of chart paper "Not Everyone Celebrates Thanksgiving" and asked my students what they thought this might mean.

Mike blurted out, "You mean like Jehovah Witnesses don't celebrate holidays?"

"Could be," I replied. "What else?"

It was not until I read aloud Elizabeth George Speare's *The Sign of the Beaver* that they began to figure out to whom the slogan referred. In the novel, Attean, an Indian boy, showed Matt the beaver signs on the tree and explained why they could not hunt there and what was happening to their hunting grounds as white men moved in.

As we got further into our Native American studies, the students worked in small groups and chose a region of the United States to research: Northeast, Northwest, Desert, or Plains. We set up categories to help gather and share information: homes, clothing, food, lifestyles, and tribes. I read aloud nonfiction (Brandt's *Indian Homes* and Bains's *Indians of the West*) and poetry (Longfellow's *Hiawatha* and Jamake Highwater's *Moonsong Lullaby*) as well as Speare's historical novel *The Sign of the Beaver*. I also shared the work of a favorite illustrator, Paul Goble, in which he depicts the plains Indians, and Byrd Baylor's poetic descriptions of life in the deserts of the Southwest. Some literature we read during reading class, some in social studies.

As each small group organized itself, with the usual arguments about assigning categories for group members to research, we gathered all our resources and set up a chart on the back bulletin board. Here the groups shared their newfound knowledge as they acquired it, adding squares of paper to a grid representing the five categories and four regions.

After the students completed their research and entered their findings on the chart, each group planned, prepared, and set up a display that they shared with a second-grade class. During this process we often discussed how and where to get appropriate resources and materials. Finally, the students evaluated their own work, an essential part of the experience of learning. I asked them to grade their group's project and their own contribution and to describe any advice they would give to another third grader attempting a similar study. "Show as much as you can," Joey advised on his evaluation.

Throughout our study of Native Americans I continued to read aloud literature in both social studies and reading that would help students with their own research: *Annie and the Old One* by Miska Miles, *I'm in Charge of Celebrations* by Byrd Baylor, *The Legend of the Indian Paintbrush* by Tomie de Paola. I blended social studies and reading curricula, and I read aloud fiction, nonfiction, and poetry to reveal the great variety of resources available to students and to show the many options of genre they might choose for their written work. We also discussed how we read differently for different purposes and described the different strategies we use to read fiction or nonfiction. And we each discovered a favorite book. Rae, now a fourth grader, asked me on the first day of school this year, as we met in the hall, if I would please read aloud to my present third-grade class Jeanne Gardner's *Mary Jemison, Indian Captive*, a book she read independently during her research on Northeast Indians. "The information was very good," she said, "but the story was great."

Literature in Science

I use literature similarly during science units from the first week of school. Our first area of study is trees. In August I began collecting books on trees from home and from the school and public libraries, putting them together in a plastic basket so students would know where to go for resources and where to return them. As we observed, identified, and classified trees during science class, I read aloud books from the basket or showed and described books that would help students identify trees or extend their own knowledge.

I also read David McCord's poem "Everytime I Climb a Tree." We brainstormed in a learning log entry a list of reasons why we need trees, followed by a read-aloud of *The Giving Tree* by Shel Silverstein. Had we mentioned in our lists all the things that Silverstein's tree gave the boy? I also read aloud nonfiction books, such as *Trees* by Illa Podendorf. We compared two stories with the same title, *Once There Was a Tree* by Phyllis Busch and *Once There Was a Tree* by Natalia Romanova, one a fiction story and one nonfiction, discussing what we learned from each and comparing the authors' messages. I read a Karla Kuskin poem shaped like a tree, and then we tried some shape poems of our own. I read *The Life Cycle of the Oak Tree* by Paula Hogan, and we drew life cycles of the trees we had adopted in the school yard, which we observed through the four seasons. We sketched our adopted trees, made monthly written observations, and read books that gave us insights into how our trees live, why we need them, and why they need us. The tree books were constantly in and out of their basket. I often browsed through the collection, highlighting different titles through read-alouds or brief book talks, in order to expose children to the wealth of literary resources available to them. As students read silently during reading class or researched during science class, I watched them pick up more and more of the forest literature and was thrilled as children brought in books from home to add to this collection.

As I moved from the forest to the sea in our science curriculum, I once again invited my class to gather materials at the library, at home, and in the classroom that had to do with marine life. Our first read-aloud during this unit was *Where the Forest Meets the Sea* by Jeannie Baker. We discussed the author's concern for the disappearing rain forest and how that message might be important to us in rural Maine: one student raised the issue of condominium construction in Boothbay Harbor.

Next, the students chose their own ocean creatures to research. We explored additional kinds of resources, writing to the Bigelow Lab for materials and arranging for someone from the Department of Marine Resources to visit our classroom. I read aloud each day from *Sea Creatures Do Amazing Things* by Arthur Myers and *Newberry: The Life and Times of a Maine Clam* by Vincent Dethier, as the students began taking notes and researching their sea creatures. And I shared with my students examples of a variety of genres in which to write and report information, from acrostics about ocean animals to their own published books about sea creatures to dioramas that displayed the habitat of their creatures.

A Love of Books

I have included in this book, as Appendix C, a list of literature arranged by theme that might be used in content-area studies. These titles, collected with the help of many teachers, are not intended as an all-inclusive list. Each year I use the resources a little differently from the year before, and I keep the list on a computer disk, which I add to annually. I invite you to search out these titles, share your favorites, discard those you find inappropriate, and add your own discoveries.

Whenever I attend a professional conference, my students ask, first thing the next morning, about the new books they know I've bought. (We even have a basket labeled *New Books* in the center of our classroom.) Through daily read-alouds, book talks, displays, collections, and recommendations to individual children, I extend my love of books to my students. Literature representing a variety of genres—fiction, nonfiction, and poetry of every kind—introduces children to exciting language and important information about the world, their place in it and responsibility to it. No textbook series could ever accomplish all that.

But immersion in literature, by itself, is not enough. I also plan activities and schedule large blocks of time that allow my students to sample the literature that might answer their questions and help them raise new ones. The students discover, sort, compare, and connect facts, and plan and develop ways to share what they learn. I expect third-grade readers to take control of and responsibility for their learning, and independently, in small groups, or as a whole class, they talk, observe, experiment, and write to learn. But underlying all of the activity in my classroom in every subject area, first and foremost, is a love of books and an appreciation of the power of literature to shape and change the world.

REFERENCES

Anno, Mitsumasa. 1975. *Anno's Counting Book.* New York: Thomas Y. Crowell.

Bains, Rae. 1985. *Indians of the West.* Mahwah, NJ: Troll Associates.

Baker, Jeannie. 1987. *Where the Forest Meets the Sea.* Sydney, Australia: Julie MacRae Books.

Baylor, Byrd. 1986. *I'm in Charge of Celebrations.* New York: Charles Scribner's Sons.

Brandt, Keith. 1985. *Indian Homes.* Mahwah, NJ: Troll Associates.

Busch, Phyllis. 1968. *Once There Was a Tree: The Story of the Tree, a Changing Home for Plants and Animals.* New York: Scholastic.

Cole, Joanna. 1986. *The Magic School Bus: At the Waterworks.* New York: Scholastic.

———. 1986. *The Magic School Bus: Journey to the Center of the Earth.* New York: Scholastic.

Cooney, Barbara. 1982. *Miss Rumphius.* New York: Viking.

de Paola, Tomie. 1983. *The Legend of the Bluebonnet.* New York: G. P. Putnam's Sons.

———. 1988. *The Legend of the Indian Paintbrush.* New York: G. P. Putnam's Sons.

Dethler, Vincent. 1981. *Newberry: The Life and Times of a Maine Clam.* Camden, ME: Downeast Books.

Gammell, Stephen. 1987. *Old Henry.* New York: William Morrow.

Gardner, Jeanne. 1966. *Mary Jemison, Indian Captive.* New York: Scholastic.

Goble, Paul. 1980. *The Gift of the Sacred Dog.* Scarsdale, NY: Bradbury Press.

———. 1984. *Buffalo Woman.* New York: Aladdin Books.

———. 1988. *Iktomi and the Boulder.* New York: Orchard Books.

Heller, Ruth. 1981. *Chickens Aren't the Only Ones.* New York: Grosset and Dunlap.

————. 1982. *Animals Born Alive and Well.* New York: Grosset and Dunlap.

————. 1984. *Plants That Never Ever Bloom.* New York: Grosset and Dunlap.

Highwater, Jamake. 1981. *Moonsong Lullaby.* New York: Lothrop, Lee and Shepard.

Hogan, Paula. 1979. *The Life Cycle of the Oak Tree.* Milwaukee, WI: Raintree Children's Books.

Hopkins, Lee Bennett, ed. 1987. *Click, Rumble, Roar: Poems About Machines.* New York: Thomas Y. Crowell.

Kennedy, X. J. 1982. *Knock at a Star.* Boston: Little, Brown.

Knowlton, Jack. 1985. *Maps and Globes.* New York: Harper & Row.

Koch, Kenneth, and Kate Farrell, ed. 1985. *Talking to the Sun.* New York: Holt, Rinehart and Winston.

Kuskin, Karla. 1980. *Dogs and Dragons, Trees and Dreams.* New York: Harper & Row.

Longfellow, Henry Wadsworth. 1983. *Hiawatha.* Ill. by Susan Jeffers. New York: Dial Books.

Maestro, Betsy, and Giulio Maestro. 1987. *A More Perfect Union: The Story of Our Constitution.* New York: Lothrop, Lee and Shepard.

McCord, David. 1967. *Everytime I Climb a Tree.* Boston: Little Brown.

Mendoza, George. 1981. *Need a House, Call Ms. Mouse.* New York: Grosset and Dunlap.

Miles, Miska. 1971. *Annie and the Old One.* Boston: Atlantic Monthly Press Book, Little, Brown.

Myers, Arthur. 1981. *Sea Creatures Do Amazing Things.* New York: Random House.

Podendorf, Illa. 1982. *Trees: A New True Book.* Chicago: Children's Press.

Romanova, Natalia. 1985. *Once There Was a Tree.* New York: Dial Books.

Schwartz, David. 1985. *How Much Is a Million?* New York: Scholastic.

Silverstein, Shel. 1964. *The Giving Tree.* New York: Harper & Row.

Speare, Elizabeth George. 1983. *The Sign of the Beaver.* Boston: Houghton Mifflin.

Spier, Peter. 1980. *People.* Garden City, NY: Doubleday.

Van Allsburg, Chris. 1982. *Ben's Dream.* Boston: Houghton Mifflin.

Teaching
and
Learning

12

Showing the Way: Using Journal Writing to Develop Learning and Teaching Strategies

NANCY S. WHEELER

It was early January, and the long-awaited report lay on my desk. Since the first of October, when the battery of psychoeducational tests had been completed, Bill's fourth-grade teacher and I had looked for this report. Together we had worried about Bill's program and the slow progress he was making, particularly in reading.

Should I read it now?

No, better to save it until evening, when I would have time to savor its findings and recommendations, time to chart a new course.

Later, after dinner, I finally took up the report. I felt confident, secure in a belief that the consulting psychologist would provide the solutions to Bill's problems. But what was this? "Possible neurological dysfunction. . . . Bill appeared helpless . . . depressed. . . . A phonics approach to reading is recommended." And on it went, a maze of verbiage in which I struggled to find the Bill I knew.

Helpless? No. Depressed—possibly. Phonics approach? Didn't they know how much phonics instruction this boy had already had? I put down the report. I was no better off than before, and neither was Bill. What would I do now? The question hung heavy for the rest of the evening.

The next day it came to me: I could write my own report. I could write about Bill as I saw him, this lively child with a twinkle in his eye who knows everything about the Wright brothers, who loves informational texts, who can't wait to take books home to share with his family—books he desperately wants to read but can't. I could write about his family and how they love and care for Bill, and I could write about my concerns, concerns that were not ad-

129

dressed in the report. How would I teach Bill? I would continue as I had from the beginning. We would read and write together, each teaching the other, each getting on with the business of learning. The pages of my journal would become my report on this special child.

Bill

Bill had entered my life that fall as a fourth-grade student. He was identified as learning-disabled—and therefore eligible for the services provided through my resource room—because of his very slow progress in reading and writing, his hyperactive behavior, and his poor socialization skills. Although I had spent the fall wishing the report would arrive so that I might better plan Bill's program, I was fortunate that it was delayed so long. During that time my own picture of Bill had begun to emerge. I understood now that the examiners had not had my advantage of observing him on a daily basis. For example, they did not seem to be aware of the effects of Ritalin, or lack of it, on Bill's learning. In fact, there was no evidence that they knew that he was taking Ritalin—this powerful drug that produces a wide range of behaviors—at the time of the testing. Nor were they aware of Bill's incredible strengths. How could they know, as I did, how alert he was to the world around him? Here was a child who would pause in his work to wonder at the meanderings of a bug across my carpet or the antics of the crows outside my window. They would never know how much Bill hates the winter snows because they keep him from building secret hideouts on the shore near his home.

During that first fall I had also learned that Bill loved to tinker with spare automobile parts and that he was an expert at figuring out what was wrong when my pencil sharpener wouldn't work or the photocopier broke down. He loved a challenge such as cleaning our room, and he carefully planned all the steps necessary to do a thorough job. He took *everything* off the shelves before he dusted and washed them, something even the custodians didn't do.

It is a regrettable fact in the world of special education that a teacher's daily observations do not carry the same weight as psychoeducational evaluations. But because my observations of Bill seemed to be at odds with the examiners' in so many instances, I felt the time had come for me to trust my own instincts. It was time to develop a program for Bill that was in tune with his life, his personality, preferences, and achievements.

Bill came to me reading at about a first-grade level. He held "baby" books in high disdain, but he loved informational books, particularly those on topics dear to his heart: Halley's comet, the Wright brothers, and dinosaurs. He had had plenty of phonics instruction; in fact, he used phonics frequently as a means of attacking unfamiliar words. Phonics, I decided, wasn't the problem. The problem was that Bill couldn't make sense of the materials he really loved. Somehow I must create a reading program that tapped his wealth of interests.

Bill and I made little progress the first year I worked with him. Much of our time was taken up figuring out the best way to get his behavior under control. His self-confidence was at such a low ebb that he could barely bring himself to put his thoughts on paper. He much preferred to dictate stories to me, which I would write down and he would copy. He enjoyed doing research on the Wright brothers, and we spent a good deal of time in the library locating information. In the process I discovered that Bill could often read labels or phrases from entries in encyclopedias, so we photocopied those pages, and I highlighted the lines for Bill to reread.

It wasn't until the following year, in the fifth grade, that Bill and I began to make some real headway. He came to the resource room only for reading, writing, and spelling; his classroom teachers were able to modify their programs so that he could remain with the rest of his class for his other subjects. His behavior was now under better control, thanks to his parents, fourth-grade teacher, and pediatrician. Bill's reading skills still remained at a first-grade level, but I began the year hopeful that things could change, given the tremendous progress he had made in other areas of his life.

In October of the new school year, Bill expressed an interest in learning more about dinosaurs. This marked the beginning of an unforgettable learning experience for us both, an experience that involved journal writing.

Dinosaurs Show Us the Way

During the previous year I had incorporated academic journals into my teaching in a number of ways. I had assigned log entries as a way for children to respond to topics in social studies or reading, and I had also become a journal writer myself, using my log to reflect on my own teaching and my students' growth as learners.

Journal writing served several purposes for me. It allowed me to write along with my students in response to the prompts I developed for them, and it gave me insights into the demands of the tasks I set. If I had difficulty responding, and I sometimes did, then I could expect that my students might also. My journal also became a place to record the children's behavior as I watched them putting their own thoughts on paper. Sometimes their words seemed to flow, but more often than not they struggled, the words coming in fits and starts.

In my journal, unlike other areas of my work where the writing and reporting are cut-and-dried, I could vent my feelings, exult in my successes, and deplore my failures. Putting my thoughts down in writing showed me both where I stood on a particular teaching issue and where I had to go. The journal enabled me to learn from and with my students.

In response to Bill's interest in dinosaurs, I went to the library in search of books and other materials with which we could work. Dinosaurs are an excellent topic for someone with Bill's limited reading ability. I found wonderful resource materials written at a first- to second-grade reading level and numerous picture books that contain vast amounts of information about these fascinating creatures. With Bill's interest in the topic well established, my plan was to have him work with the materials in several ways. He would read to me or I would read to him. In addition, he was to keep a learning log in which he would respond to my carefully devised prompts.

In the library I had found an excellent filmstrip, *Dinosaurs*. As an introduction to the project on dinosaurs, Bill was to view the film and then respond in his journal to my question "What did you learn about dinosaurs from this filmstrip?" The following is an excerpt from my hastily recorded log entry of that morning:

> 9/23
> 10:32
>
> When I asked him to write what he had learned from the filmstrip he had just viewed, he replied, "I didn't learn anything, but I KNOW a lot about dinosaurs. Can I write what I know?"
> I replied, "Go ahead and write what you know."
> At first Bill wanted to get his books, so that he could check for spelling, but I told him just to go ahead and write or spell the best he could. Later, when he thought he had written all he knew, I told him to read it over while I finished my log entry. The result: he read his entry over twice and added information each time. My modeling helps!

Bill had written in his journal:

1 They are colde blooded
2 They did dring the ise adg.
3 They fownd a DINOSAUR egg with a Dinosaur in it.
4 Dinosaur Rewd the erth millonse of years Ago.
5 No Body RiLy NOWS wiy they did

Bill revealed some significant information about himself in my class that day. First, he believed he knew something about dinosaurs. This is hardly unusual for someone of his years. What was important was that he could affirm his knowledge from viewing the filmstrip and listening to the accompanying tape, thus boosting his self-esteem. Children who have difficulty reading often feel that they are dumb and do not know anything. Bill had proved otherwise to me and, more importantly, to himself.

I also learned that Bill was unsure of his knowledge. His question, "Can I write what I know?", and his desire to refer to his books made it clear that he needed assurances from me that his knowledge was worth recording and that I would accept it, no matter how it was worded or spelled. Learning disabled children, in particular, need to be reassured in this regard. Too often we teachers convey the impression that children must find and record the information the teacher is looking for, and that it must be in the correct form from the beginning. Bill's actions warned me that I had to continually show him through my own actions and writing that I valued his knowledge, however he chose to show it.

Finally, Bill showed me he was willing to read, even reread, and to revise his own writing in order to make sure it contained everything he wanted to say. My discovery of his willingness to revise came about only because I was still writing in my journal when he had finished, and he felt compelled to fill up the time. There was obviously no need for me to rush—my modeling showed Bill that writing takes time. In the future I would be sure to allow him the time to reread and revise his writing.

The next three days' entries in my journal demonstrate how both Bill and I approached journal writing and how our logs helped us as learners.

9/24
10:30

Today Bill and I looked through another book by Aliki, *Digging Up Dinosaurs*. This book, in addition to her *Wild and Woolly Mammoths*, is excellent for a youngster like Bill—full of factual information written at a level he can read and absorb.

In the process Bill became smitten with Ankylosaurus. He is now attempting to trace its picture into his journal. Pictures are so important to LD kids, long after the point when most children will give them up in favor of just writing. I can see this will be a longer process than I originally anticipated.

9/25
10:35

Bill continues to work on his journal entry about Ankylosaurus. First, he used a ruler to draw lines around his picture. Then he drew a box for his name (which he wrote with extreme care). He explained to me that he did this to provide space for his writing.

He asked if he should copy the information on A. out of the book. I replied, "Why don't you write what you already know?"

We had to stop, but he tells me he is planning to write about ALL the dinosaurs he knows.

9/29
10:32

Bill continues work on Ankylosaurus. He began by locating Ankylo-saurus in all of the books we have used. Smart idea, it seems to me —have all your references handy. Then he began writing.

I was called out of the room before he finished, but my volunteer reported that Bill told her he was planning to write about all the dinosaurs, taking them up in alphabetical order—A for Ankylosaurus, B for Brontosaurus, etc.

Bill managed to change my original plans for the project in a number of ways. Sometimes I provided the lead, as I did when we explored the books by Aliki. As often as not, however, Bill took the lead, as he did when he chose to investigate Ankylosaurus and then write about all the dinosaurs he knew. His decision to take them up in alphabetical order provided an overall structure for the project that guided me in planning daily activities.

In subsequent days Bill's journal entries became the first draft of a dinosaur alphabet book. Together we explored a wide variety of dinosaurs, and in the process I learned a great deal about his reading and writing skills, skills that standardized reading tests don't measure. In my journal I described how Bill was growing as a reader and writer, and I recorded the strategies he had developed to help him gather information.

9/30
10:35

"Indent," Bill remarked, as he started work. He then proceeded to rule out a space for his name and the name of the dinosaur— B R O N T O S A U R U S D. (D. for dinosaur, he told me).

10/1
9:30

Bill and I have just finished reading about Brontosaurus in preparation for his journal writing today. I had Bill do all the reading. (In the past we had shared this experience.) In so doing I noticed some very interesting coping mechanisms on his part. He knows how to use the table of contents and, because he can read "Brontosaurus," he was able to locate the chapter on that dinosaur. Once he found the pages, he scanned them, reading the words or phrases he was familiar with. Thus he was able to gather several facts that interested him, which he ultimately incorporated into his journal entry.

10/2
10:20

Bill read the page from the book almost unaided. I sense he is on the verge. The words he figured out today really speak to his ability to use context. He slipped on "fat" and "run" but got "enemies" and "close by."

10/15
10:33

I notice that more and more he is using print to gather information. For example, he has long been interested in a horse-like creature that existed around the time of the dinosaurs. In one book it appeared to be known as the Beast of Baluchistan, in another, Baluchitherium. He was able to pick up the differences in the words.

10/16
10:27

I am elated! Today Bill read about Diplodocus in four sources—books we both have gathered from home and school. His reading went very smoothly. I hardly had to supply any words. I think this happened because of several things: 1.) He is now familiar enough with the material to be able to predict with a fair amount of certainty and 2.) He is really "catching on" to the business of reading. As he read each of the sources, he compared the information, remarking on any similarities and differences or even "lack of information" (his words).

10/20
10:29

Although I can't say for sure, I believe he reread the information on his own before he wrote. He remarked that there was very little information on Edaphosaurus, and I know I hadn't read about this dinosaur with him.

Observing him slightly later: I am assured that Bill is reading parts of this book on his own to gather the information he wants. I just heard him reading the text to himself.

When I reread my journal entries one evening in November, it was clear to me that Bill had acquired a number of skills. He could use a variety of resources at his level, and even beyond, to gather information, and he was able to read the information to himself. Further, in developing means to cope with the various texts, he had acquired some excellent study skills. He could locate a source in a table of contents or an index, and he could skim and scan a page of print to find pertinent information. He could also read critically, as demonstrated by his remarks about similarities, differences, and insufficient information. Despite his desire to have his sources close at hand when he was recording in his journal, what he wrote there was entirely his own work. He used sources largely as spelling references, not as information to be paraphrased or plagiarized. He always had a clear idea of the kind of information he was looking for, and once he found it, the act of recording it in the journal in his own words somehow made it a part of him.

The act of recording Bill's activity in my journal, in my own words, was also crucial. Because I was writing down what he did, I could reflect on his behavior and theorize about why he did what he did. Some days Bill was restless when he came to class, and it seemed to me that we made little progress. But my log revealed the slow growth that is often obscured by the dailiness of teaching and allowed me to speculate about the behaviors I captured. Following is a typical entry from one of those times:

1/12
10:16

Bill talks his way through problems in his writing. For example, I heard him say, "Better use WAS instead of IS because there are no more dinosaurs."
I wonder if talking his way through a problem, especially talking out loud or under his breath, isn't one way Bill copes with some of his reading and writing difficulties—a sort of prewriting or prereading activity.

Bill finished his alphabet book in January. His twenty-one-page journal represented his first draft. He used a word processor for subsequent drafts, penning his revisions on the printouts and transferring them later to the computer; it was easier for him to revise and edit in this fashion. I took charge of editing, typing, and, ultimately, publishing the final copy. Figure 12–1 shows the first four pages of Bill's published book.

Conclusions

We were now roughly halfway through the school year, a good time for me to take stock of what Bill and I had gained from our experience with *Dinos Sauros*, Latin for "Terrible Lizards" and the title he had chosen for his book. As a special education teacher, I had developed goals for Bill based on his individual education plan, which included the following:

1. To improve Bill's reading ability to a second-grade reading level.
2. To develop the reading skills necessary for Bill to become an efficient reader of informational material at his level.
3. To develop his ability to write about what he knew or had learned about a given topic.
4. To improve his confidence in his reading and writing abilities.

To some extent I had met all of my goals. Testing conducted shortly before Christmas revealed that Bill could now read material at a second-grade level. In fact, he had made one half-year's growth since the beginning of the school year, his greatest gain ever. And although this could not be tested by conventional means, I had observed Bill repeatedly locate and evaluate information he wanted in a variety of sources. He may have struggled to read it, but he

FIGURE 12–1 ● PAGES 1–4 OF BILL'S BOOK ABOUT DINOSAURS

Ankylosaurus

Ankylosaurus was a plant-eater.
He lived on land and laid eggs.
He had a very hard back.

Brachiosaurus

Brachiosaurus was the biggest dinosaur. He
was a plant-eater and spent most of his life
in the water. He felt safe in the water.
His enemies couldn't get him. He was too
fat to run.

Corythosaurus

Corythosaurus was a plant-eater.
He could swim very well. He was
found in Canada. He had a helmet.

Diplodocus

Diplodocus was the longest dinosaur.
He was ninety feet long. He was a
plant-eater, and he had a small brain.
He had dull teeth. He was as long as
three buses.

could readily utilize the information in his journal and later in his book. Further, his teachers reported that he was using these skills in his other subjects as well.

It is difficult to say who gained the most from our adventure with journal writing, Bill or I. I had only recently begun to use a journal as a means of discovering what I knew or needed to know. Responding to questions or situations in my journal afforded me an opportunity to reflect on my knowledge, thus pointing the way to future inquiry. As I recorded Bill's progress in gathering information about dinosaurs, I reflected on my own learning and teaching. How had I grown?

I had not stated personal goals, as I had done for Bill, but had I, they might have read as follows:

1. To improve my teaching skills.
2. To discover innovative ways of helping Bill grow as a learner.

Keeping a journal of my teaching and Bill's learning allowed me to meet these goals. By rereading the log entries that recorded his behavior, I could reflect on the ways he learned and develop lessons that really tapped his strengths and interests. My log entries also provided a record, unlike any rank book, test, or psychoeducational report, that showed his growth over a period of time, thus providing a true measure of what he could do. The teaching strategies I developed were innovative in that they were unique to Bill and his situation at a particular point in time. They probably were not novel methods, but they were my own, developed through tentative and unpolished writing that served as a reflection of my knowledge.

Bill and I still have a long way to go. What I was not able to accomplish with the dinosaur project will become goals for our next undertaking. The way is rarely clear to me at a point like this, but one thing is clear: we will work and write together, Bill and I, and Bill and my journal will show me the way.

REFERENCES

Aliki. 1977. *Wild and Woolly Mammoths*. New York: Thomas Y. Crowell.
———. 1981. *Digging Up Dinosaurs*. New York: Thomas Y. Crowell.
National Geographic Society. 1978. *Dinosaurs* (filmstrip and cassette). Washington, DC: National Geographic Educational Services.

13

A Puffin Is a Bird, I Think

JO HANEY

Four junior high students armed with masking tape and a roll of brown paper descended upon the tranquillity of our hallway. They were here on a mission, at my request.

The third graders' curiosity was piqued as the older kids taped wads of brown paper, then sheets of it, to the wall outside our door. Suddenly everyone needed a drink of water, and out to the water fountain they went, one by one, trying to discover the answer to the riddle of the brown paper. They learned that we were about to begin a special unit of study. The big kids had volunteered to transform our room to represent the rugged island that is summer home to the Atlantic puffin.

The idea for a third-grade puffin study came to me when I attended National Audubon's Ecology Camp in Maine. I was impressed by the efforts of Audubon biologists to re-establish the puffin colony on Eastern Egg Rock, a small island six miles offshore, and I saw a way I might expose my students to an aspect of their own environment. A puffin project could cover a scientific review of our near environment and also delve into the impact of people on our surroundings. Puffins seemed a natural vehicle for study since we live on the coast of Maine, only a few miles from where the seabirds once lived and are now living again. I knew that most of my students would have been exposed to the puffin souvenirs available in local stores, but I wondered if they really knew what a puffin is and why it is so special.

There are no packaged programs for conducting a study of puffins with third graders—at least none that I'm aware of. And even if some publisher did offer a ready-made puffin unit, I'm pretty certain that I would pass it by. The Bread Loaf project had opened a door for me. I'd joined because I wanted to explore new approaches to writing in the content areas, and during the first year my initial skepticism about third graders as researchers dissolved as I watched them devour opportunities to conduct research. I showed them how and they, in turn, showed me what was possible when an individual was set free to intensively pursue a topic of personal interest. My interest in the puffin recolonization effort, coupled with my new confidence as a researcher, writer, and designer of curriculum, was the impetus for creating a new unit of study for my kids. I didn't need a textbook, skills masters, a teacher's manual, or someone else's lesson plans. I did have to ensure that sufficient resources existed to bring the project to life for my students—trade books, films, local experts, and opportunities for firsthand experience. I had to allow myself plenty of lead time, to gather resources and to develop and revise a plan. And I had to write: to use my own learning log to help me organize, analyze, and reassure myself about the new unit.

8 AUGUST

I'm interested in using puffins as a focus for study, but what resources are there? I know of a few magazine articles and one film. Can I base a unit of study for third graders on that? It doesn't seem possible that I'll locate what I need, but I won't know what's possible if I don't start looking.

The Audubon Camp store was my first stop. I found two children's books about puffins. Searching a local bookstore and the book section at L. L. Bean, I turned up three additional volumes. I even had the good fortune to stumble across a book in our school library. One day as I was waiting for the laminating press to heat, I casually scanned the spines of nearby books until a title caught my attention. It was a puffin book by Frank and Ada Graham that I had not seen before. With six trade books to read and lend to students, as well as access to the Audubon film, I felt that I had the core resources for a puffin study.

10 SEPTEMBER

I know that photographs of puffins appear on postcards. Puffin illustrations appear on everything from t-shirts to "No Puffin" signs. My next task will be to be selective. I want materials that will enhance the kids' understanding. This means that I'll have to weed out all the cute touristy items, like puffin toilet plungers. I want my students to appreciate puffins, not their exploitation.

As excerpts from my log show, I began planning the unit months before I presented it to the class in the spring. In addition to allowing myself time to develop a plan and establish resources, I also felt that the study should coincide with the puffin's biological rhythms. Puffins spend eight months of the year at sea and come home to our waters in the spring to mate. Their return to the local habitat, as well as the timing of any field trip to Eastern Egg Rock, would be crucial to the success of the unit. My planning log helped me to keep track of my thoughts throughout the school year.

11 NOVEMBER

I've been pondering the timing of this study off and on for weeks now—months actually. I want to start soon enough that students have time to write to organizations and individuals for specific information. Yet I need to be careful that I don't begin too early. Maybe I shouldn't worry about starting too soon, but look at the study as an ongoing unit begun under my impetus but carried on by the students through their input. Then I need to help guide their interest and provide the appropriate resources. Timing is the key.

I did a lot of thinking—about puffins, materials to use, possible resources, activities. I made rough lists of my ideas:

16 NOVEMBER

Set the stage—classroom door as a puffin burrow
  First log prompt—What is a puffin?
  Read Aloud: *Wee Peter Puffin*, Jane Weinberger
    Puffin, Bird of the Open Seas, Lynne Martin
    Puffin, Deborah King
    Puffins Come Back!, Judi Friedman
    Miracle at Egg Rock, Doris Gove
  Film: "Project Puffin"—Call Mid-Coast Audubon
  Puffin skin—borrow from Mid-Coast Audubon
  Write Steve Kress—a few students
  Adopt puffin chick: $$$$$$
    —bake sale?
    —raffle?
  Nautical charts—locate nesting sites
  Students' research—during writing workshop
  Puffin banners
  Field trip to Eastern Egg Rock—a must

Eventually I incorporated some of these ideas as part of the study. The list allowed me to assess whether I had adequate materials for my students. I also made separate planning pages in the back of my log for each feature of the project: people to contact, books, possible log prompts, fund-raising ideas for puffin adoption, films, anticipated costs, research projects. As I found new resources or came up with ideas for activities, I noted each on the appropriate page. Having specific places to record data helped me to see and revise the shape of the project once I began to plan in earnest.

"Where do I begin?" was a question that I asked myself often that fall. The answer was the same one I give student researchers:

begin with what you know. I knew that Mid-Coast Audubon had a film on puffins. I knew, too, that Stephen Kress, the Audubon scientist in charge of the puffin project, might be a resource. I wrote to him and received a favorable response as well as some useful suggestions. Steve's letter was one incentive for me to move ahead. Another was the personal satisfaction I began to feel as I became a researcher of puffins. I tracked down resources much as my students would during their own research. At times it seemed as if resources jumped out at me from bookshelves and newsstands.

Did *Maine Fish and Wildlife* magazine publish a puffin poster in the fall issue because they knew I needed it? Of course not, but how opportune. I wasn't sure that I could obtain a poster for each student in my class, but a letter I sent to the address on the poster was forwarded to someone who could answer my request, and most generously. Enough posters arrived so that each child would have his or her own.

I had a similar experience with The National Geographic Society. How did they know I needed a film on puffins? Here was an opportunity that I knew I had to seize, even though a small obstacle stood in my way. The film was going to be shown on cable television, and I don't have cable. But I remembered my parents, living in Ohio, did and surely would be able to record the program for me. I made a quick phone call, and a few days later the film was on my desk. I found the resources I needed *because* I was looking. The curriculum was in my hands, and I became more and more excited about taking responsibility for its design.

I also began to explore the possibility of a field trip to Eastern Egg Rock. I felt that a field trip would be an important factor in this study because nothing teaches as well as firsthand experience. From the first contact I made in the fall, long before my students ever knew about the puffin study, it appeared that all was set for a May excursion to the island.

My own curiosity about puffins helped, but my students were the main reason I worked so hard. I wanted them to learn. Each time I found new information that I could share with my class, I felt more confident that the puffin study would become an opportunity for them to understand more about their environment. I thought about the ramifications of the study in the pages of my log.

2 JANUARY

Puffins are a prism through which to look at the natural environment—past, present, and future. My students might only be eight and nine, but their surroundings will be affected by the decisions they make when they grow up. Those decisions need to be based on knowledge, and the resources I present might affect that knowledge.

Another log entry shows an ebb in my self-confidence. Since I was starting from scratch, I worried about planning a rigorous and worthwhile unit while in the midst of everyday teaching.

3 FEBRUARY

Don't give in to "I can't" or else I won't. Taking the attitude of doing this with and for the kids must be the driving force behind my planning. A new unit of study will never happen if I say "It isn't part of the curriculum," or if I stop when I encounter a hurdle. I will have to mull things over before I can continue: I have to accept, even invite, the uncertainty. Over and over I find myself saying, "I will make this work."

I also had to consider the third-grade curriculum as I planned the new unit. In my log I brainstormed activities and plotted them according to subject areas, to organize my thoughts and to assess the feasibility of the puffin study. I added to the list as I planned through the winter.

4 DECEMBER

ART

puffins on door
posters for fund-raising
Audubon illustrations
postcard photos
puffin illustrations

SOCIAL STUDIES

economic—   impact of man
                       past and present
political—   bird relationships
                       gulls and terns
socio-cultural—puffin life
mapping—   nautical charts
                       locate colonies

PUFFINS

SCIENCE

view films
log entries
research projects
puffin skin
adopt a puffin
bird banding/sightings
environmental issues
field trip

LANGUAGE ARTS

read books and articles
   —aloud for information
   —share log entries
writing
   —log entries
   —research
   —stories
news clippings about puffins

As I planned the puffin study, I set the stage for it with other units. I read a biography of John James Audubon to the class so they would understand the scientist/artist and a quest for accuracy of detail. I asked Joe Gray, an environmental educator from Mid-Coast Audubon, to present a talk and slide show on "Birds in Our Lives." A specialist on raptors came to school to speak to our kids, and the opportunity to see a live saw-whet owl and a sharp-shinned hawk enhanced their appreciation of birds of prey. And all the while I asked myself in the pages of my log, "Will this fit? How do I use it?"

28 MARCH

And so we have begun. Now my anxieties revolve around accomplishing the goals I've set for myself and the kids. I worry about whether they'll be able to follow through. *Relax.* I've seen them do it before. Third graders are eager for the opportunity to do research, to learn new things and explore new territory. If I allow it, their energy will carry them.

The beginning was exciting. A week had passed since the junior high students had turned our classroom into a puffin burrow. My students were curious, and now they would begin to act. On a tranquil afternoon in March, I asked them to take out their science logs and respond to the prompt "What is a puffin?" Kerry's and Tony's log entries showed me the scope of knowledge among my kids.

3/25   1:48

I think a puffin is
a puffin is a bird.

3/25   1:48

A Puffin is a atlantic bird. It's eyes look strange. It's beake has different colors. They spend most of there life in the sea. They have a big beake. They are small.

Kerry's uncertainty contrasted with Tony's knowledge about puffins. The log entries allowed me to see the kind of ongoing planning that would now be necessary. I had laid the groundwork months before the study began, but day-to-day planning depended on the children. I have learned that it isn't possible to lay out all the details and then say, "Okay. This is it, folks, step by step from beginning to end." As the teacher I have to remain flexible, to recognize and seize opportunities as they present themselves, and to build on what my students know and want to know and do.

And I have to involve the kids. When I organized the puffin study there were definite things I wanted to happen, but I knew they could only happen if my students were sufficiently interested. They took responsibility for the study in several ways. In April I approached them with information about "Project Puffin." During science class I asked, "How would you like to adopt a puffin?"

"Yes!"

"A real one?"

"Where will we keep it?"

"Well, we wouldn't keep it. And we may not ever see it," I answered.

"Awwww."

"Why not?"

I explained, "Adopting a puffin is a little different from adopting a person. We'd be helping Audubon biologists bring the puffin back to Eastern Egg Rock and Seal Island. They'll tell us when our chick is transplanted from Newfoundland and when it fledges. Our chick will have bands on its legs so that the scientists will be able to tell us if our chick is sighted, even if it's two or three years from now. The question is, how do we raise the money? We need a hundred dollars."

The class voted to start with a bake sale and made a list of what each person would contribute. The first—and only—bake sale was a huge success, raising ninety-four dollars. A benefactor provided the six dollars needed to reach our goal, and we put our adoption papers in the mail that day. Puffin #200 was ours.

I also involved students in planning individual research on puffins. They wrote a log entry each time they or I read one of the books about puffins and whenever I showed a film. Students shared their entries with the whole group, and I recorded the information on a large chart so that I could verify individual students' knowledge and correct any misinformation. This was also a foundation for the research that individual students would continue on their own.

Once the children had absorbed a wealth of information about puffins, it was time to do something with their knowledge. A group discussion led to another vote and the decision to write a collection of stories about puffins, with the type of story to be determined by the individual writer. I knew that the kids would need solid chunks of time to research and write, so I drew on methods described by Mary Ellen Giacobbe (1986): the hour designated for writing workshop was turned over to my puffin researchers, and science, social studies, reading, and writing became one. I managed the time as I would for writing workshop by taking a daily "status of the class" poll (Atwell 1987) to follow their progress. Then I circulated and conferred with children about their research and writing. My role as facilitator allowed the students to begin to see themselves as experts about puffins. This was the role I assumed during much of the puffin study. But I still had to organize the field trip, so that students might see the puffin recolonization project firsthand.

When I called the boat captain in April to confirm the trip, I discovered that he had forgotten about us and made another commitment. I felt that my class had earned a field trip and was determined to find a way to get them to Eastern Egg Rock, even if I had to take them there myself. I had visions of myself vigorously paddling, seventeen inner tubes strung out behind me.

28 APRIL

OK, one possibility is out, but there has got to be another way to the island. There are two other sources to check, Jim and Vern. I'll start with them tomorrow.

I spent two weeks trying to make arrangements. One possibility I eliminated due to its cost, but that still left one to pursue, and pursue I did. I called and called and called. Then, one evening as I thumbed through a local paper, I noticed an ad for the boat I was trying to contact. There was a second phone number listed: success at last. Captain Vern Lewis had a group scheduled to go out to Eastern Egg Rock the following week, if I didn't mind joining them. I was elated and could hardly wait to tell my students, who still knew nothing of the trip. I had not wanted to disappoint them, but now I could share my excitement. Their research was about to gain a new dimension. They were going to visit the puffin island that they had read, written, and talked about and seen on film. If luck was with us, we might see a live puffin or two.

30 MAY

The morning was crystal blue with a light breeze. The weather report said land temperature would be in the upper seventies and seas would run two to four feet—possibly rough for children. Would we make the trip? I called Vern as planned, and the answer was yes.

Everyone was excited as we left school, me included. I had prepared the kids by discussing the trip all week long. They couldn't stop talking about it. They were to bring warm clothing and plenty of crackers because the ocean air can be downright cold, and crackers would help to combat queasy stomachs unused to the pitch and roll of the sea. I was glad we had plenty for the trip.

Once on the water, the anticipation of seeing a puffin kept everyone in good spirits, even though it was chilly and the seas were choppy. Then Eastern Egg Rock came into view. We scanned the horizon for puffins. I spotted one in flight and then another and then a guillemot. Soon the kids could tell what a puffin looked like in flight. They were excited but frustrated and hoped for a closer look.

Suddenly, Vern spotted one in the water just thirty feet off the bow. Now the kids were excited! I thought they might jump out of the boat trying to get a closer look. And then there was another. We circled the island three times in our search and then headed off to hunt for seals before returning to the dock.

I'm more than content. Eastern Egg Rock was there. The puffins were there. My students had been there too, and they will surely remember this day.

At the beginning of June, I typed and published students' research as an anthology of short stories about puffins. The study was a success on every level: the children had read, observed, and written because they wanted to make meaning of a topic that had captured their imaginations. The elements that contributed to the success of the project are easier for me to see now that the school year is over and I have the luxury of time to reflect on what we did.

In creating a new unit, it was important to choose an area of study that I found interesting and that I believed the children would, too. Our third-grade curriculum emphasizes concepts of environment and community, and the topic I selected fit the curriculum as well as me, my students, and our location on the coast of Maine. Because I was compelled as a learner, my students trusted and responded to my invitation to them to learn with me.

I also began early and built in plenty of time to think and organize. Over seven months I generated and revised a plan in my log, searched for appropriate resources, sought the help of experts, and arranged for guest speakers and a field trip so that some of the children's research might be firsthand. I drew on children's literature and found relevant trade books that I read aloud to the whole class, so that everyone could appreciate the content and its presentation. When the project required funds that the school couldn't provide, I turned to my class and the children worked together to raise the money. Whenever possible, I let them take the initiative in determining their roles in the project. And I persisted. I wrestled with questions and problems rather than giving up on the new unit because I know that this is what learners do, and because I want curriculum design to be an occasion for learning. I'll follow a similar process with the next unit I design, whatever its focus.

"Will you do the puffin study again?" Stephen Kress asked me in June.

The answer is yes, but it will be different. This year I established a framework; next year I'll discover new resources. I'll also encounter a new group of third graders with their own needs and interests. One thing is certain: I will continue to share news of sightings with the fourth-grade students who have a special interest in puffin #200.

REFERENCES

Atwell, Nancie. 1987. *In the Middle: Writing, Reading, and Learning with Adolescents.* Portsmouth, NH: Boynton/Cook.

Egg Rock Update. 1986, 1987. Newsletter of the Fratercula Fund of the National Audubon Society. Stephen Kress, Director. Ithaca, NY.

Friedman, Judi. 1981. *Puffins Come Back!* New York: Dodd, Mead.

Giacobbe, Mary Ellen. 1986. "Learning to Write and Writing to Learn in the Elementary School." In *The Teaching of Writing: Eighty-fifth Yearbook of the National Society for the Study of Education,* ed. Anthony R. Petrosky and David Bartholomae. Chicago: University of Chicago Press.

Gove, Doris. 1985. *Miracle at Egg Rock.* Camden, ME: Down East Books.

Graham, Ada, and Frank Graham, Jr. 1971. *Puffin Island*. Thorndike, ME: Thorndike Press.

King, Deborah. 1984. *Puffin*. New York: Lothrop, Lee and Shepard.

Martin, Lynne. 1976. *Puffin, Bird of the Open Seas*. New York: William Morrow.

Weinberger, Jane. 1984. *Wee Peter Puffin*. Mt. Desert, ME: Windswept House.

14

Taking Charge of Curriculum

CINDY GREENLEAF

It was hot. It was the middle of July. The wall across from me was covered with strips of paper and large post-it notes.

"Don't you think we ought to move this over here?" Jo Haney asked, standing on her dormitory bed and pointing to one of the fluttering pieces of paper.

The fan sent me a blast of steamy air as I pondered her question from my side of the room. We were trying to find ways to enrich our science curriculum through art, and from there to make connections with social studies and the other subjects we teach. We wanted our third graders to learn to observe and appreciate both natural and man-made art. It was mind-boggling work, but moving our notes and ideas around on a wall was easier than cutting and pasting legal pads, at least as a start.

Jo, Donna Maxim, and I were finishing our second week at Confratute, an institute on gifted and talented education held at the University of Connecticut. We didn't realize it at the moment, but we were beginning a two-year process that would profoundly change our curriculum, how we teach, and how our third graders learn.

A New Curriculum Emerges and a Team Is Forged

The first two years that Jo, Donna, and I taught third grade we each worked in a self-contained classroom and teamed only for occasional social studies and science activities. Since our time together in Connecticut, we have worked as a team to develop a new curriculum for grade three, one that integrates writing and literature with content-area studies and the fine arts. Each of us became concerned about the traditional approach to social studies and science, which treats them as mutually exclusive entities rather than interdependent facets of our lives. We were also frustrated with textbook and curriculum guides that frequently assume two things: that the only facts learned from year to year are those covered in the text or guide, and that those facts are learned in a preordained sequence.

We knew that our students brought with them a whole body of information—and some misinformation—related to a given subject. In many textbooks, children's experience is either ignored or dealt with superficially, with an end-of-the-unit "thinker" question for extra credit. There is little opportunity to assess and confirm a student's real knowledge of a subject, or for teacher and student to identify and deal with misconceptions that can become effective barriers to learning.

Through working together toward our common goals, Donna, Jo, and I became a team. The three of us have many things in common: teaching literature-based reading and process writing, volunteering to participate in the Bread Loaf project on writing to learn, and attending Confratute. Just as important, each of us has different but complementary interests, talents, and areas of expertise that we are willing to share with the others. Jo is our naturalist and graphics artist, Donna our authority on children's literature, and I am our fine arts resource and assistant naturalist.

In this chapter I'll share how our roles as teachers have changed, from following scripted texts to guiding our students through hands-on experiences and independent research. To the extent that it is possible within the constraints of a traditional public school system, we have made explicit our theories about learning, learned together, and negotiated our own curriculum. This is our story—so far.

The First Year

Our new curriculum and model for planning began to take shape in the weeks that followed Confratute and our introduction to the Bread Loaf project. As we began our preparations for the new school year, we had high expectations and a lot of hope. Everything, it seemed, was new.

Near the end of the first grading period I realized that while we had been doing many hands-on activities in our study of plants, the students hadn't yet read our science textbook. Feeling a little anxious, I reviewed the chapters, fearing that we might have overlooked important information. I was greatly relieved, and then elated, when I confirmed that we had not only covered everything in the text but had gone well beyond it. Our kids had experienced, discussed, and written about plants for five weeks. Their knowledge of plants was far greater than the information found in the text. We asked them to read the unit, but as a brief review. This experience gave us confidence to go forward with our new curriculum.

Three months into the school year, we realized that we had a tiger by the tail. We had been gathering new resources since July but lacked a system for organizing them, and had already made a lot of changes in our curriculum but without a sense of where we were headed. We recognized the symptoms of overload and the need for time to sift through what we were learning, review where we had come from, and decide where we wanted to go. In December we met with Nancie Atwell to sort ourselves out and plan new directions.

Using "community" as our overall curricular theme, we were attempting to develop three new areas of study: the forest community, marine life, and the local community of the Boothbay region. Our goal was to provide our students with experiences that would allow them to observe these communities from the perspectives of social studies, science, and art, and for students to use learning logs to record their observations and explore the connections they found among the communities.

At our planning session we used the format shown in Figure 14–1 to organize all the information and resources we had gathered so far. Then we brainstormed additional ideas for each area of study. Seeing all of our resources separated into categories on planning pages helped us to identify many facets of each community. We saw additional connections, as well as some obvious gaps that we were able to fill. Then we chose the resources that best met our needs, leaving us with a good list of alternative sources if we needed them. We began to see our theme planning pages as a group learning log, a way for us to use writing to capture ideas, make sense of them, and come up with new ones.

A month later we met again, with two goals: to firm up our plans for the rest of the year and to develop a list of resource materials we needed. We had already set our themes for the second half of the year: matter, the solar system, and nutrition. This time we planned additional programs and activities to help establish connections among the themes.

For example, we extended our nutrition unit to include connections to Maine's land and sea harvests (science and social studies), food sources and eating customs in other countries (geography, literature, environment, and habitat), labels on packaged foods (reading and science), and making vegetable prints and studying still lifes (art). We developed learning log prompts, too: "How do

FIGURE 14–1 ● THEME PLANNING PAGE

Theme Planning Page

TOPIC: *Forest Community*

People:	Organizations:
Joe Gray	University of Maine Cooperative
Science Resource Teacher	Extension Service
Arborist	Pulp Industry - Augusta Office
Artisans: sculptors	Maine Audubon Society
model ship builders	4-H Camp
furniture builders	Environmental / Ecology Camp
Shipbuilders	Bath Marine Museum
	Long Tryst
	Garden Club

Print Resources:	Field Trips:
Woodworking Magazine	Maine State Museum
NatureScope	Mt. Battie State Park
Connections to the Forest (4H)	local lumberyard
BRES Library	local skipyard
Town Library	Marine Museum
Plants That Never Bloom by Ruth Heller	
Foxfire Books	
Find A Place, Show your Face	

Oak & Co.
A Forest Year
Project Learning Tree
Hug A Tree
Ring of Life

Other:

Maine State Media Guide
Portland Museum of Art - tree slides (art)

you think humans fit into the food chain?'' ''How does where you live affect the foods you eat?'' ''What do you think you can learn from reading the labels on food packages?''

Our list of resource materials included many books, both factual and fiction; specimens for our science centers and materials for experiments, such as bowls, measuring cups and spoons, pans and trays, maps, charts, and posters; and classroom subscriptions to *Owl, Geographic World, Nature Scope, Ranger Rick,* and *Odyssey.*

Then we reflected on what had occurred from September through January and began to talk about changes for the following fall. It was then that we realized that we wanted to plan a whole year in advance and in much greater detail than we had in the past. And, at the same time, we could budget jointly for the supplies and equipment we needed.

That May the three of us spent a whole day in the school's conference room, surrounded by all of our content-area materials and catalogs. We sorted through them, discarding some and setting others aside to review later. Then we settled in to plan for the coming school year.

Creating a Master Plan for a School Year

Planning for a whole year took a lot of organization. We did several things before we even began.

First, we met with our principal to schedule the third grade's art, music, and physical education classes. Our goal was to have a common block of time two afternoons a week for programs and activities, and two days a week when all three of us were free at the same time to plan and prepare for group activities. Our principal was able to accommodate our needs.

Next, we developed a master schedule for the week, blocking out times for language arts and math and identifying any other time that all three classes would have in common. We found four blocks of time that we could use for whole-group activities.

We also pulled together all of the materials we would need to have with us as we planned. We brought our lists of programs, speakers, slides, and films, including names, addresses, and phone numbers. We brought lists of activities, projects and products, field trips, and experiments we wanted to include. We brought text-books, trade books, curriculum guides, and catalogs for ordering materials. And, of course, we brought our theme planning pages for each area of study.

We organized all of this information in a loose-leaf notebook with sections dedicated to each major area of study. We began by listing the materials already available—where to find them, how they connect to the topic, and what other areas of study they relate to—then added new resources as we found them.

We began by creating a month-by-month calendar for the whole year, noting holidays, in-service days, parent conference dates, and the ends of the grading periods. Then we filled in the dates of meetings and conferences that each of us planned to attend and sketched in holiday celebrations and anticipated concert rehearsals. Having mapped out the basic school year, we were ready to begin planning in earnest.

The third grade has a good, but limited, science text, a locally developed social studies curriculum guide that allows us some freedom in implementation, and a Maine studies text. We used these as the bare bones, the skeleton that supported our enriched content-area curriculum. Beginning with September's calendar, we penciled in major curricular themes, related activities, and field trips for each month of the school year. In the process, we reviewed the past year and discussed any changes we wished to make.

For example, as we planned for our second field trip to Mt. Battie, we knew we wanted to repeat some activities. We also wanted to add new ones that would help the kids to focus on specific aspects of their experience. The trip begins with a mile-and-a-half nature hike through the woods to the tablelands that make up the summit of Mt. Battie. The reward is a bird's-eye view of the town of Camden and its harbor. Sitting together around a table in the conference room, we negotiated the changes:

CINDY: . . . and we want to use two-column log entries again . . . "What *will* you see close up? Far away?" on the day before we go, and "What *did* you see close up? Far away?" on the day after the trip, then compare the lists.

JO: We want to take clipboards, too, so they can do some sketching.

CINDY: Yes . . . and there were some other things we wanted to do there . . .

DONNA: We want to do more of a geography lesson . . .

CINDY: Which would be great with the poem by Edna St. Vincent Millay. It's on the bronze tablet . . .

DONNA: We could set up three different stations . . . if we did a sketching activity . . .

JO: . . . and the poem . . .

CINDY: When they look down, they'll see a town, a harbor. They'll see shops, churches, homes . . . that's perfect. It leads right into our study of Boothbay Harbor.

Time was a major issue as we planned. We knew that this year we had to allow for such schedule demons as storm days and assemblies—and to be cautious about planning too much, especially at the beginning of the school year. In order to accomplish everything we set our sights on, we needed to be flexible. Sometimes we had to revamp the schedule for an entire day. For example, when Joe Gray, our Audubon volunteer, presented his programs on nature trails and the forest floor, the third grades saw his slide presentations together. Then Joe took each class on a nature hike in the woods for about forty-five minutes. On those days we rescheduled math and used our language arts time to write and share log entries about what the kids had seen and learned, in place of writing workshop.

As we planned, we tried to set specific dates for programs, speakers, and field trips, and we divvied up the responsibilities:

DONNA: Can we confirm Joe Gray right away?

JO: I'll write down the dates and confirm them with him this week. We shouldn't have any problem.

DONNA: There's no point calling the Planetarium right now. I'll have to wait until September when they have their new schedule set up. I'll call the Maine State Museum then, too: they may have some different gallery programs.

CINDY: Well, we should get firm dates for the nutrition films now. We usually get the confirmation slips right back. And I can set up the slide programs with the Portland Museum of Art now. What about "Moveable Moose"?

JO: We were given choices for dates. I'll check with Tom to see what he's done with that.

CINDY: What about the films and programs from the Department of Marine Resources—shouldn't we confirm those now?

DONNA: Yes, they're usually booked way ahead . . .

JO: I'll call them. We want them to bring the two slide shows "Rocky Shore" and "Sandy Shore" and the video about the ocean floor with them when they bring the sea critters, right?

A major advantage to planning early was that we usually got the programs when we wanted them, allowing for smooth transitions from theme to theme during the year.

Figure 14–2 shows part of the results of our efforts: our monthly planning calendar for September. These calendar pages are our blueprint for an entire year and represent our efforts to weave reading, writing, science, social studies, and art into the overall theme of community. The planning calendar is the place where we record and organize a thousand important pieces of information into a cohesive, functional, living document. We use pencil because this is a working draft, open to frequent revisions—changing the time frame, adding new activities, and even dropping activities when necessary. It is another kind of entry in our group log. We discovered as we drafted, conferred, and revised together that yearly planning is very much like process writing: it is definitely a recursive process.

We met again in August, prior to beginning our second year as a team, to confirm our plans, make adjustments due to schedule changes, and establish a new tradition to help us stay on track.

FIGURE 14–2 ● MONTHLY PLANNING CALENDAR

Patterns in Nature: leaves
shapes of trees
flower shapes

Month __September__

Sunday	Monday	Tuesday	Wednesday	Thursday	Friday	Saturday
		1	*2* In-Service	*3* →	*4*	*5*
6 Poetry 6	*7*	*8* Writing + Reading Surveys Take a Closer Look 2 Tree drawings 1ST Day	*9* Log prompt Tell me what you Know about trees	*10* Bark Rubbings - Characteristics of bark - Log ① Tell me about bark ② what new - did you learn?	*11* Tree Adoption	*12*
13 Art - leaf impressions - fired clay -	*14* ① Leaf transpiration experiment ② All about leaves ③ Food Chain	*15* Anatomy of a tree - roots - crown Find museum slides - trees	*16* Joe Gray Nature Trails	*17* Jello Leaves photosynthesis	*18* Build a Tree	*19*
20 Read Co. Oak & Year A forest Community	*21* Log prompt what will you see in the woods from close up- far away - 2 column list ✓	*22* Find A Place - Show Your Face ✓	*23* Mt. Battie Camden	*24* Mt. Battie Rain date Log prompt: what did you see close up - far away?	*25* Tree Community Poster - begin	*26*
27	*28* Letter illumination tree - leaves	*29*	*30* Joe Gray Maine Coast			

JO: We need to find a regular time when we can sit down with our calendars and use this time for our planning . . . keep it sacred. Nobody make doctor's appointments for those days. It will help us a lot next year.

DONNA: What we need to do is find one day . . . obviously, Mondays and Fridays are bad because of holidays . . .

JO: Right now we don't know for sure on what days we'll have staff meetings.

DONNA: So we'll set this up later . . . at the beginning of the year. But definitely a time for us to plan together.

We eventually decided on Thursday, after school, as our sacred time to review and fine-tune our plans. Usually we met for about an hour, but occasionally we needed more time, especially when making a transition to a new area of study. By January we were so familiar with our Thursday format that we were able to accomplish a lot in an hour. In this conversation about setting up a science unit on matter, Donna's question about tree observations didn't cause us to skip a beat:

JO: What we need to do now is to plan the experiments we want to use, since we saw the filmstrip on matter today and the next chapter in the science book has the "mystery goop" experiment in it.

CINDY: We want to do the balloon experiment for the kids again. It's a good one—it has all three phases of matter.

JO: We actually did it twice last year, remember? So they could see the difference? It was good for log entries—they could make comparisons . . .

DONNA: Are we going to do our tree observations right after lunch tomorrow? Good.

JO: If we're going to grow sugar crystals we'll have to start them soon. They take a long time. It ties in with the filmstrip we saw today, too.

CINDY: We'll need a large block of time on Wednesday . . .

DONNA: I'll try to switch my art to the morning.

CINDY: I can change our library to nine o'clock, I'm pretty sure.

DONNA: We need to plan two times for Jean Meggison to come in to talk about rocks and crystals next week.

CINDY: We can do that on Tuesday and Thursday afternoon next week. I'll call her to be sure.

Working Toward a Seamless Curriculum

Three years ago anyone looking at our lesson plans could easily identify separate curricula for language arts, science, and social studies. It is not so easy now. The content areas, language arts, and art have converged and melded together—no longer separate, no longer taught in isolation. Other changes are more subtle.

Jo, Donna, and I have become active learners ourselves. We have learned much about a wide range of subjects as we research ahead of and with our kids, sharing materials, resources, and discoveries. We even take our own field trips. We spent one day at the museums at Harvard and another at the Boston Museum of Fine Arts and came home from these trips richer in knowledge and poorer of pocket.

We no longer teach to ability groups, except for math, nor do we frustrate ourselves and many of our students by teaching to the middle. We want the children to participate in all of the activities at their own levels and to be able to work to the limits of their abilities. We monitor their progress, teach directly to individuals or small groups (Hansen 1987), and address larger issues through minilessons (Calkins 1986). We find that even the kids who have great difficulty writing—and reading what they have written—are eager to share their knowledge. By writing log entries based on their own experiences and observations during hands-on activities, these students are able to participate in content-area studies, too.

We three also work closely with our resource room teacher so that she is aware of what we are doing in the classroom and can incorporate and adapt our curriculum to the specific needs of the kids. Our Chapter I teachers work with us in the classroom, helping students to work independently or in heterogeneous groups with the support they need (Hansen 1987).

We use the spaces in our classrooms differently now, as well, to accommodate our new program. Jo Haney and I share one large space, with the folding wall between our classrooms permanently open. We use the central area where our classrooms join for gathering all three classes together and for shared learning centers in fine arts, applied arts, and geography. Donna has a self-contained classroom across the hall, which allows us to separate groups and activities when we need to. There are times when Jo's class and mine join forces for major research projects, and other times when Donna's class joins as well. Then we pool all of the available resources in the central area, and the kids are free to work anywhere in either room, collaboratively in teams or individually.

Our new curriculum also places different demands on our equipment and resources. Each spring Jo, Donna, and I meet to plan our budgets for the following year. Through planning together we are building an inventory of equipment, resources, and materials. This way we share some things and can pool our resources for expensive items; this past year we purchased our own library carts. We also continue to build our library of children's literature. Just as kids who learn to read through literature need incredible quantities of books, kids who become researchers and write to learn consume incredible quantities of resource materials. We never seem to have enough, even though we use both the school and town libraries.

Our accumulation of specimens continues to grow, too. It is widely known at Boothbay Elementary that any natural treasure will find a home in the third grade. Our collection includes sand samples from many parts of the world, shells, skeletons, bird and wasp nests, beaver logs, seeds and pods, rocks and minerals—all the better to observe the beauty and art in nature.

And writing continues to play a major role in every area of the curriculum. Using writing to learn allows our kids to actively engage in science, social studies, and art. They are discovering how these subjects are related—through observing, experimenting, reading, pursuing answers to their own questions, and recording all of these data in their learning logs. Writing to learn was the key that gave us the freedom to open up our curriculum—to implement an enrichment model and begin to explore connections among the content areas, language arts, and art.

Jo, Donna, and I enjoy working and teaching as a team. We are always learning and discovering new connections, and we never do anything exactly the way we did it the year before. We know now how to collaborate as planners, how to organize and share resources, how to use talk and writing to help move our thinking, and how to tap each other's strengths as teachers. We have a functioning, flexible model for designing, negotiating, and revising curriculum that makes anything possible for us and our kids. And we have a power as professionals that we lacked when we allowed textbooks and teacher's guides to do our thinking and writing for us. I look back at the experiences we have shared, beginning with Confratute that steamy July, and see how a team of committed teachers *can* take charge of curriculum.

REFERENCES

The American Forest Institute. 1977. *Project Learning Tree*. Washington, DC: The American Forest Institute.

Anderson, Gary. 1981. *Find a Place, Show Your Face*. Augusta, ME: Department of Inland Fisheries and Wildlife. (Pamphlet and video.)

Calkins, Lucy McCormick. 1986. *The Art of Teaching Writing*. Portsmouth, NH: Heinemann.

Fine Woodworking Magazine. Newton, CT: Taunton Press.

Hansen, Jane. 1987. *When Writers Read*. Portsmouth, NH: Heinemann.

Heller, Ruth. 1984. *Plants That Never Bloom*. New York: Grosset and Dunlap.

Lerner, Carol. 1987. *A Forest Year*. New York: William Morrow.

Maybay, Richard. 1983. *Oak and Co*. New York: Greenwillow.

Ranger Rick's Nature Scope. Washington, DC: National Wildlife Federation.

Rockwell, Robert E., Elizabeth A. Sherwood, and Robert A. Williams. 1983. *Hug a Tree and Other Things To Do Outdoors with Young Children*. Mt. Ranier, MD: Gryphon House.

Wigginton, Eliot, ed. 1972–86. *The Foxfire Books*. Garden City, NY: Anchor Press, Doubleday.

Yolen, Jane. 1986. *Ring of Life*. New York: Harcourt, Brace, Jovanovich.

Appendices

Appendices

Appendix A

Genres for Report Writing

Peter Medway (1988) has written: "Maybe it will be through the pleasure of the text and not the lessons of the text that our students may best be brought into motivated engagement with reading and writing" (176). When teachers admit the many possible forms that school reports might take, they also admit the strong possibility that writers will enjoy writing as well as learn from it.

This appendix presents all of the options for reporting knowledge across the disciplines generated by the children and teachers in the writing to learn project. Teachers who plan to invite multi-genre reports might wish to review these modes and select those most appropriate for their students and subject areas. It is not a list to hand to children, but a starting point for the teacher who is considering options to present to students and is willing to show children, in conferences and minilessons, how the genres work.

1. *Individual, bound books* for the classroom library. Giacobbe's book-binding technique, described in Graves (1983, 59–61), is one that children can manage independently from around third grade.
2. *Picture books* that introduce younger children to a topic and are based on students' knowledge of good, content-area literature for children (e.g., illustrated books about electricity, black bears, local architecture, the human skeleton).
3. *Textbooks* for which each student in the class writes a chapter (e.g., the results of statistical surveys conducted by students in a math class, an anthology about life in Ancient Greece, an examination of the effects of World War II on the local community).
4. *Correspondence* between two real or imagined historical person-ages (e.g., a woman from ancient Sparta and one from Athens,

Thomas Paine and a twentieth-century fifth grader, Harriet Tubman and a young slave).

5. *Journals or diaries* of real or imagined historical personages (e.g., the diary of a serf, the journal of a young survivor of the flu epidemic of 1918).

6. *Oral histories and interviews*, transcribed and supplemented by background information, photographs, drawings, poetry, etc. Linda Rief's (1985) eighth-grade study of aging is a lovely example, as are oral histories published in the *Foxfire* collections edited by Eliot Wigginton (1972–1986).

7. *Scripts*: radio and television plays to be tape recorded or videotaped; speeches, plays, and skits to be performed; interviews; and film strips.

8. *Historical fiction*: short stories about historical personages or about imagined people taking part in important historical events (e.g., a day in a child's life during the plague or on a wagon train, a fictional account of Anne Hutchinson's trial).

9. *Autobiographical sketches* of real or imagined historical personages or living things (e.g., a first-person account of the boyhood of Alexander the Great, a deciduous tree describes a year in its life).

10. *Poetry*: collections of poems about a topic—free verse, rhymed, counted syllable and/or acrostic formats—in which information about a topic is embedded.

11. *Science fiction*: short stories or novellas set in the future or on another planet in which contemporary issues are explored.

12. *Animal stories*: a favorite genre of third through fifth graders; the stories must strike a balance between presenting the animal as a character and giving an accurate account of its existence without anthropomorphizing it (see Wilde 1988).

13. *How-to books* in which students pass on specialized knowledge related to a unit of study (e.g., blacksmithing, trapping, tapestry weaving, stargazing, reducing fractions).

14. *Field guides* that describe characteristics of a particular species or community.

15. *Class or individual newspapers* in which each article, column, advertisement, editorial, interview, want ad, and cartoon is related to a time and place in history (e.g., a Boston newspaper of 1776, a Gettysburg paper from 1863).

16. *Columns or feature articles* published in the local newspaper (e.g., an interview with a local artist, a story about the nesting habits of the osprey, Christmas in Maine in Colonial times).

17. *Math concept books*: short stories or picture books in which mathematical information is embedded. Appendix C includes many titles of trade books that could serve as models for young mathematicians.

18. *Recipes* of a period or people: foods eaten in ancient Rome, during Medieval times, by Native Americans, etc.

19. *Games and puzzles* that demonstrate and require a knowledge of a time, place, or unit of study (e.g., a trivia game about Portland, a crossword puzzle with the solar system as its theme).

20. *Annotated catalogs* of artifacts (e.g., the dress of men and women of ancient Greece; cooking implements found in the kitchen at Sturbridge Village).

21. *Annotated family trees* of real or imagined historical personages (e.g., Greek gods and goddesses, a passenger on the May-flower).

22. *Friendly letters* to individuals outside the classroom in which students describe their new knowledge and what it means to them (e.g., letters to pen pals from another school, grandparents, cousins, and other relatives).

23. *Bulletin boards* of drawings or photos with accompanying text (e.g., plants that grow in the desert, Portland then and now).

24. *Choose-your-own-adventure stories* in which success in proceeding through the story is based on specific knowledge of math or science concepts.

25. *Posters, murals, time lines, and mobiles* that include text (e.g., a dinosaur mobile, a mural depicting the destruction of Pompeii, a poster showing a plant's life cycle).

26. *Coloring books* with accompanying text, to be photocopied for classmates and/or younger children (e.g., scenes from New England states, the Underground Railroad, the life of a hermit crab).

27. *Calendars*, each page annotated with a drawing and text related to the topic (e.g., a Medieval knight's calendar, a calendar for stargazers, a puffin calendar).

28. *Alphabet books* in which each letter supplies relevant information about the topic (e.g., a Beverly Cleary ABC, an astronaut's ABC, a geologist's ABC).

29. *Pop-up books* in which the format replicates a natural phenomenon (e.g., the solar system, the earth's layers).

30. *Shadow boxes and dioramas* with accompanying text (e.g., the habitat of the eastern panther, Anne Frank's secret annex, the parts of a stem).

REFERENCES

Graves, Donald H. 1983. *Writing: Teachers & Children at Work.* Portsmouth, NH: Heinemann.

Medway, Peter. 1988. "Reality, Play and Pleasure in English." In *The Word for Teaching Is Learning*, ed. Martin Lightfoot and Nancy Martin. Portsmouth, NH: Boynton/Cook.

Rief, Linda. 1985. "Why Can't We Live Like the Monarch Butterfly?" In *Breaking Ground: Teachers Relate Reading and Writing in the Elementary School*, ed. Jane Hansen, Thomas Newkirk, and Donald Graves. Portsmouth, NH: Heinemann.

Wigginton, Eliot, ed. 1972–1986. *The Foxfire Books 1–9*. Garden City, NY: Anchor Press, Doubleday.

Wilde, Jack. 1988. "The Written Report: Old Wine in New Bottles." In *Understanding Writing: Ways of Observing, Learning, and Teaching*, 2nd ed., ed. Thomas Newkirk and Nancie Atwell. Portsmouth, NH: Heinemann.

Appendix B

Prompts for Learning
Log Entries

The learning log prompts included in this appendix were designed by teachers of grades three through six. We judged a prompt successful if it engaged young writers and helped them to think and learn about the subject at hand. The best prompts were open-ended and avoided right or wrong answers. They personally involved writers by asking children to discover their own opinions, draw on their prior experiences, or *envision* (Martin et al. 1976) the experiences of other people or living things. And they involved children in many kinds of writing and drawing so that learning log entries remained fresh and unpredictable for both teacher and writer.

Although the prompts are arranged by topic, they can also be categorized by type. Across the curriculum, teachers asked log writers to list, brainstorm, chart, map, sketch, pose questions, set goals, guess, predict, express opinions, note observations, summarize, role-play, envision, correspond, and shift to a new mode, such as poetry or fiction. This good range led to a diversity of responses and a fluid definition of what it means to use writing to learn; it also allowed students to find their particular strengths as writers.

The list of prompts is representative rather than definitive. We hope that it exemplifies ways that teachers can help students make constructive, imaginative use of learning logs and how teachers can put logs to work in many subject areas.

REFERENCE

Martin, Nancy, et al. 1976. *Writing and Learning Across the Curriculum 11–16*. Portsmouth, NH: Boynton/Cook.

LEARNING LOG PROMPTS BY TOPIC

American Indians

Draw and/or write everything you know about American Indians.

How do you think that geography affected the life-styles of the different Indian groups? List as many ways as you can think of.

How are today's Native Americans different from their ancestors?

"Not all Americans celebrate Thanksgiving." What does this mean to you?

Ancient Greece and Rome

List everything you know about ancient Greece. What would you like to know about ancient Greece?

Pretend you are the son or daughter of a Spartan or Athenian warrior during the Persian Wars. Write either a letter or a diary entry telling your feelings.

List ten questions that you'd like to have answered in our study of Rome.

Daily response to the novel *A Triumph for Flavius* (Caroline Dale Snedeker), which the teacher is reading aloud: students may either list facts they learned about Roman life or respond to the story in a personal way.

Animals in Living Communities/Habitats

What is a habitat?

List as many habitats as you can.

Choose a habitat and draw it, including any living things found in it.

What habitats will you see outside when we take a walk around the school? What habitats *did* you see outside? Compare your two lists.

Think of a habitat. In three minutes, list all the animals you can that live in that habitat. (Then students, in small groups, read their lists of animals while others guess the habitat.)

Guess: How do you think colonies of animals form?

Write a short story that shows a food chain.

What do you think is meant by a cold-blooded animal?

Why can't a polar bear survive in the jungle?

Adapt your animal to a totally different environment.

Community

What do you think a community is?

How have you seen people work together in a community?

What does "interdependence" mean to you?

List some things that are special about our community.

Why did your family decide to live in this community?

If you could change one thing about our community, what would it be?

List the advantages/disadvantages of living here.

What do you think was the most important news event in our community during the past year?

Desert Regions

Brainstorm a list of words that have to do with deserts.

What would you do if you were left alone in a desert?

How do you think desert plants survive?

Guess: What causes a desert to form?

Earth

Describe how you think the earth moves.

Guess how ancient people used the sun to help them tell time.

Write a telephone conversation between you and your Aunt Rose, who lives [across the country]. What will she be doing right now?

Write a short story that explains how day and night came to be.

How is planet Earth like a magnet?

Write a poem as if you are one of the four seasons.

List three things about winter in Maine and three things about winter in Florida. Who can list three more?

List five places in the northern hemisphere and five in the southern hemisphere. Who can list five more?

Why do you think the earth is hottest at the equator?

What are some differences between natural light and artificial light?

Electricity

How do you think our town gets the electricity it needs?

Explain to a second grader the difference between a battery and a solar cell.

If you were outside during a lightning storm, what would you do? Why?

Endangered Species

What does "endangered" mean to you?

Many animals have become endangered on our earth. What might have caused this?

List all the animals or plants you believe may be endangered.

Choose an endangered species and become that animal. Tell which changes in your habitat are making your life difficult.

"The best time to protect a species is before it becomes endangered." What does this mean to you? Think of a species you wish to protect.

Explorers

What would you be thinking to yourself if you were a member of Columbus's crew and you were just leaving port?

What would you be thinking to yourself if you were Columbus, after being thirty days out to sea with no land in sight?

Pretend that you are sailing with Columbus to the New World. Write an entry in your log as if it were the ship's log.

List the names of the explorers we've read about so far. Which is your favorite?

Pretend a new continent was discovered and you are going to settle there. What are five things you'll need to do?

Field Trips, Visitors, and Films

Make a list of things you think you may see at ——.

What kinds of things will you be looking for tomorrow? Make a list.

Make a plan for viewing the exhibits at ——.

What do you think it will be like? (Before)
What was it really like? (After)

Make a list of things you know about ——. (Before)
What did you learn today about ——? (After)

What questions do you think will be answered by this film? (Before)
Cross off the questions that were answered by the film. (After)

What was most memorable or meaningful to you?

Make a list of what you saw at ——, then star the parts that stand out in your mind.

Write a poem about your experience yesterday.

A range of choices for afterward:
  1. Tell about an interesting discovery you made.
  2. Tell about one thing that really interested you and that you'd like to know more about.
  3. Write any new questions that you have.
  4. Did you find answers to any questions you had before you went?

What did you see that's different from what you're accustomed to?

Write and tell [an absent classmate] about what he/she missed.

Write a letter to a friend in another class, telling about our visitor and what you learned today.

After listening to [an author]: How has he/she influenced you as a writer? Will you do anything differently now?

Fire Prevention and Safety

Your clothes have caught on fire. Tell what you must do to put the fire out and avoid making the burns worse.

Draw the upstairs floor plan of our school. Label as many fire exits as you can identify.

Draw the floor plan of your house. Put an X on your bedroom. Show two ways to escape a house fire from your room.

Write a script of a conversation you would have with an operator if you were calling 911 about a fire.

After talking to a friend, list as many home fire hazards as the two of you can think of.

What can you do to prevent a fire? List as many things as you can think of.

What would you do if there were a fire drill at our school? List your steps.

After a demonstration on how to help a choking victim: Write the steps that you can recall. Then work with a friend and revise your steps.

Geography and Maps

What is geography?

What would you like to know about maps and making them?

What do we use maps for? List as many reasons as you can think of.

We'll be taking an imaginary trip to Yellowstone National Park. List at least five questions you'd need to have answered before our trip.

Choose any two cities on the U.S. map. Figure out the distance between the two and write about how you did it.

List or draw any land forms you can remember from our reading.

How does a legend help you?

Draw a simple map with a key.

List all the water bodies/land forms that you can think of.

Historical Evidence/Archaeology

Write about the cave painting depicted in your social studies book. You are the artist. What will you say about your creation?

Write a poem about historical evidence.

Brainstorm a list of all the words you think of when you say the word "archaeology."

Construct an archaeology web.

Write a description of your antique object [obscure antiquities that the teacher distributed] and guess what it was used for.

Choose a position as one of the workers on the Great Pyramid. Tell about the problems you have carrying out your job.

Holidays

Before our discussion, list all the safety rules you can think of for Halloween. After, you may go back and add to your list.

Through the voice of your apple doll [a social studies project], tell about your safety plans for Halloween night.

Write about or draw how you celebrated Thanksgiving.

What are you thankful for?

Write your Christmas wish list.

Tell me about something you did or something that happened to you over our vacation.

What do you know about the Civil Rights movement and Martin Luther King, Jr.?

Children who go on family excursions: Write log entries about your trip while on the road.

Magnets

Tell how magnets and Krazy Glue are the same and different.

How is the Earth like a magnet?

List ten things that will stick to a magnet and ten that won't.

Mathematics

What is time?

What is money? Why do we use it?

Why do you think our number system is base ten?

Explain prime numbers to a friend.

Write a letter to me that takes me step by step through your solution to this long division problem: $3420 \div 209$.

In two minutes, how many multiples of 11 can you list?

Write a word problem that will give your classmates practice with the concept of ———.

Write a poem about numerators and denominators.

Make a list of math vocabulary words. How many can you think of? Can you find others in your math text and in the materials in the math center?

Make a chart to classify/categorize/sort the stuff in the junk box in your desk.

What is one pattern you discovered during today's lesson?

$R + O + B + E + R = T$ and T is < 10. Solve the problem in as many ways as you can.

Using the ROBERT problem as a model, solve your own name. (If you have an impossible name, use a nickname, last name, or someone else's name.)

Write the directions for playing a favorite math game.

Write the directions for doing one of the math programs on the computer.

Using a pencil and a protractor, draw three angles and measure them.

Using what you know about points, line segments, lines, rays, and angles, draw a spider web.

Explain what the terms "parallel" and "perpendicular" mean to you.

Make a list of figures in the classroom that have a line of symmetry.

Make a chart to show figures in the classroom that have one, two, three, or more infinite lines of symmetry.

Using the supermarket circulars from the newspaper, select three items that are sold by the pound. Figure out how much it would cost for 2½ pounds, 2¼ pounds, and 3¾ pounds of each item.

Take your journal to the grocery store. Find examples of multiple pricing. Observe the shoppers. Interview a clerk. Does such pricing encourage buying in multiples? Record your data and observations, and report back to the class on Monday.

Write down ten things you do every day and the times these things happen (e.g., "Get up: 7:15 A.M."). Then calculate the amount of time between each activity or event.

Make a list of ten items in the room that are less than six centimeters in length. List each item and its length.

Make a blueprint of your home.

Find the height (in centimeters) of each person in your group. What is the average height for your group?

Read one of the literature books in the math center (*The Doorbell Rang, Alexander Who Used To Be Rich Last Sunday, When Sheep Cannot Sleep, The Philharmonic Gets Dressed*, etc.) and write your own version.

Take your journal to the library. Make a list of picture books that could be used to teach math concepts. Categorize the books: numbers, place value, shapes, addition and subtraction, multiplication and division, telling time, probability/estimation/prediction, fractions and decimals, measurement, and money.

Matter

What do you think matter is? (Thirty minutes later, after a reading assignment: Now, tell me again about matter.)

List all of the things you do or use every day that involve water.

Students are given an ice cube in a clear cup: Describe what you see, feel, and smell over the next fifteen minutes.

In three columns, quickly list as many solids, liquids, and gases as you can think of.

Describe our "mystery matter" (cornstarch and water). Is it a solid, liquid, or gas? Explain.

The Middle Ages

After a day in which kids kept a vow of silence and dressed as monks (in old choir robes): What did you think of being a monk? What was life like for you?

Do you think Charlemagne should have been called "Charles the Great"? Why or why not?

In response to the novel *Otto of the Silver Hand* (Howard Pyle), which the teacher is reading aloud: What did you learn about the Middle Ages from the story today?

During a filmstrip on feudalism, stop the film in three places to ask:

1. How does the filmstrip version of what it was like to be a noble differ from the fairy-tale image of kings?
2. How does your image of a knight differ from the filmstrip's?
3. What are some differences that you see between the peasant class and the middle or merchant class?

Why could the Middle Ages also be called the "dark ages"?

Nutrition and Health

Pretend you are my mother or father. Convince me that I need to eat well.

Write a list of important things that [an ill classmate] can do for his/her health.

Choose your favorite of the four food groups and tell why you think it's the best. (Share with kids who chose other groups.)

Pretend you are flouride. Tell how you help children.

Where do humans fit in the food chain?

Oceans and Marine Animals

If you could stand on the ocean floor, what do you think you'd see?

Draw two pictures of Charlie the Tuna, one standing on the continental slope and the other on the continental shelf.

Half the class, you are currents. The rest of you are tides. Write a letter to the other group explaining why you're important. (Then, in pairs, read your letters to each other.)

What is ocean water good for? List as many uses as you can think of.

Draw a diagram of a way ocean water could be used to generate electricity.

Brainstorm a list of foods from the sea.

If you lived in the ocean, what would you be and why? Where would you live? Draw yourself.

Write a daily observation of one of our live sea animals.

Sketch and make notes about the sea creatures in today's collection (several times, over a period of six weeks).

How do you think the animals in a salt marsh feed?

What might be the effects of high and low tides on the plants and animals that live in the salt marsh?

How do you think that fish adapt to where they live in the ocean (top, middle, bottom)?

If I were a [sea creature of the writer's choice] . . .

The best part of the ocean is ———.

How do you think that chemical/biological/physical factors influence the lives of sea creatures?

Sketch the top, side, and bottom of a sand dollar and a basket sea star.

Compare land animals and sea animals.

Why did our hermit crab die? What do you think contributed to its death?

After a read-aloud of the first half of *Newberry: Life and Times of a Maine Clam* (Vincent Dethier):

> List any facts you heard.
>
> List any questions you might have.
>
> What do you think Newberry will do to get out of this mess?

Plants and Trees

What is a plant?

We all need trees. Why? List as many reasons as you can think of.

How are trees good community members?

Draw your own diagram of the process of pollination to fertilization.

Write a letter to me telling me as much as you can about how a leaf makes its own food.

After an experiment adding water to raisins: Write down your observations of what happened. Why do you think this happened?

Pretend you're a tree in a forest and can see and talk. Tell me what is happening in the forest around you.

Draw a kind of tree you know well. Write and tell a friend all that you know about the tree you drew.

Why do you think that some of the plants in our room are closer to the window?

How does a flower get to be a flower?

Why do you think the leaves change color in the fall?

Draw a picture that shows how water travels in a plant.

You are a seed. Tell all the ways you might travel in order to start a new plant.

Draw the life cycle of a plant.

In four groups: If a tree could talk, what would it tell you about its trunk, leaves, roots, and crown?

Each student "adopts" a tree in the area around the school. Periodically, through the school year, they write an observation of the tree and make a rubbing of one of its leaves.

Pollution

What are your feelings about pollution?

As you walk through the habitat around our school, list all the pollution you're aware of. Categorize your list. Who is responsible for creating each category?

Portland, Maine

Where is Portland?

Tell me all you know about Portland.

How do you think that Portland became a city?

Describe your neighborhood.

Make a list of places to go in the Portland area.

What kinds of buildings are on our Reiche School block? What are their uses?

Draw sketches of the buildings on the Reiche block.

Tell about the Longfellow House. Tell about the Dow House. Compare the two houses.

Make a list of local places of architectural or historical significance we might visit on field trips this spring.

Reading and Literature

AUTHORS AND ILLUSTRATORS

Who is your favorite author so far this school year? What do you like about this author's writing?

Who is the narrator of the story you're reading? Why do you think the author chose this narrator?

Finish this sentence: I love the way the author . . .

Have you read any other books by the author you're reading now? If yes, how does this one compare? If no, would you like to?

Did you learn anything about the author of the book you're reading? If yes, what? If no, what would you like to know about the author?

Who is one of your favorite illustrators? Why?

Tell about a book you've read where you think that the author had a message. What was the message?

CHARACTERS

Who is the main character in your book? How do you know?

Tell me about your favorite character in the book you're reading. What kind of person is your character, and why is he/she your favorite?

How did your main character change?

Is your main character believable?

How did you get to know the main character in your story? (Through what he/she said or did? Through description? How?)

Write a brief interview with the main character of your book.

EXTENDING A READ-ALOUD

What do you think will happen next? What would you like to happen next?

Write your own solution to the chapter mystery in *Encyclopedia Brown*.

List your favorite read-alouds.

What book should I read aloud next? Why this one?

Attean and Matt, our main characters, have changed in this story [Elizabeth Speare's *The Sign of the Beaver*]. Choose one and tell me how you think he has changed.

GENRES

Write a letter to me about the kind of story you like best. Why do you like this type?

Set aside several pages to keep a list of folktales and fairy tales that you read during the school year.

Compare the movie of *The Lion, the Witch, and the Wardrobe* with the book.

How do you classify fiction and nonfiction?

How do you think a poem is different from prose?

How often do you read poetry? Name a favorite poet and tell why you like him or her.

What do you think are the elements that make up a tall tale? A myth?

List as many kinds of reading/writing as you know.

LEADS AND CONCLUSIONS

How did the author of your book get you interested in the story? What was there about the lead that worked for you?

Were you satisfied with the ending of your book?

Why do you think the author chose this conclusion?

OPEN-ENDED

Respond in any way you'd like to the book you're reading now.

Write a letter to me about the book you're reading now.

Write a poem about your book.

How would you advertise your book?

Does your book remind you of other stories?

How does this book make you feel?

Did you ever feel like laughing or crying when you were reading this book?

Finish the sentence: I was surprised . . .

Finish the sentence: I wonder . . .

Finish the sentence: I wish . . .

THE READER'S TASTES

How do you decide whether you'll read a particular book?

Write a letter to me telling me about a book you really liked.

What was the best book you read this quarter? What made it best?

What was your favorite part of this book/story/poem?

Write a letter to someone who says he or she doesn't like to read, convincing him or her to read your book.

Would you recommend your book to another? Why or why not?

How do you rate books? That is, what makes a book one of the best you've ever read?

What kind of person do you think would like the book you're reading?

THE READER'S WRITING

Is there anything about this book that you don't like? Tell how you would write it differently.

Have you ever gotten an idea from a book you were reading that you used in your own writing?

Which authors that you've read have influenced the way that you write?

READING HABITS

Why do you read?

When do you read?

Where do you read?

Have you ever bought a book?

How do you feel about being read to by me?

READING STRATEGIES

What do you do when you're reading and you come up against a word you don't know?

How do you decide to abandon a book?

How do you decide when to skip or skim?

Try to predict what will happen next in your story.

Have you ever reread a book or a part of a book? Why or why not?

What makes a good reader?

Tell a bit about your reading rate: when do you speed up or slow down?

What clues does the author of your book use to help you understand the story?

How did you learn to read?

Why is there a table of contents in a book?

What would you use an index for? What kind of book would have an index?

SETTING

Write a letter telling me about the setting of the book you're reading. Why do you think the author chose this time and place?

Is the setting of your story more or less important than the characters? Why do you think this is so?

TITLES

Do you think the title of your book is appropriate?

Did the title of your book "grab" you?

How do you think the author chose this title?

School Life

What did you think of your first day of school? What did you enjoy? What has you worried?

List five things that you did in school today.

What could we do to make our room better?

Where would you like to go on a school field trip this year?

What can you do, as an individual, to improve behavior in our classroom?

Now that you've heard a little bit about writing workshop, what are some questions that you have?

How would you explain writing workshop to a new student?

How do you feel about the quiz you just took?

How was it helpful or unhelpful to study today with a partner?

What happened in our classroom when the substitute was here this morning?

Make a list of our school activities we could write about in a booklet for our Florida pen pals.

Pretend you're the teacher. Make up a quiz for our class about ———.

What's your favorite subject? Why? Your least favorite? Why?

Who was your favorite teacher ever? What made him/her the best?

What would you change about our school building?

Evaluate your role in your group's project.

Evaluate your own project. What worked? What didn't? What advice would you give to next year's students?

The Senses

How does each of our senses help us survive?

Our classroom is silent, and I have just set this timer for five minutes. List as many sounds as you can hear during the five minutes.

The Solar System

What do you know about our solar system? (After the unit: What were you mistaken about?)

Choose a planet that you'd like to live on. Write a letter to a friend inviting him/her to your planet. Tell about what you would see there.

What are some differences between Earth and our moon?

List as many of the nine planets as you can remember. Which is your favorite?

What do you think the Christmas star really is?

Brainstorm as many reasons as you can for why we need the sun.

Make a list of everything you'd need to pack for a trip to the moon.

The U.S. Constitution and Colonies

List three things you'd like to know about the Constitution.

You're George Washington. Explain to a group of fifth graders why we have a Constitution.

Write a "Who Am I?" as one of the original Amendments.

Write a poem about the Constitution.

Who do you think runs our country?

List the rights you have as a U.S. citizen.

Which of the first colonies would you like to have lived in? Why?

Why do you think we have laws?

Do you think the Americans were justified in using violence against England?

What is the U.S. Constitution to you?

List some things you can do because of the Constitution.

U.S. States

Write the names of the New England states that you can remember. (The following day: List the New England states. Did you think of more today than you did yesterday?)

If someone offered you a free airline ticket to any New England state, which would you choose? Why?

Make a list of scenes of [state or region] for a coloring book.

Weather

What would you like to know about the weather?

How do we observe weather?

How do we measure weather?

Pretend you're a meteorologist. Explain to a class of third graders what a barometer does.

Why do you think people's hair gets frizzy when the weather is humid?

Write a dialogue between a warm front and a cold front in which each introduces himself or herself to the other.

Choose one type of precipitation and write a poem about it.

How can you tell what the weather will be like? List as many ways as you can think of.

Write your own *Poor Richard's Almanac* entry on weather.

If you could talk to [local television meteorologist], what questions would you have about how he/she does his/her job?

What do you know about ice?

Guess why parts of the earth are hot and other parts are cold.

Draw the three kinds of clouds. List three words beneath each drawing to describe the cloud.

Appendix C

Bury Yourself in Books: Children's Literature for Content-Area Study

ABC Books

A Is for Angry: An Animal and Adjective Alphabet, Boynton, Workman Publishing, 1983

A Is for Australia, Brennan, J. M. Dent Pty Ltd., 1985

A My Name Is Alice, Bayer, Dial Books, 1984

The ABC Bunny, Gag, Coward-McCann, 1933

ABC: Museum of Fine Arts, Boston, Mayers, Harry N. Abrams, 1986

Alphabatics, MacDonald, Bradbury Press, 1986

The Alphabet Book, Eastman, Random House, 1974

The Alphabet Symphony, McMillan, Greenwillow Books, 1977

Animalia, Base, Viking Kestrel, 1986

Anno's Alphabet, Anno, Thomas Y. Crowell, 1974

The Ark in the Attic: An Alphabet Adventure, Ockenga, David R. Godine, 1987

Ashanti to Zulu: African Traditions, Musgrove, Dial Books, 1976

The Bird Alphabet Book, Pallotta, Quinlan Press, 1986

Caribou Alphabet, Owens, Dog Ear Press, 1988

David McPhail's Animals A to Z, McPhail, Scholastic, 1988

An Edward Lear Alphabet, Newson (illus.), Mulberry Books, 1983

Farm Alphabet Book, Miller, Scholastic, 1981

A Farmer's Alphabet, Azarian, David R. Godine, 1981

The Icky Bug Alphabet Book, Pallotta, Quinlan Press, 1986

Ocean Alphabet Book, Pallotta, Quinlan Press, 1986

Pig from A to Z, Geisert, Houghton Mifflin, 1986

Q is for Duck: An Alphabet Guessing Game, Eiting/Folsom, Clarion Books, 1980

Spot's Alphabet, Hill, G. P. Putnam's Sons, 1983
What's Inside? The Alphabet Book, Kitamura, Farrar, Straus & Giroux, 1985

Ancient Egypt

Mummies Made in Egypt, Aliki, Thomas Y. Crowell, 1979
Tut's Mummy Lost . . . and Found, Donnelly, Random House, 1988

Ancient Greece

The Greek Gods, Evslin, Evslin, and Hoopes, Scholastic, 1966
Hercules and Other Tales from Greek Myths, Coolidge, Scholastic, 1949
Jason and the Golden Fleece, Gunther, Scholastic, 1959
The Macmillan Book of Greek Gods and Heros, Low, Macmillan, 1985

Ancient Rome

The Bronze Bow, Speare, Houghton Mifflin, 1961
City: A Story of Rome Planning and Construction, Macaulay, Houghton Mifflin, 1974

Colonial Times

The Adventures of George Washington, Davidson, Scholastic, 1965
And Then What Happened, Paul Revere?, Fritz, Scholastic, 1973
A Gathering of Days, Bios, Macmillan, 1979
Rachel and Obadiah, Turkle, E. P. Dutton, 1978
The Root Cellar, Lunn, Puffin Books, 1981
Thy Friend, Obadiah, Turkle, Viking Press, 1969
Where Was Patrick Henry on the 29th of May?, Fritz, Coward, McCann & Geoghegan, 1975

Communities

Baa, Macaulay, Houghton Mifflin, 1985
The Butter Battle Book, Suess, Random House, 1984

Hugh Pine and the Good Place, van de Wetering, Houghton Mifflin, 1986

The Mushroom Center Disaster, Bodecker, Atheneum, 1974

New Providence: A Changing Cityscape, Von Tscharner, Harcourt Brace Jovanovich, 1987

Sing a Song of People, Lenski, Little, Brown, 1987

The Constitution

The Bill of Rights, Colman, Childrens Press, 1987

The Constitution, Colman, Childrens Press, 1987

A More Perfect Union: The Story of Our Constitution, Maestro, Lothrop, Lee & Shepard, 1987

Shh! We're Writing the Constitution, Fritz, Scholastic, 1987

The Spirit of 1787: The Making of Our Constitution, Lomask, Ballantine, 1980

We the People, Spier, Doubleday, 1987

Creatures

IN GENERAL

Amazing Animal Groups, Venino, National Geographic Society, 1981

Amazing World of Ants, Sabin, Troll Associates, 1982

Amazing World of Butterflies and Moths, Sabin, Troll Associates, 1982

Animal Fact/Animal Fable, Simon, Crown Publishers, 1979

Animals and Their Hiding Places, McCauley, National Geographic Society, 1986

Animals Born Alive and Well, Heller, Grosset & Dunlap, 1982

Animals in Danger, National Geographic Society, 1978

Animals: My Picture Library, Jules Books, 1986

Animals Should Definitely Not Act Like People, Barrett, Atheneum, 1980

Animals Should Definitely Not Wear Clothing, Barrett, Atheneum, 1970

Animals That Live in Trees, McCauley, National Geographic Society, 1986

Annie and the Wild Animals, Brett, Houghton Mifflin, 1985

Baby Animals, Shapiro, Intervisual Communications, 1979

Baby Farm Animals, Windsor, National Geographic Society, 1984

Bugs, Parker/Wright, Greenwillow Books, 1987

Chickens Aren't the Only Ones, Heller, Grosset & Dunlap, 1981

Creatures of Darkness, Waters, Scholastic, 1975

Creatures of the Desert, Gibson (illus.), National Geographic Society, 1987

Creatures of the Night, Rinard, National Geographic Society, 1977
Creatures of the Woods, Eugene, National Geographic Society, 1985
Exploring Animal Homes, Rowland-Entwistle, Willowisp Press, 1984
A Forest Year, Lerner, William Morrow, 1987
Have You Seen the Birds? Oppenheim, Scholastic, 1968
Helping Our Animal Friends, Rinard, National Geographic Society, 1985
Hide and Seek, Gibson (illus.), National Geographic Society, 1985
How Animals Behave, National Geographic Society, 1984
How Animals Live, Civardi and Kilpatrick, Usborne Publishing Ltd., 1976
How Speedy Is a Cheetah? Knapp, Platt & Munk, Publishers, 1987
How to Draw Forest Animals, Soloff-Levy, Watermill Press, 1985
How to Hide a Butterfly and Other Insects, Heller, Grosset & Dunlap, 1985
How to Hide a Crocodile and Other Reptiles, Heller, Grosset & Dunlap, 1986
How to Hide a Gray Treefrog and Other Amphibians, Heller, Grosset & Dunlap, 1986
How to Hide a Whippoorwill and Other Birds, Heller, Grosset & Dunlap, 1986
I Can Read About Birds, Schultz, Troll Associates, 1979
I Can Read About Creepy Crawly Creatures, Naden, Troll Associates, 1979
I Can Read About Frogs and Toads, Schultz, Troll Associates, 1979
I Can Read About Horses, Harris, Troll Associates, 1973
I Can Read About Insects, Merrians, Troll Associates, 1977
I Can Read About Reptiles, Cutts, Troll Associates, 1973
I Can Read About Spiders, Merrians, Troll Associates, 1977
Icky Bug Alphabet Book, Pallotta, Quinlan Press, 1986
In My Garden, Eldridge, The Medici Society, 1983
Incredible Animals A to Z, National Wildlife Federation, 1985
Insects and Their Relatives, Burton, Facts on File Publications, 1984
A Kettle of Hawks and Other Wildlife Groups, Arnosky, Coward, McCann & Geoghegan, 1979
Life in Ponds and Streams, Amos, National Geographic Society, 1981
The Magic Finger, DuBois, Harper & Row, 1966
Mammals, Sabin, Troll Associates, 1985
Meat Eaters, Latham/Sloan, Rigby, 1986
Mysteries and Marvels of the Animal World, Goaman and Amery, Usborne Publishing Ltd., 1983
Mysteries and Marvels of Bird Life, Wallace, Hume, and Morris, Usborne Publishing Ltd., 1984
Mysteries and Marvels of Insect Life, Owen, Usborne Publishing Ltd., 1984
Mysteries and Marvels of the Reptile World, Spellerberg and McKerchar, Usborne Publishing Ltd., 1984

National Geographic Book of Mammals, National Geographic Society, 1981

A Natural History Notebook of North American Animals, Douglas (illus.), Spectrum Book, Prentice Hall, 1985

Need a House? Call Ms. Mouse!, Mendoza, Grosset & Dunlap, 1981

A New True Book: Endangered Animals, Stone, Children's Press, 1984

A New True Book: Predators, Rosenthal, Children's Press, 1983

A New True Book: Underground Life, Roberts, Children's Press, 1983

Now You Can Read About Creatures of the Night, Griange, Brimax Books, 1988

Our Changing World, Selberg, Philomel Books, 1982

Peterson First Guides, Houghton Mifflin

    Birds, Peterson, 1986

    Insects, Leahy, 1987

    Mammals, Alden, 1987

    Wildflowers, Peterson, 1986

Pets in a Jar, Simon, Puffin Books, 1975

Prehistoric Animals, Gibbons, Holiday House, 1988

Reader's Digest North American Wildlife, Wernert, Reader's Digest Association, 1982

Saving Our Animal Friends, McGrath, National Geographic Society, 1986

The Secret World of Animals, National Geographic Society, 1986

Secrets of Nature, Cochrane, Scholastic, 1979

Small Pets, Hill, Usborne Publishing Ltd., 1982

Strange Animals of Australla, Eugene, National Geographic Society, 1981

The Tenth Good Thing About Barney, Viorst, Atheneum, 1971

Tooth and Claw, Freedman, Scholastic, 1980

Usborne First Nature Birds, Cox and Cork, Usborne Publishing Ltd., 1980

Usborne First Nature Butterflies and Moths, Cox and Cork, Usborne Publishing Ltd., 1980

Usborne First Nature Creepy Crawlers, Kilpatrick, Usborne Publishing Ltd., 1982

Usborne First Nature Wild Animals, Cork, Usborne Publishing Ltd., 1982

Vanishing Animals, Current, 1981

Wake Up—It's Night, Reigot, Scholastic, 1978

What Do Animals Eat?, Gross, Scholastic, 1971

What Happens at the Zoo, Rinard, National Geographic Society, 1984

What Makes a Bird?, Garelick, Follett Publishing, 1969

Where Do They Go? Insects in Winter, Selsam, Scholastic, 1981

Wild Animal Families, Davidson, Scholastic, 1980

Wildcats, Winston, National Geographic Society, 1981

Wonders of Wildlife, Walt Disney Studios, Grolier Enterprises, 1980

    Introduction to Animals

Raising the Young
Rhythms in Nature
Zoo Animals in Color, Kilpatrick, Octupus Books Ltd., 1981
Zoo Babies, Grosvenor, National Geographic Society, 1978

IN PARTICULAR

The Adventures of Maynard . . . A Maine Moose, Baker, Gannett Books, 1984
Alligators & Crocodiles, Blassingame, Scholastic, 1973
Amazing Monkeys, National Geographic Society, 1985
Baby Bears and How They Grow, Buxton, National Geographic Society, 1986
Bats in the Dark, Kaufmann, Thomas Y. Crowell, 1972
Bears in the Wild, Graham, Dell, 1981
The Beaver, Lane, Dial Books, 1981
Caterpillar Diary, Drew, Rigby, 1987
My Daddy Longlegs, Hawes, Thomas Y. Crowell, 1972
The First Dog, Brett, Harcourt Brace Jovanovich, 1988
The Giant Panda, Xugi, G. P. Putnam's Sons, 1986
The Goose Family Book, Kalas, Verlag Neugebauer Press, 1986
Great Gorillas, McGovern, Scholastic, 1980
Green Grass and White Milk, Aliki, Thomas Y. Crowell, 1974
The New Baby Calf, Chase, Scholastic, 1984
Owl Moon, Yolen, Philomel Books, 1987
Owls in the Family, Mowatt, Bantam Skylark Book, 1962
Panda, Bonners, Yearling, 1978
Questions and Answers About Ants, Selsam, Scholastic, 1967
Raccoons, Kostyal, National Geographic Society, 1987
Raccoons and Ripe Corn, Arnosky, Lothrop, Lee & Shepard, 1987
Rascal, North, Avon, 1963
Tadpole Diary, Drew, Rigby, 1987
Watch Honey Bees with Me, Hawes, Thomas Y. Crowell, 1964
What Is the Alligator Saying?, Gross, Scholastic, 1972
Wolves, Reigot, Scholastic, 1980

IN PARTICULAR: DINOSAURS

The Age of Dinosaurs, Lambert, Random House, 1987
All About Dinosaurs, Lambert, Nutmeg Press, 1978
The Brontosaurus, Redhead, Scholastic TAB Publications Ltd., 1985
Dinosaur Bones, Aliki, Thomas Y. Crowell, 1988
Dinosaur Time, Parish, Scholastic, 1974
Dinosaurs, Daly, Western Publishing, 1977
Dinosaurs Walked Here and Other Stories Fossils Tell, Lauber, Bradbury Press, 1987
Extinct Animals, Burton, Grosset & Dunlap, 1976
Finding Out About Dinosaurs, Petty, Willowisp Press, 1988

First Days of the World, Ames and Wyler, Scholastic, 1958
The First Men of the World, White, Scholastic, 1953
Flying Dragons, Eldridge, Troll Associates, 1980
Fossils Tell of Long Ago, Aliki, Scholastic, 1972
The Giant Dinosaur, Eldridge, Troll Associates, 1980
Giants from the Past, Bailey, National Geographic Society, 1983
How Big Is a Brachiosaurus?, Carroll, Platt & Munk, Publishers, 1986
I Can Read About Dinosaurs, Howard, Troll Associates, 1972
I Can Read About Prehistoric Animals, Eastman, Troll Associates, 1977
Last of the Dinosaurs, Eldridge, Troll Associates, 1980
My Visit to the Dinosaurs, Aliki, Thomas Y. Crowell, 1969
Patrick's Dinosaurs, Carrick, Clarion Books, 1983
Sea Monsters, Eldridge, Troll Associates, 1980
Search for a Living Fossil, Clymer, Scholastic, 1963
Story of Dinosaurs, Eastman, Troll Associates, 1982

IN PARTICULAR: MARINE LIFE

ABC Fish of the Gulf of Maine, State of Maine Department of Marine
    Resources
All About Islands, Rydell, Troll Associates, 1984
Along the Seashore, Buck, Abingdon Press, 1964
Amazing Animals of the Sea, National Geographic Society, 1981
Animals Nobody Loves, Simon, Scholastic, 1980
Animals of the Sea, Selsam, Four Winds Press, 1975
Animals of the Sea, Verite, Children's Press, 1964
Animals of the Seashore, Roux, Silver Burdett, 1981
Animals that Live in the Sea, Straker, National Geographic Society,
    1979
Animals That Live in Shells, Morris, Raintree Children's Books, 1977
Beach Bird, Carrick, Dial Books, 1973
Beneath the Cold Waters: The Marine Life of New England, Bavendam,
    Down East Books, 1980
Biography of a Killer Whale, Steiner, G. P. Putnam's Sons, 1978
The Blue Lobster, A Life Cycle, Carrick, Dial Books, 1975
The Blue Whale, Grosvenor, National Geographic Society, 1977
Burt Dow: Deep Water Man, McCloskey, Viking Press, 1963
The Castle Builder, Nolan, Macmillan, 1987
Corals, Ronai, Thomas Y. Crowell, 1976
Creatures of the Sea, Apy, Current, 1982
Crystal: The Story of a Real Baby Whale, Smyth, Down East Books,
    1986
Discovering Seashells, Florian, Charles Scribner's Sons, 1986
Does Anyone Know Where a Hermit Crab Goes?, Glaser, Knickerbocker
    Publishing, 1983
Dolphins: Our Friends in the Sea, Rinard, National Geographic Society,
    1986
Ducks Don't Get Wet, Goldin, Thomas Y. Crowell, 1965

The Emperor Penguins, Mizumura, Thomas Y. Crowell, 1969

Exploring an Ocean Tide Pool, Bendick, Garrard Publishing, 1976

Exploring the Seashore, Amos, National Geographic Society, 1984

A Field Guide to Fishes: Coloring Book, Peterson, Houghton Mifflin, 1987

A Field Guide to Shells: Coloring Book, Peterson, Houghton Mifflin, 1985

51 Questions and Answers About the Sea, Limburg, Random House, 1975

Fish Is Fish, Lionni, Pantheon, 1970

Fishes and Other Sea Creatures in Their Environments, Stewart, Marlborough Ltd., 1988

The Friendly Dolphins, Lauber, Scholastic, 1963

The Great Whales, Zim, Scholastic, 1951

Hidden Treasures of the Sea, A National Geographic Book for World Explorers, 1988

Houses from the Sea, Goudey, Charles Scribner's Sons, 1959

I Can Read About the Octopus, Schultz, Troll Associates, 1979

I Can Read About Sharks, Naden, Troll Associates, 1979

I Can Read About Whales and Dolphins, Anderson, Troll Associates, 1973

The Incredible Atlantic Herring, Cook, Dodd, Mead, 1979

Jellyfish and Other Sea Creatures, Oxford Scientific Films, G. P. Putnam's Sons, 1982

A Jellyfish Is Not a Fish, Waters, Thomas Y. Crowell, 1979

Kermit the Hermit, Peet, Houghton Mifflin, 1965

The Legend of the Whale, Stansfield, David R. Godine, 1985

Life on the Seashore, Angel, Silver Burdett, 1976

The Little Island, MacDonald, Doubleday, 1946

Little Whale, McGovern, Four Winds Press, 1979

Mysteries and Marvels of Ocean Life, Morris, Usborne Publishing Ltd., 1983

Nature Hide & Seek Oceans, Wood, Alfred A. Knopf, 1985

A New True Book: Animals of Sea and Shore, Pondendorf, Children's Press, 1982

A New True Book: Dangerous Fish, Broekel, Children's Press, 1982

A New True Book: Oceans, Carter, Children's Press, 1982

A New True Book: Penguins, Lepthien, Children's Press, 1983

A New True Book: Tropical Fish, Broekel, Children's Press, 1983

A New True Book: Whales and Other Sea Mammals, Posell, Children's Press, 1982

Newberry: The Life and Times of a Maine Clam, Dethier, Down East Books, 1981

The Nocturnal World of the Lobster, Cook, Dodd, Mead, 1972

Now You Can Read About . . . Creatures of the Deep, Stanton, Brimax Books, 1984

Now You Can Read About Sharks and Whales, Hoffman, Brimax Books, 1986

Ocean Alphabet Book, Pallotta, Quinlan Press, 1986

Ocean Dwellers, Roux, Silver Burdett, 1982

The Ocean World of Jacques Cousteau: Pharaohs of the Sea, Volume 9, Danbury Press, 1973

One Morning in Maine, McCloskey, Viking Press, 1952

Our Amazing Ocean, Adler, Troll Associates, 1983

Pagoo, Holling, Houghton Mifflin, 1957

Penguins and Polar Bears, Crow, National Geographic Society, 1985

Plankton, Drifting Life of Waters, May, Holiday House, 1972

Puffins Come Back, Friedman, Dodd, Mead, 1981

Questions and Answers About Seashore Life, List, Scholastic, 1970

Round Fish, Flat Fish and Other Animal Changes, Graham/Barber, Crown Publishers, 1982

The Sea, Life Nature Library, Engel, Time Life Books, 1969

The Sea Around Us, Carson, Golden Press, 1958

Sea Creatures Do Amazing Things, Myers, Random House, 1981

The Sea Is Calling Me, Hopkins (ed.), Harcourt Brace Jovanovich, 1986

Sea Otters—Little Clowns of the Sea, Davidson, Scholastic, 1984

Sea Songs, Livingston, Holiday House, 1986

Seabird, Holling, Houghton Mifflin, 1948

The Sealphabet Encyclopedia Coloring Book, McConnell, Stemmer House, 1982

The Seashore, Action Series, Pope, Franklin Watts, 1985

Seashore, Lambert, Warwick Press, 1977

Seashore Life, Kirkpatrick, Raintree Children's Books, 1985

The Seaside Naturalist, Coulombe, Phalarope Books, Prentice Hall, 1984

Shark Lady, McGovern, Scholastic, 1978

Sharks, McGovern, Scholastic, 1976

The Shell, Stix and Abbott, Harry N. Abrams, 1978

Shells Are Skeletons, Victor, Thomas Y. Crowell, 1977

Starfish, Bloch, Thomas Y. Crowell, 1962

Strange Animals of the Sea, Pinkney (illus.), National Geographic Society, 1987

The Sunlit Sea, Goldin, Thomas Y. Crowell, 1968

Swimmy, Lionni, Pantheon, 1968

Tidal Zones, Bouthillette, Delorme Publishing, 1983

Time of Wonder, McCloskey, Viking Press, 1957

Tracks Between the Tides, Shepard, Lothrop, Lee & Shepard, 1972

The True Story of Corky the Blind Seal, Irvine, Scholastic, 1987

Underwater Life: The Oceans, Morris, Raintree Children's Books, 1977

Usborne First Nature Fishes, Wheeler, Usborne Publishing Ltd., 1982

Whale Song, Johnston, G. P. Putnam's Sons, 1987

What the Sea Left Behind, Carpenter, Down East Books, 1981

What's Down There? Questions and Answers About the Ocean, Moche, Scholastic, 1984

What's Under the Ocean, Craig, Troll Associates, 1982

When the Whale Came to My Town, Young, Scholastic, 1974
Where the Waves Break: Life at the Edge of the Sea, Malnig, Carolrhoda Books, 1985
The Wonderful World of Seals and Whales, Crow, National Geographic Society, 1984
Wonders of Sea Gulls, Schreiber, Dodd, Mead, 1975
Wonders of the Seashore, Berrill, Dodd, Mead, 1951
Wonders of Starfish, Jacobson/Emerson, Dodd, Mead, 1977
Wonders of Terns, Schreiber, Dodd, Mead, 1978
World Beneath the Sea, National Geographic Society, 1967
Zachary Goes Ground Fishing, Larkin, Down East Books, 1982

The Environment

The Giving Tree, Silverstein, Harper & Row, 1964
The Kweeks of Kookatumdee, Peet, Houghton Mifflin, 1985
The Lorax, Seuss, Random House, 1971
The Mushroom Center Disaster, Bodecker, Atheneum, 1974
Professor Noah's Space Ship, Wildsmith, Oxford University Press, 1980
Where the Forest Meets the Sea, Baker, Julia MacRae Books, 1987
The Wump World, Peet, Houghton Mifflin, 1970

Exploration

I Can Read About Magellan, Schecter, Troll Associates, 1979
Where Do You Think You're Going Christopher Columbus?, Fritz, G. P. Putnam's Sons, 1980

Famous Americans

A Book About Benjamin Franklin, Gross, Scholastic, 1975
40 Presidents Facts & Fun, Bumann/Patterson, Willowisp Press, 1981
If You Grew Up with George Washington, Gross, Scholastic, 1982
The Incredible Journey of Lewis and Clark, Blumberg, Lothrop, Lee & Shepard 1987
John F. Kennedy, Smith, Simon & Schuster, 1987
Lincoln: A Photobiography, Freedman, Clarion Books, 1987
The Story of George Washington Carver, Moore, Scholastic, 1971
The Story of Martin Luther King: I Have a Dream, Davidson, Scholastic, 1986
The Wright Brothers at Kitty Hawk, Sobol, Scholastic, 1961

Geography

All About Mountains & Volcanoes, Marcus, Troll Associates, 1984
All About Ponds, Rockwell, Troll Associates, 1984
All About Rivers, Emil, Troll Associates, 1984
America, Lippman, Crown Publishers, 1985
Antarctica, Stone, Children's Press, 1986
Asia, Georges, Children's Press, 1986
Ben's Dream, Allsburg, Houghton Mifflin, 1982
The Children's Book of the Earth, Watts and Tyler, Usborne Publishing
    Ltd., 1976
The Children's Book of the Seas, Tyler, Usborne Publishing Ltd., 1976
Continents, Fradin, Children's Press, 1986
Countries of the World, Facts, Champion, EDC, 1986
Deserts, Wilkes, Usborne Publishing Ltd., 1980
Exploring the 50 States, Andersen, Willowisp Press, 1983
Florida in Words and Pictures, Fradin, Children's Press, 1980
Geo-Whiz, Tejada, National Geographic Society, 1988
The Harbor, Dapasquier, Grosset & Dunlap, 1984
Hawaii in Words and Pictures, Fradin, Children's Press, 1980
The Instant Answer Book of Countries, Warrender and Tyler, Usborne
    Publishing Ltd., 1978
Little Fox Goes to the End of the World, Tompert, Crown Publishers,
    1976
Maps and Globes, Broekel, Children's Press, 1983
Maps and Globes, Knowlton, Harper & Row, 1985
Marshes and Swamps, Stone, Children's Press, 1983
Mojave Siebert, Thomas Y. Crowell, 1988
Mountains, Wilkes, Usborne Publishing Ltd., 1980
A New True Book: Deserts, Posell, Children's Press, 1982
A New True Book: Volcanoes, Challand, Children's Press, 1983
Our Living Earth, Osband and Clifton-Dey, G. P. Putnam's Sons,
    1987
People, Spier, Doubleday, 1980
Picture Atlas, Tyler and Watts, Usborne Publishing Ltd., 1976
Secrets of the Earth, Dixon, Willowisp Press, 1987
The Usborne Book of World Geography, Tyler, Watts, Bowyer, Trundle,
    and Warrender, Usborne Publishing Ltd., 1978
Volcano, Lauber, Bradbury Press, 1987
Wonders of the Pond, Sabin, Troll Associates, 1982
Wonders of Rivers, Bains, Troll Associates, 1982
Wonders of Water, Dickinson, Troll Associates, 1983

AUSTRALIA

A Is for Australia, Brennan, J. M. Dent Pty Ltd., 1985

Aboriginal Lore, Mullins/Cook/Gerritsen, Shepp Books, 1987

Animalia, Base, Viking Kestrel, 1986

Animals in the Wild: Kangaroo, Serventy, Scholastic, 1983

Animals in the Wild: Koala, Serventy, Scholastic, 1983

Australian Wildlife and Flowers, Curran, Bartel Photography Pty Ltd., 1986

Australia's Great Barrier Reef, Bennett, Collins, 1987

The Bad-Tempered Ladybird, Carle, Puffin Books, 1977

The Bat and the Crocodile, Dolumyu/Sandaloo/Lofts, Ashton Scholastic, 1987

Bertie and the Bear, Allen, Nelson, 1983

The Bunyip of Berkeley's Creek, Wagner, Puffin Books, 1975

Click Go the Shears, Ingpen (illus.), Fontana Picture Lions, 1984

The Drover's Dream, Niland (illus.), Fontana Picture Lions, 1979

Dunbi the Owl, Utemorrah/Lofts, Ashton Scholastic, 1983

Educating Arthur, Graham, Era Publications, 1987

Enoch the Emu, Winch, Childerset, 1986

The Fed Up Family Album, Macleod, Puffin Books, 1983

The Great Piratical Rumbustification and the Librarian and the Robbers, Mahy, Puffin Books, 1978

The Great Tasmanian Tiger Hunt, Salmon, Lamont, 1986

How the Birds Got Their Colours, Albert/Lofts, Ashton Scholastic, 1983

Koala, Condit, Scholastic, 1981

A Koala Grows Up, Gelman, Scholastic, 1986

Koalas, Wexo, Zoobooks, National Education, Ltd., 1988

Koala's Book of Poems, Fossard, Edward Arnold, 1984

The Kookaburra That Helps at the Nest, Reilly, Kangaroo Press, 1987

A Lake in the Forest, Russell, G. K. Bolton, 1980

The Legend of the Whale, Stansfield, David R. Godine, 1986

The Long Red Scarf, Hilton, Omnibus Books, 1987

The Magpie and the Crow, Coulthard and McKenzie, Harcourt Brace Jovanovich, 1987

The Man from Ironbank, Paterson, Fontana Picture Lions, 1974

The Man from Snowy River, Paterson, Collins, 1977

Moon Man, Coulthard and McKenzie, Harcourt Brace Jovanovich, 1987

Mulga Bill's Bicycle, Paterson, Collins, 1973

Nice and Nasty: A Book of Opposites, Butterworth and Inkpen, Picture Knicht, 1987

One Woolly Wombat, Argent, Omnibus Books, 1982

Penny Pollards Diary, Klein, Oxford University Press, 1983

Platypus and Kookaburra, Ingamells, Collins, 1987

Possum Magic, Fox, Abingdon Press, 1983

Sail Away: The Ballad of Skip and Nell, Fox, Ashton Scholastic, 1986

17 Kings and 42 Elephants, Mahy, J. M. Dent and Sons Ltd., 1972

Strange Animals of Australia, Eugene, National Geographic Society, 1981

Ten Monster Islands, Macleod, Omnibus Books, 1987

Trucks, Ottley, Hodder and Stoughton, 1985

Waltzing Matilda, Paterson, Fontana Picture Lions, 1979

What Do You Do with a Kangaroo? Mayer, Scholastic, 1973

Where the Forest Meets the Sea, Baker, Julia MacRae Books, 1987

Wilfrid Gordon McDonald Partridge, Fox, Kane Miller Book Publishers, 1985

The Witch in the Cherry Tree, Mahy, Puffin Books, 1974

Wombat Stew, Vaugham, Ashton Scholastic, 1984

Young Imagination, Roy and Steele (eds.), Primary English Teaching Association, 1988 (distributed by Heinemann)

Yulu's Coal, Coulthard and McKenzie, Harcourt Brace Jovanovich, 1987

CHINA

A Book About Pandas, Gross, Scholastic, 1980

Chasing the Moon to China, McLean, Redbird Press, 1987

Chen Ping and His Magic Axe, Demi, Dodd, Mead, 1987

Chin Chiang & the Dragon's Dance, Wallace, Atheneum, 1984

China, Adshead, Multimedia Publications, 1986

China, Here We Come, Yungmei, G. P. Putnam's Sons, 1981

China Homecoming, Fritz, G. P. Putnam's Sons, 1985

China's Long March, Fritz, G. P. Putnam's Sons, 1988

Chinese New Year, Brown/Ortiz, Henry Holt, 1987

Chinese Word for Horse, Lewis, Schocken Books, 1980

Chinese Written Characters, Quong, Cobble Hill Press, 1968

A Chinese Zoo: Fables and Proverbs, Demi, Harcourt Brace Jovanovich, 1987

Count Your Way to China, Haskins, Carolrhoda Books, 1987

Cricket Boy, Ziner, Doubleday, 1977

Dragon Kites and Dragonflies, Demi, Harcourt Brace Jovanovich, 1986

Dragonwings, Yep, Harper & Row, 1975

The Emperor and the Kite, Yolen, Philomel Books, 1988

The Emperor's New Clothes, Anderson, Scholastic, 1971

Enchanted Tapestry, San Souci, Dial Books, 1987

Everyone Knows What a Dragon Looks Like, Williams, Four Winds Press, 1976

Eyes of the Dragon, Leaf, Lothrop, Lee & Shepard, 1987

A Family in China, Fyson/Greenhill, Lerner Publications, 1985

The Five Chinese Brothers, Bishop, Coward-McCann, 1983

Golden Conch, Qizhong, Foreign Languages Press, Bejing

Great Wall of China, Fisher, Macmillan, 1986

Gung Hay Fat Choy, Behrens, Children's Press, 1982

Homesick: My Own Story, Fritz, G. P. Putnam's Sons, 1982

In the Year of the Boar and Jackie Robinson, Lord, Harper & Row, 1984
Liang and the Magic Paintbrush, Demi, Henry Holt, 1980
Little Chen and the Dragon Brothers, Xi/Wen, Foreign Languages Press, Bejing
Lu Ban Learns Carpentry, Hua, Foreign Languages Press, Bejing
Ma Liang and His Magic Brush, Xing, Foreign Languages Press, Bejing
The Magic Wings, Wolkstein, E. P. Dutton, 1983
Mao, Carter, Viking Press, 1979
Mao for Beginners, Rius & Friends, Pantheon, 1980
Mei Li, Handforth, Doubleday, 1938
Ming Lo Moves the Mountain, Lobel, Scholastic, 1982
Monkey and the White Bone Demon, adapted by Shi, Viking/Kestrel, 1984
The Mountains of Tibet, Gerstein, Harper & Row, 1987
Nezha Stirs Up the Sea, Hongen, Foreign Languages Press, Bejing
Nightingale, Anderson, Picture Book Studio, 1984
The Nightingale, Anderson, Harcourt Brace Jovanovich, 1985
Once There Were No Pandas, Greaves, E. P. Dutton, 1985
Panda, Bonners, Delacorte, 1978
Paper Through the Ages, Cosner, Carolrhoda Books, 1984
Princess & Sun, Moon & Stars, Reuter, Pelham Books, 1985
The Seeing Stick, Yolen, Thomas Y. Crowell, 1977
Seven Clam Sisters, Niang, Zhaohua Publishing, Bejing
Shen of the Sea, Chrisman, E. P. Dutton, 1925
Spring of Butterflies, Ligi, Lothrop, Lee & Shepard, 1985
Story About Ping, Flack, Viking Press, 1961
Tikki Tikki Tembo, Mosel, Scholastic, 1968
Ts'ao Chung Weighs an Elephant, Ludwig, Creative Arts Books, 1983
Weaving of a Dream, Heyer, Viking Kestrel, 1986
The White Wave, Wolkstein, Thomas Y. Crowell, 1979
Xiao Ming & Katie Visit the Zoo, Li, People's Publishing House, China
Yeh Shen, Louie, Philomel Books, 1982
Young Fu of the Upper Yangtze, Lewis, Henry Holt, 1960

JAPAN

The Crane Wife, Patterson, Mulberry Books, 1987
Crow Boy, Yashima, Scholastic, 1965
The Dream Eater, Garrison, Aladdin Books, 1986
The Funny Little Woman, Mosel, E. P. Dutton, 1972
The Paper Crane, Bang, Greenwillow Books, 1985
Sedako and the Thousand Paper Cranes, Coerr, Dell, 1977

MAINE

Abbie Burgess, Lighthouse Heroine, Jones/Sargent, Down East Books, 1969

The Adventures of Maynard . . . A Maine Moose, Baker, Gannett Books, 1984

Bimsi and Bamsi: An Adventure in the Maine Woods, Derevitzky, Gannett Books, 1985

Blueberries for Sal, McCloskey, Viking Press, 1948

Island Boy, Cooney, Viking Kestrel, 1988

The Island Merry-Go-Round, Sargent, Windswept House, 1988

Island Winter, Martin, Greenwillow Books, 1984

Jem's Island, Lasky, Charles Scribner's Sons, 1982

Keep the Lights Burning Abbie, Roop, Carolrhoda Books, 1985

The Littlest Lighthouse, Sargent, Down East Books, 1981

Maine in Words and Pictures, Fradin, Children's Press, 1980

Miss Rumphius, Cooney, Viking Press, 1982

A New Friend for Morganfield: The Adventures of a Maine Mouse, Hobart, Gannett Books, 1985

One Morning in Maine, McCloskey, Viking Press, 1952

Time of Wonder, McCloskey, Viking Press, 1957

RUSSIA

Babushka, Mikolaycak, Holiday House, 1984

The Month Brothers, Marshak, William Morrow, 1983

Once There Was a Tree, Romanova, Dial Books, 1985

Peter and the Wolf, Mikolaycak, Viking Press, 1982

Peter and the Wolf, Prokofiev, Viking Penguin, 1985

Holidays

The Holiday Song Book, Quackenbush, Lothrop, Lee & Shepard, 1977

ARBOR DAY

Arborday, Fisher, Thomas Y. Crowell, 1965

Johnny Appleseed, Moore, Scholastic, 1964

Johnny Appleseed, York, Troll Associates, 1980

CHRISTMAS

A Child's Christmas in Wales, Thomas, Holiday House, 1954

Christmas, Plenkowski, Alfred A. Knopf, 1984

Christmas in the Barn, Brown, Thomas Y. Crowell, 1952

An Early American Christmas, de Paola, Holiday House, 1987

The Little Fir Tree, Brown, Thomas Y. Crowell, 1954

The Night Before Christmas, Moore, Holiday House, 1980

The Polar Express, Allsburg, Houghton Mifflin, 1985

The Story of Holly and Ivy, Godden, Viking Kestrel, 1985

Tomie de Paola's Book of Christmas Carols, de Paola, G. P. Putnam's Sons, 1987

The Twelve Days of Christmas, Brett, Dodd, Mead, 1986

What a Morning: The Christmas Story in Black Spirituals, Langstaff (ed.), Macmillan, 1987

COLUMBUS DAY

Christopher Columbus, Goodnough, Troll Associates, 1979

The Columbus Story, Dalgliesh, Charles Scribner's Sons, 1955

I Christopher Columbus, Weil, Atheneum, 1983

"Our Search for the True Columbus Landfall," *National Geographic*, November 1986

The Story of Christopher Columbus: Admiral of the Ocean Sea, Osborne, Dell, 1987

The Story of the New Lands, Peattie, Grossett & Dunlap, 1987

Where Do You Think You're Going Christopher Columbus? Fritz, G. P. Putnam's Sons, 1980

World Explorer Christopher Columbus, Kaufman, Garrad Publishing, 1963

EASTER

The Big Bunny and the Easter Eggs, Kroll, Scholastic, 1982

The Carrot Seed, Krauss, Scholastic, 1945

Chickens Aren't the Only Ones, Heller, Grosset & Dunlap, 1981

The Country Bunny and the Little Gold Shoes, Heyward, Scholastic, 1939

The Easter Bear, Barrett, Children's Press, 1981

The Golden Egg Book, Brown, Golden Press, 1947

The Great Big Especially Beautiful Easter Egg, Stevenson, Scholastic, 1983

Horton Hatches the Egg, Suess, Random House, 1940

Mouskin's Easter Basket, Miller, Prentice-Hall, 1986

The Runaway Bunny, Brown, Harper & Row, 1942

Seven Little Rabbits, Becker, Scholastic, 1973

The Tale of the Bunny Picnic, Gikow, Scholastic, 1987

The Tale of Peter Rabbit, Potter, Scholastic, 1986

FOURTH OF JULY

I Can Read About July 4, 1776, Schultz, Troll Associates, 1979

HALLOWEEN

Arthur's Halloween, Brown, Little, Brown, 1982

The Blue-Nosed Witch, Embry, Bantam Skylark, 1956

Bumps in the Night, Allard, Bantam Skylark, 1979
Clifford's Halloween, Bridwell, Scholastic, 1986
Do Not Open, Turkle, E. P. Dutton, 1981
Funny Bones, Atilberg, Scholastic, 1980
Georgie and the Robbers, Bright, Doubleday, 1963
The Ghost Eye Tree, Martin Jr./Archambault, Henry Holt, 1985
Knee-Knock Rise, Babbitt, Farrar, Straus & Giroux, 1970
Millions of Cats, Gag, Coward-McCann, 1928
Pumpkin Pumpkin, Titherington, Greenwillow Books, 1986
The Rabbi and 29 Witches, Hirsh, Scholastic, 1986
Scary Scary Halloween, Bunting, Clarion Books, 1986
That Terrible Halloween Night, Stevenson, Scholastic, 1980
The Vanishing Pumpkin, Johnston, G. P. Putnam's Sons, 1983

HANUKKAH

A Picture Book of Hanukkah, Adler, Scholastic, 1982

THANKSGIVING

Alligator Arrived with Apples: A Potluck Alphabet Feast, Dragonwagon, Macmillan, 1987
Boy on the Mayflower, Vinton, Scholastic, 1957
Constance: A Story of Early Plymouth, Clapp, Puffin Penguin, 1968
Cranberry Thanksgiving, Devlin, Four Winds Press, 1971
I Can Read About the First Thanksgiving, Anderson, Troll Associates, 1977
If You Sailed on the Mayflower, McGovern, Scholastic, 1969
It's Thanksgiving, Prelutsky, Scholastic, 1982
Let's Celebrate Thanksgiving: A Book of Drawing Fun, Watermill Press, 1988
Oh What a Thanksgiving, Kroll, Scholastic, 1988
An Old Fashion Thanksgiving, Alcott, J. B. Lippincott, 1970
Over the River and Through the Woods, Turkle, Coward-McCann, 1974
Pilgrims and Thanksgiving, Bains, Troll Associates, 1985
The Pilgrims of Plymouth, Sewall, Atheneum, 1986
Sailing to America: Colonist at Sea, Knight, Troll Associates, 1982
Squanto Friend of the Pilgrims, Bulla, Scholastic, 1954
The Thanksgiving Story, Dalgliesh, Atheneum, 1954
The Thanksgiving Treasure, Rock, Dell, 1974
Turkeys, Pilgrims, & Indian Corn: The Story of Thanksgiving Symbols, Barth, Clarion Books, 1975

Math

Anno's Counting Book, Anno, Thomas Y. Crowell, 1975
Anno's Counting House, Anno, Philomel Books, 1982
Anno's Math Games, Anno, G. P. Putnam's Sons, 1982
Anno's Mysterious Multiplying Jar, Anno, Philomel Books, 1983
The Bears' Counting Book, Wild, Harper & Row, 1978
Bears on Wheels, Berenstain, Random House, 1969
Beginning to Learn About Shapes, Allington, Raintree Children's Books, 1979
Bunches and Bunches of Bunnies, Matthews, Scholastic, 1978
Count the Cats, Weihs, Doubleday, 1976
Count Down Til Christmas, Peet, Golden Gate Jr. Books, 1972
The Counting Book, Hindley & King, Hayes Books, 1979
The Doorbell Rang, Hutchins, Scholastic, 1986
A Dozen Dogs, Zlifert, Random House, 1985
Farmer Goff and His Turkey Sam, Schatell, Lippincott, 1982
Father Foxe's Penny Rhymes, Watson, Harper & Row, 1971
The Grouchy Ladybug, Carle, Harper & Row, 1977
How Much Is a Million?, Schwartz, Scholastic, 1985
Lucy and Tom's 1,2,3, Hughes, Lothrop, Lee & Shepard, 1987
The Man Who Tried to Save Time, Krasilousky, Doubleday, 1979
Marmalade's Picnic, Wheeler, Alfred A. Knopf, 1983
Marmalade's Snowy Day, Wheeler, Alfred A. Knopf, 1982
Marmalade's Yellow Leaf, Wheeler, Alfred A. Knopf, 1982
Mary Alice, Operator Number Nine, Jeffrey Allen, Little, Brown, 1975
May I Bring a Friend? De Regniers, Atheneum, 1964
The Midnight Farm, Lindbergh, Dial Books, 1987
Millions of Cats, Gay, Coward-McCann, 1928
Moja Means One: Swahili Counting Book, Feelings, Dial Books, 1971
The Month Brothers, Marshak, William Morrow, 1983
Mother Goose Nursery Rhymes, various authors, illustrators
My Very First Book of Numbers, Carle, Thomas Y. Crowell, 1974
My Very First Book of Shapes, Carle, Thomas Y. Crowell, 1974
The Nine Crying Dolls, Peilowski, G. P. Putnam's Sons, 1980
On Sunday I Lost My Cat, Demers, Willowisp Press, 1986
One Duck, Another Duck, Pomerantz, Greenwillow Books, 1984
One Fish, Two Fish, Red Fish, Blue Fish, Seuss, Random House, 1960
One Hunter, Hutchins, Mulberry Books, 1982
One Monday Morning, Shuleritz, Macmillan, 1967
Pezzettino, Lionni, Pantheon, 1975
Seasons on the Farm, Miller, Prentice Hall, 1986
Six Dogs, Twenty Three Cats, Forty Five Mice, Chalmers, Harper & Row, 1986
The Song, Zolotow, William Morrow, 1982
Spot Learns to Count, Hill, G. P. Putnam's Sons, 1983

Ten, Nine, Eight, Bang, Greenwillow Books, 1983
The Twelve Days of Christmas, Brett, Dodd, Mead, 1986
Twelve Days of Christmas, Ets, Golden Press, 1963
The Very Hungry Caterpillar, Carle, Philomel Books, 1983
Wacky Wednesday, LeSieg, Beginner Books, 1974
Whale Song, Johnston, G. P. Putnam's Sons, 1987
Why We Went to the Park, Hughes, Lothrop, Lee & Shepard, 1985
The Year at Maple Farm, Provensen, Atheneum, 1978
A Year of Beasts, Wolff, Dodd, Mead, 1984
A Year of Birds, Wolff, E. P. Dutton, 1986

The Middle Ages

Adam of the Road, Gray, Viking Press, 1942
The Age of Chivalry: English Society 1200–1400, Wright, Warwick Press, 1988
Anno's Medieval World, Anno, Philomel Books, 1980
Arms and Armor, Byam, Alfred A. Knopf, 1988
Arms and Armor, Wilkinson, Franklin Watts, 1984
Castle, Macaulay, Houghton Mifflin, 1977
Castles, Smith, Franklin Watts, 1988
Cross and Crescent: The Story of the Crusades, Suskind, W. W. Norton, 1967
Datelines of World History, Arnold, Warwick Press, 1983
Do You Know? About Castles and Crusaders, Suavain, Warwick Press, 1986
The Door in the Wall, de Angeli, Scholastic, 1949
The Encyclopedia of World Costume, Yarwood, Charles Scribner's Sons, 1978
From Hand to Mouth, Giblin, Thomas Y. Crowell, 1987
Kings Queens Knights & Jesters: Making Medieval Costumes, Schnurnberger, Harper & Row, 1978
Knights of the Round Table, Gross, Scholastic, 1985
Learning About: Castles and Palaces, Odor, Children's Press, 1982
Let's Look At: Castles, Matthews, Bookwright Press, 1988
The Luttrell Village: Country Life in the Middle Ages, Sancha, Thomas Y. Crowell, 1982
Max and Me and the Time Machine, Greer/Ruddick, Harcourt Brace Jovanovich, 1983
Medieval Days and Ways, Hartman, Macmillan, 1937
Medieval Europe, filmstrips with cassettes, Society for Visual Education, 1977
A Medieval Feast, Aliki, Thomas Y. Crowell, 1983
A Medieval Monk, Caselli, Peter Bedrick Books, 1986
The Middle Ages, Cairns, Lerner Publications, 1975

Oars, Sails and Steam: A Picture Book of Ships, Tunis, Thomas Y. Crowell, 1952

Pearl in the Egg, Van Woerkom, Thomas Y. Crowell, 1980

The Pied Piper of Hamelin, Diamond, Holiday House, 1981

The Reluctant Dragon, Grahame, Holt, Rinehart and Winston, 1983

Robin Hood of Sherwood Forest, McGovern, Scholastic, 1968

Saint George and the Dragon, Hodges, Little, Brown, 1984

The Search for Delicious, Babbit, Farrar, Straus & Giroux, 1969

See Inside: A Castle, Unstead, Warwick Press, 1986

See Inside: A Galleon, Rutland, Warwick Press, 1986

The Soldier Through the Ages: The Medieval Knight, Windrow, Franklin Watts, 1985

The Story of the Champions of the Round Table, Pyle, Charles Scribner's Sons (no date)

The Time Traveller Book of Knights and Castles, Hindley, Hayes Books, 1979

What Happened in Hamelin, Skurzynski, Four Winds Press, 1979

Wheels: A Pictorial History, Tunis, Thomas Y. Crowell, 1955

The Whipping Boy, Fleischman, Greenwillow Books, 1986

Young People's Story of Our Heritage: The Medieval World, Hillyer/Huey, Meredity Press, 1966

National Geographic Books

Africa's Animal Giants, McCauley, 1987

Amazing Animal Groups, Venino, 1981

Amazing Mysteries of the World, O'Neill, 1983

Animal Architects, 1987

Animals and Their Hiding Places, McCauley, 1986

Animals in Danger: Trying to Save Our Wildlife, 1978

Animals That Live in the Sea, Straker, 1978

Animals That Live in Trees, McCauley, 1986

Baby Bears and How They Grow, Buxton, 1986

Baby Farm Animals, Windsor, 1984

The Blue Whale, Grosvenor, 1977

Book of Mammals, 1981, 2 volumes

Builders of the Ancient World, 1986

Computers Those Amazing Machines, O'Neill, 1985

Creatures of the Night, Rinard, 1977

Creatures of the Woods, Eugene, 1985

Dogs on Duty, O'Neill, 1988

Explore a Spooky Swamp, Cortesi, 1978

Exploring the Seashore, Amos, 1984

Far-Out Facts, 1980

Fun with Physics, McGrath, 1986

Giants from the Past, Bailey, 1983
Helping Our Animal Friends, Rinard, 1985
Hidden Treasures of the Sea, 1988
How Animals Behave, 1984
How Animals Care for Their Babies, Hirschland, 1987
How Animals Talk, McGrath, 1987
How Things Work, 1983
Let's Go to the Moon, Wheat, 1977
Life in Ponds and Streams, Amos, 1981
Messengers to the Brain, Martin, 1984
More Far-Out Facts, 1982
Our Violent Earth, 1982
Penguins and Polar Bears, Crow, 1985
Raccoons, Kostyal, 1987
Safari, Stuart, 1982
Saving Our Animal Friends, McGrath, 1986
The Secret World of Animals, 1986
Small Inventions That Make a Big Difference, 1984
Strange Animals of Australia, Eugene, 1981
What Happens at the Zoo, Rinard, 1984
Why in the World, 1985
Why on Earth, 1988
Wild Animals of North America, 1987
Wildcats, Winston, 1981
Wildlife Making a Comeback, Rinard, 1987
The Wonderful World of Whales and Seals, Crow, 1984
The World Beneath Your Feet, 1985
You Won't Believe Your Eyes, 1987
Your Wonderful Body, 1982
Zoo Babies, Grosvenor, 1978

Native Americans

America's Fascinating Indian Heritage, Reader's Digest, Reader's Digest Association, 1978
Annie and the Old One, Miles, Atlantic Monthly Press, 1971
Berry Ripe Moon, Day, Tide Grass Press, 1977
Buffalo Women, Goble, Bradbury Press, 1984
Corn Is Maize, Aliki, Thomas Y. Crowell, 1976
The Defenders, McGovern, Scholastic, 1970
The Desert Is Theirs, Baylor, Charles Scribner's Sons, 1975
The Gift of the Sacred Dog, Goble, Bradbury Press, 1980
The Girl Who Cried Flowers and Other Tales, Yolen, Schocken Books, 1974
The Girl Who Loved Wild Horses, Goble, Bradbury Press, 1978

Hiawatha, Longfellow, Dial Books, 1983
I Can Read About Eskimos, Schultz, Troll Associates, 1979
I Can Read About Indians, Warren, Troll Associates, 1975
If You Are a Hunter of Fossils, Baylor, Charles Scribner's Sons, 1980
Iktomi and the Boulder, Goble, Orchard Books, 1988
I'm in Charge of Celebrations, Baylor, Charles Scribner's Sons, 1986
Indian Chiefs, Freedman, Holiday House, 1987
Indian Homes, Brandt, Troll Associates, 1985
Indian Two Feet and His Horse, Friskey, Scholastic, 1959
Indians of the West, Bains, Troll Associates, 1985
Knots on a Counting Rope, Martin, Jr./Archambault, Henry Holt, 1987
The Legend of Bluebonnet, de Paola, G. P. Putnam's Sons, 1983
The Legend of the Indian Paintbrush, de Paola, G. P. Putnam's Sons, 1988
Maine Folk History, Day and Whitmore, Tide Grass Press, 1978
Moonsong Lullaby, Highwater, Lothrop, Lee & Shepard, 1981
The New England Indians, Wilbur, Globe Pequot Press, 1978
A New True Book: Indians, Martini, Children's Press, 1982
Osceola Seminole Warrior, Oppenheim, Troll Associates, 1979
Paddle to the Sea, Holling, Houghton Mifflin, 1969
Pocahontas Girl of Jamestown, Jassem, Troll Associates, 1979
Pontiac Chief of the Ottawas, Fleischer, Troll Associates, 1979
Pride, Project Indian Pride, 1978
Rainbow Rider, Yolen, Thomas Y. Crowell, 1974
The Sign of the Beaver, George, Houghton Mifflin, 1983
Squanto: Friend of the Pilgrims, Bulla, Scholastic, 1954
Squanto: The Pilgrim Adventure, Jassem, Troll Associates, 1979
Startales, Mayo, Walker and Company, 1987
The Story of Buffalo Bill, Collier, Grosset & Dunlap, 1952
The Story of Crazy Horse, Meadowcroft, Grosset & Dunlap, 1954
The Story of Daniel Boone, Steele, Grosset & Dunlap, 1953
The Story of Davy Crockett, Meadowcroft, Grosset & Dunlap, 1952
The Story of General Custer, Leighton, Grosset & Dunlap, 1954
The Story of Geronimo, Kjelgaard, Grosset & Dunlap, 1958
Tecumseh: Shawnee War Chief, Fleischer, Troll Associates, 1979
Trouble at Otter Creek, Hays, Xerox Education Publications, 1978
The Way to Start a Day, Baylor, Macmillan, 1978
Whale in the Sky, Siberell, E. P. Dutton, 1982
Where the Buffalo Begin, Baker, Frederick Warne, 1981
Why the Possum's Tail Is Bare and Other North American Indian Nature Tales, Connolly, Stemmer House, 1985

Pioneers

The Cabin That Faced West, Fritz, Puffin Books, 1958
Caddie Woodlawn, Brink, Macmillan, 1973

The Courage of Sarah Noble, Dalgliesh, Scholastic, 1954
Dakota Dugout, Turner, Macmillan, 1985
If You Traveled West in a Covered Wagon, Levine, Scholastic, 1986
Little House (collection), Wilder, Harper & Row, 1971
Nettie's Trip South, Turner, Macmillan, 1987
Pioneer Life on the American Prairie, Scholastic, 1977
Sarah, Plain and Tall, MacLachlan, Harper & Row, 1985
Trouble for Lucy, Stevens, Clarion Books, 1979

Plants/Trees

Amazing World of Plants, Marcus, Troll Associates, 1984
Animals That Live in Trees, McCauley, National Geographic Society, 1986
Arbor Day, Fisher, Thomas Y. Crowell, 1965
Bimsi and Bamsi: An Adventure in the Maine Woods, Derevitzky, Gannett Books, 1985
Cactus in the Desert, Busch, Thomas Y. Crowell, 1979
Counting Wildflowers, McMillan, Lothrop, Lee & Shepard, 1986
Creatures of the Woods, Eugene, National Geographic Society, 1985
The Curious Naturalists, Mitchell, Prentice-Hall, 1980
Discovering Acadia: A Guide for Young Naturalists, Scheild, Bever Tale Productions, 1987
Discovering Trees, Brandt, Troll Associates, 1982
Everytime I Climb a Tree, McCord, Little, Brown, 1967
Exploring Animal Homes, Rowland-Entwistle, Willowisp Press, 1984
Eyewitness Books: Tree, Burnie, Alfred A. Knopf, 1988
A Field Guide to Forests Coloring Book, Peterson, Houghton Mifflin, 1983
A Field Guide to Wildflowers Coloring Book, Peterson, Houghton Mifflin, 1982
Forest of Dreams, Wells, Dial Books, 1988
A Forest Year, Lerner, William Morrow, 1987
The Giving Tree, Silverstein, Harper & Row, 1964
The Great Dimpole Oak, Lisle, Orchard Books, 1987
Growing Vegetable Soup, Ehlert, Harcourt Brace Jovanovich, 1987
How to Draw Forest Animals, Soloff-Levy, Watermill Press, 1985
How to Make Things Grow, Wickers/Tuey, Scholastic, 1972
I Can Read About Trees and Plants, Warren, Troll Associates, 1975
I Was Born in a Tree and Raised by Bees, Arnosky, Bradbury Press, 1977
The Leaf Book, Orange, Lerner Publications, 1975
The Life Cycle of the Oak Tree, Hogan, Raintree Childrens Books, 1979
The Lorax, Seuss, Random House, 1971
The Mare on the Hill, Locker, Dial Books, 1985

Mouskin's Woodland Sleepers, Miller, Prentice Hall, 1970
Mysteries and Marvels of Plant Life, Cork, Usborne Publishing Ltd., 1983
Nature Hide and Seek: Jungles, Wood, Willowisp Press, 1987
Nature Scope: Trees Are Terrific!, National Wildlife Federation, 1985
Nature with Children of All Ages, Sisson, Prentice-Hall, 1982
A New True Book: Trees, Podendorf, Children's Press, 1982
Oak and Company, Mabey, Greenwillow Books, 1983
Once There Was a Tree, Busch, Scholastic, 1968
Once There Was a Tree, Romanova, Dial Books, 1985
One Day in the Woods, George, Thomas Y. Crowell, 1988
Plants in Winter, Mizumara, Thomas Y. Crowell, 1973
Plants That Never Ever Bloom, Heller, Grosset & Dunlap, 1984
The Reason for a Flower, Heller, Grosset & Dunlap, 1986
Redwoods Are the Tallest Trees in the World, Adler, Thomas Y. Crowell, 1978
Sailing with the Wind, Locker, Dial Books, 1986
Seeds by Wind and Water, Jordan, Thomas Y. Crowell, 1962
Sketching Outdoors in Autumn, Arnosky, Lothrop, Lee & Shepard, 1988
Sketching Outdoors in Spring, Arnosky, Lothrop, Lee & Shepard, 1987
Sketching Outdoors in Summer, Arnosky, Lothrop, Lee & Shepard, 1988
Sketching Outdoors in Winter, Arnosky, Lothrop, Lee & Shepard, 1988
The Tiny Seed, Carle, Picture Book Studio, 1987
Tree Flowers, Lerner, William Morrow, 1984
A Tree Is a Plant, Bulla, Thomas Y. Crowell, 1960
Trees, Kirkpatrick, Raintree Children's Books, 1985
Trees, Podendorf, Children's Press, 1982
Trees: My Picture Library, Jules Books, 1986
Usborne First Nature—Flowers, Cox and Cork, EDC Publishing, 1980
Usborne First Nature—Trees, Thomson, EDC Publishing, 1980
Where Does Your Garden Grow, Goldin, Thomas Y. Crowell, 1967
Where the River Begins, Locker, Dial Books, 1984
Wonders of the Forest, Sabin, Troll Associates, 1982
The World Beneath Your Feet, Rinard, National Geographic Society, 1985

Poetry

All Day Long, McCord, Dell, 1965
All Small, McCord, Little, Brown, 1986
All the Small Poems, Worth, Sunburst Book, 1987
Arrow Book of Poetry, McGovern, Scholastic, 1965
Best Friends, Hopkins, Harper & Row, 1986

Blackberry Ink, Merriam, William Morrow, 1985

Brats, Kennedy, Atheneum, 1986

A Child's Garden of Verse, Stevenson, Exeter Books, 1979

Click, Rumble, Roar, Hopkins (ed.), Thomas Y. Crowell, 1987

A Concise Treasury of Great Poems, Untermeyer, Simon and Schuster, 1942

Dinosaurs, Hopkins, Harcourt Brace Jovanovich, 1987

Dirty Beasts, Dahl, Farrar, Straus & Giroux, 1983

Dogs & Dragons—Trees & Dreams, Kuskin, Harper & Row, 1980

Earth Story, Maddern, Barron's, 1988

Everytime I Climb a Tree, McCord, Little, Brown, 1967

Father Fox's Penny Rhymes, Watson, Scholastic, 1971

First Poems of Childhood, Tudor, Platt & Munk, Publishers, 1967

A First [Second, Third, Fourth] Poetry Book, Foster (ed.), Oxford University Press, 1980–84

The Forgetful Wishing Well, Kennedy, Atheneum, 1985

Fragile as Butterflies, Patterson, Good Apple, 1983

Fresh Paint, Merriam, Macmillan, 1986

The Giving Tree, Silverstein, Harper & Row, 1964

The Golden Treasury of Poetry, Untermeyer, Golden Press, 1959

Good Morning to You, Valentine, Hopkins, Xerox Education Publications, 1976

Hailstones and Halibut Bones, O'Neill, Doubleday, 1961

Hurry, Hurry Mary Dear, Bodecker, Atheneum, 1978

If I Were in Charge of the World, Viorst, Atheneum, 1981

I'm Nobody! Who Are You?, Dickinson, Stemmer House, 1978

In My Garden, Eldridge, The Medici Society, 1983

It's Raining Said John Twaining, Bodecker, Atheneum, 1973

Jamberry, Degen, Harper & Row, 1983

Jamboree, Merriam, Dell, 1962

Joyful Noise: Poems for Two Voices, Fleischman, Harper & Row, 1988

Knock at a Star, Kennedy, Little, Brown, 1982

Laughing Time: Nonsense Poems, Smith, Dell, 1953

Let's Marry Said the Cherry, Bodecker, Atheneum, 1974

A Light in the Attic, Silverstein, Harper & Row, 1981

A Lollygag of Limericks, Livingston, Atheneum, 1978

Long Ago in Oregon, Lewis, Trumpet, 1987

Mojave, Siebert, Thomas Y. Crowell, 1988

More Mother Moose Rhymes, Palmer, Gannett Books, 1987

More Poems, Untermeyer, Western Publishing, 1959

Mother Goose, de Paola, G. P. Putnam's Sons, 1985

Mother Moose Rhymes, Palmer, Gannett Books, 1986

The New Kid on the Block, Prelutsky, Greenwillow Books, 1984

Now We Are Six, Milne, Dell, 1927

Owl Moon, Yolen, Philomel Books, 1987

The Oxford Book of Children's Verse in America, Hall, Oxford University Press, 1985

The Pelican Chorus & the Quangle Wangle's Hat, Lear, Viking Press, 1981

Phoebe's Revolt, Babbitt, Farrar, Straus & Giroux, 1968

Pigeon Cubes, Bodecker, Atheneum, 1982

Poem Stew, Cole, J. B. Lippincott, 1981

Poems Children Will Sit Still For: A Selection for Primary Grades, Citation Press, 1969

Poetry Place Anthology, Instructor Books, Instructor Publications, 1983

Potato Chips and a Slice of the Moon, Hopkins/Arensten, Scholastic, 1976

The Random House Book of Poetry for Children, Prelutsky, Random House, 1983

Read-Aloud Rhymes for the Very Young, Prelutsky, Alfred A. Knopf, 1986

Reflection on a Gift of Watermelon Pickle, Dunning, Scholastic, 1966

Ride a Purple Pelican, Prelutsky, Greenwillow Books, 1986

Ring of Earth, Yolen, Harcourt Brace Jovanovich, 1986

Roses, Where Did You Get That Red? Koch, Random House, 1974

The Sea Is Calling Me, Hopkins (ed.), Harcourt Brace Jovanovich, 1986

Sea Songs, Livingston, Holiday House, 1986

Side by Side, collected by Hopkins, Simon & Schuster, 1988

Sing a Song of Popcorn, selected by de Regniers/Moore/White/Car, Scholastic, 1988

A Sky Full of Poems, Merriam, Dell, 1986

Small Poems Again, Worth, Farrar, Straus & Giroux, 1986

Speak Up, McCord, Little, Brown, 1979

Stopping by Woods on a Snowy Evening, Frost, E. P. Dutton, 1978

The Stuff You Couldn't Find, Sparks, Sparkie Stuff, 1985

A Swinger of Birches, Frost, Stemmer House, 1982

Talking to the Sun, Koch and Farrell, Holt, Rinehart and Winston, 1985

Time to Shout, Hopkins, Scholastic, 1973

Where the Sidewalk Ends, Silverstein, Harper & Row, 1974

Whiskers & Rhymes, Lobel, Greenwillow Books, 1985

Wind Song, Sandburg, Harcourt Brace and World, 1953

You Read to Me, I'll Read to You, Ciardi, Harper & Row, 1962

The Renaissance

King Bidgood's in the Bathtub, Wood, Harcourt Brace Jovanovich, 1985

Space

All About the Moon, Alder, Troll Associates, 1983
All About the Stars, Jefferies, Troll Associates, 1983
Arrow Book of Space, Freeman, Scholastic, 1976
Autumn: Discovering the Seasons, Santry, Troll Associates, 1983
The Big Dipper, Branley, Thomas Y. Crowell, 1962
A Book About Planets, Reigot, Scholastic, 1981
A Book of Seasons, Provensen, Random House, 1976
The Comet and You, Krupp, Macmillan, 1985
Comets, Petty, Franklin Watts, 1985
The Complete Paper Airplane Book, Shulan, Watermill Press, 1979
Dangerous Adventure!, Gross, Scholastic, 1977
Discovering the Stars, Santrey, Troll Associates, 1982
Earth Story, Maddern, Barrons, 1988
Find the Constellations, Rey, Houghton Mifflin, 1976
The First Travel Guide to the Moon, Blumberg, Scholastic, 1980
Fun with Astronomy, Freeman, Scholastic, 1968
The Glorious Flight, Provensen, Viking Press, 1983
The Great Flight Book of Games and Things to Do, Scholastic, 1979
How Did We Find Out About Comets?, Asimov, Walker and Co., 1981
I Can Read About Planets, Schecter, Troll Associates, 1979
Let's Go to the Moon, Wheat, National Geographic Society, 1977
A Look Around Space, Holland, Willowisp Press, 1986
Look to the Night Sky, Simon, Puffin Press, 1979
Lost Race of Mars, Silverberg, Scholastic, 1960
Moon Madness, Wall, Watermill Press, 1983
My First Book About Space, Moche, Western Publishing, 1982
My First Book of Space, Hansen and Bell, Simon & Schuster, 1985
A New True Book: Airports, Petersen, Children's Press, 1981
A New True Book: Astronomy, Fradin, Children's Press, 1983
A New True Book: Space, Podendorf, Children's Press, 1982
A New True Book: Space Shuttles, Friskey, Children's Press, 1982
The Night Sky Book, Jobb, Little, Brown, 1977
Now You Can Read About Spacecraft, Attmore, Willowisp Press, 1985
Our Universe, Gallant, National Geographic Society, 1986
Our Wonderful Seasons, Marcus, Troll Associates, 1983
Our Wonderful Solar System, Adams, Troll Associates, 1983
Papa, Please Get the Moon for Me, Carle, Picture Book Studio USA, 1986
Ring of Earth, Yolen, Harcourt Brace Jovanovich, 1986
Skylab, Latham/Sloan, Rigby, 1986
Space Exploration and Travel, Sabin, Troll Associates, 1985
The Space Shuttle Story, Begarnie, Scholastic, 1985
Spring: Discovering the Seasons, Santrey, Troll Associates, 1983
Summer: Discovering the Seasons, Santrey, Troll Associates, 1983

The Sun, the Moon, and the Stars, Freeman, Random House, 1979
What Happens in the Spring, Beer, National Geographic Society, 1977
What Makes Day and Night, Branley, Thomas Y. Crowell, 1961
What's Up There, Moche, Scholastic, 1975
Wonders of the Seasons, Brandt, Troll Associates, 1982
The Wright Brothers at Kitty Hawk, Sobol, Scholastic, 1961
The Young Astronomer, Snowden, Usborne Publishing Ltd., 1983
The Young Scientist Book of Stars and Planets, Maynard, Usborne Publishing Ltd., 1977

U.S. History

Across Five Aprils, Hunt, Follett, 1964
And Then What Happened, Paul Revere?, Fritz, Scholastic, 1973
Can't You Make Them Behave, King George?, Fritz, Scholastic, 1977
The Drinking Gourd, Monjo, Harper & Row, 1970
First Farm in the Valley: Anna's Story, Pellowski, Philomel Books, 1982
Freedom Train: The Story of Harriet Tubman, Sterling, Scholastic, 1954
From Path to Highway: The Story of the Boston Post Road, Gibbons, Thomas Y. Crowell, 1986
I Go With My Family to Grandma's, Levinson, E. P. Dutton, 1986
Jack Jouett's Ride, Haley, Viking Press, 1973
Johnny Tremain, Forbes, Dell, 1943
Jump: The Adventures of Brer Rabbit, adapted by Parks/Jones, Harcourt Brace Jovanovich, 1986
The Little Red, White, and Blue Book, Ageland, Shulman, Trumpet, 1987
My Brother Sam Is Dead, Collier, Scholastic, 1974
Runaway to Freedom, Smucker, Harper & Row, 1978
Slave Dancer, Fox, Bradbury Press, 1973
The Star Spangled Banner, Spier, Doubleday, 1973
Susanna of the Alamo, Jakes, Harcourt Brace Jovanovich, 1986
Uncle Tom's Cabin, Stowe, Macmillan, 1962
Watch the Stars Come Out, Levinson, E. P. Dutton, 1985
What's the Big Idea Ben Franklin?, Fritz, Scholastic, 1976
When I Was Young in the Mountains, Rylant, E. P. Dutton, 1982
Who Really Discovered America, Kvensky, Scholastic, 1987
Will You Sign Here John Hancock?, Fritz, Scholastic, 1976
Willow Wind Farm: Betsy's Story, Pellowski, Philomel Books, 1981
Winding Valley Farm: Annie's Story, Pellowski, Philomel Books, 1982
The Witch of Blackbird Pond, Speare, Dell, 1958

Weather

Air, Air, Air, Jefferies, Troll Associates, 1983
Air Is All Around Us, Branley, Thomas Y. Crowell, 1962
Bringing the Rain to Kapiti Plain, Aardema, Dial Books, 1981
The Cloud Book, de Paola, Scholastic, 1975
Cloudy with a Chance of Meatballs, Barett, Scholastic, 1978
Discovering the Seasons: Autumn, Santry, Troll Associates, 1983
Discovering the Seasons: Spring, Santry, Troll Associates, 1983
Discovering the Seasons: Summer, Santry, Troll Associates, 1983
Dreams, Spier, Doubleday, 1986
Energy from the Sun, Berger, Thomas Y. Crowell, 1976
50 Below Zero, Munsch, Annick Press Limited, 1986
Four Stories for Four Seasons, de Paola, Prentice-Hall, 1977
Hot as an Ice Cube, Balestrino, Thomas Y. Crowell, 1971
I Can Read About Weather, Supraner, Troll Associates, 1975
Into Winter: Discovering a Season, Nestor, Houghton Mifflin, 1982
January Brings the Snow, Coleridge, Dial Books, 1986
A New True Book: Astronomy, Fradin, Children's Press, 1982
A New True Book: Seasons, Martini, Children's Press, 1982
A New True Book: Weather Experiments, Children's Press, 1982
Night of the Twisters, Ruckman, Thomas Y. Crowell, 1984
Noah's Ark, Lorimer, Random House, 1978
Noah's Ark, Spier, Doubleday, 1977
Our Wonderful Seasons, Marcus, Troll Associates, 1983
Questions and Answers About Weather, Craig, Scholastic, 1969
Rain, Spiers, Doubleday, 1982
Rain and Hail, Branley, Thomas Y. Crowell, 1963
A Regular Rolling Noah, Lyon, Bradbury Press, 1986
Spotter's Guide to the Weather, Wilson/Mansfield, Mayflower Books,
    1979
The Weather Pop-Up Book, Wilson, Simon & Schuster, 1987
What Happens in Spring, Beer, National Geographic Society, 1977
What Makes It Rain? The Story of a Raindrop, Brandt, Troll Associates,
    1982
What Makes Wind? Santrey, Troll Associates, 1982
What the Wind Told, Boegehold, Scholastic, 1974
The Wind Blew, Hutchins, Puffin Books, 1974
Wonders of the Season, Brandt, Troll Associates, 1982

Words

Amelia Bedelia, Parish, Harper & Row, 1963
A Chocolate Moose for Dinner, Gwynne, Prentice-Hall, 1976

Easy as Pie: A Guessing Game of Sayings, Folsom, Clarion Books, 1985
Eight Ate a Feast of Homonym Riddles, Terban, Clarion Books, 1982
How a Book Is Made, Aliki, Thomas Y. Crowell, 1986
I Think I Thought and Other Tricky Verbs, Terban, Clarion Books, 1984
In a Pickle and Other Funny Idioms, Terban, Clarion Books, 1983
The King Who Rained, Gwynne, Prentice-Hall, 1970
Pundiddles, McMillan, Houghton Mifflin, 1982
17 Kings and 42 Elephants, Mahy, Dial Books, 1987
Sniglets for Kids, Hall, Antioch Publishing, 1985
Too Hot to Hoot: Funny Palindrome Riddles, Terban, Clarion Books, 1985

Miscellaneous

All About Sound, Knight, Troll Associates, 1983
Amazing Magnets, Alder, Troll Associates, 1983
Auks, Rocks, and the Odd Dinosaur: Inside Stories from the Smithsonian's Museum of Natural History, Thomson, Thomas Y. Crowell, 1985
The Berenstain Bears' Nature Guide, Berenstain, Random House, 1985
The Book of Foolish Machinery, Page, Scholastic, 1988
The Butter Battle Book, Seuss, Random House, 1984
Charlie Needs a Cloak, de Paola, Scholastic, 1973
Check It Out: The Book About Libraries, Gibbons, Harcourt Brace Jovanovich, 1985
Dinosaurs, Dragonflies and Diamonds, Gibbons, Four Winds Press, 1988
Energy from the Sun, Berger, Thomas Y, Crowell, 1976
Finding Out About Everyday Things, Humberstone, Usborne Publishing Ltd., 1981
The Glorious Flight Across the Channel with Louis Bleriot, Provenson, Viking Press, 1983
A House Is a House for Me, Hoberman, Viking Press, 1978
How Come. . . ? Easy Answers to Hard Questions, Richards, Platt & Munk, Publishers, 1975
Invention Book, Caney, Workman Publishing, 1985
Living Things: A Simple Introduction, Claridge/Shackell, Usborne Publishing Ltd., 1985
The Magic School Bus: At the Waterworks, Cole, Scholastic, 1986
The Magic School Bus: Inside the Earth, Cole, Scholastic, 1987
Mysteries of the Ancient Americas, Reader's Digest Association, 1986
The Popcorn Book, de Paola, Scholastic, 1978
The Pottery Place, Gibbons, Harcourt Brace Jovanovich, 1987
Quest for the Past, Reader's Digest Association, 1984
Rocks & Minerals, Marcus, Troll Associates, 1983
Secret Magnets, Schneider, Scholastic, 1979

Secrets of Nature, Cochrane, Scholastic, 1979

Secrets in Stone, Wyler/Ames, Scholastic, 1970

The Skeleton Book: An Inside Look at Animals, Livaudais/Dunne, Scholastic, 1972

The Story of the Ice Age, Wyler, Scholastic, 1967

Trains, Gibbons, Holiday House, 1987

Understanding and Collecting Rocks and Fossils, Bramwell, Usborne Publishing Ltd., 1983

Up Goes the Sky Scraper, Gibbons, Four Winds Press, 1986

When, Shemi and Kerman, Sterling Publishing, 1985

Where, Shemi and Kerman, Sterling Publishing, 1985

Where Does the Garbage Go?, Showers, Thomas Y. Crowell, 1974

Why, Shemi and Kerman, Sterling Publishing, 1985

The World's Last Mysteries, Reader's Digest Association, 1982

The Young Naturalist, Mitchell, Usborne Publishing Ltd., 1982

The Young Scientist Book of Archaeology, Cord/Reid, Usborne Publishing Ltd., 1984

The Young Scientist Book of Evolution, Cork/Bresler, Usborne Publishing Ltd., 1985

Zoo, Gibbons, Thomas Y. Crowell, 1987

Appendix D

Resources for Writing and Reading to Learn

I. Children's Literature: Sources and Resources

Adams News Company
1555 West Galer Street
Seattle, Washington 98119
(800) 533-7617

Warehouse source for paperback literature at a 35 percent discount; free catalog.

Appraisal
605 Commonwealth Avenue
Boston, Massachusetts 02215

A quarterly magazine devoted to reviews of math and science books by librarians and subject area specialists. Subscription: $20 per year.

Bookmen
525 North Third Street
Minneapolis, Minnesota 55401
(800) 328-8411

A children's literature paperback warehouse; 40 percent discount; free catalog.

A Child's Collection
611 Broadway, Suite 708
New York, New York 10012

An annual collection of fine children's literature, mostly hardcover; free catalog.

Children's Book Council
67 Irving Place
New York, New York 10003

A lifetime subscription to *CBC Features* costs $25.00 and includes author and illustrator brochures, posters and bookmarks, and annual bibliographies of recommended fiction, science, and social studies books for children.

Children's Press
1224 West Van Buren Street
Chicago, Illinois 60607

A superb collection of children's content-area literature; free catalog.

Chinaberry Book Service
3760 30th Street
San Diego, California 92104

Well-annotated catalog of children's literature, both paperback and hardcover; free.

The Civilization Library
The Take a Trip Series
Franklin Watts, Inc.
387 Park Avenue, South
New York, New York 10016

Two sources for literature on social studies topics; free catalogs.

EDC Publishing
Division of Educational Development Corporation
P.O. Box 470663
Tulsa, Oklahoma 74147
(800) 331-4418

Content-area resource books for children, including the Usborne series; free catalog.

The Five Owls
2004 Sheridan Avenue South
Minneapolis, Minnesota 55405

A bimonthly pamphlet of articles about children's literature, both fiction and nonfiction. Subscription: $18 per year.

The Horn Book
Park Square Building
31 St. James Avenue
Boston, Massachusetts 02116

A bimonthly magazine that has reviewed books for children and young adults since 1924. Also, feature articles about authors and recent trends in children's literature and announcements of meetings and conferences. Subscription: $36 per year.

Kobrin, Beverly, 1988. *Eyeopeners*! New York: Viking Penguin.

A practical review of more than five hundred nonfiction books with advice about how to integrate them into classroom teaching, encourage reading, enhance learning, and choose books for children.

The Kobrin Letter
732 Greer Road
Palo Alto, California 94303

A newsletter featuring discussions and reviews of children's books about real people, places, and things. Each issue is themed (e.g., Australia, volcanoes and glaciers, time, poetry, U.S. Constitution). Back issues available. Subscription: $12 per year for 8 issues.

Magpies
The Singing Tree
10 Armagh Street
Victoria Park, Western Australia

A magazine filled with articles about children's authors and thematic teaching ideas using children's literature. Subscription: U.S. Air $35 per year.

The New Advocate
P.O. Box 809
Needham Heights, Massachusetts 02194-0006

A quarterly for teachers and parents about literature for children and young adults. Includes articles by and about children's authors and illustrators, reviews, and discussions of practical implications for the home and classroom. Subscription: $27 per year.

New York Times Book Review

Each year the *NYTBR*, in the second weeks of May and November, features a comprehensive review of recent children's books. Available at chain bookstores and newsstands.

Richard C. Owen Publishers, Inc.
Rockefeller Center Box 819
New York, New York 10185

U.S. distributor of Ready to Read, the national reading program of New Zealand, and materials developed by The Whole Language Consultants; free catalog features "big books," predictable books, and audiotapes.

Rigby
P.O. Box 797
Crystal Lake, Illinois 60014
(800) 822-8661

A source for "big books" including exceptional beginning content-area books; free catalog.

Teachers Networking
Richard C. Owen Publishers, Inc.
Rockefeller Center Box 819
New York, New York 10185

A quarterly newsletter devoted to whole language issues: teaching strategies, reviews of new children's books, and a calendar of meetings and conferences. Subscription: $12 per year.

Telltales
P.O. Box 614
Bath, Maine 04530

A twice-yearly collection of exceptional children's literature; free catalogue with precise, helpful descriptions of the books.

Trumpet Book Clubs
P.O. Box 604
Holmes, Pennsylvania 19043

Two monthly book clubs, for primary and middle grade children, that feature Dell/Laurel-Leaf/Yearling paperbacks at reasonable prices; also includes letters from authors and taped author interviews.

The Web: Wonderfully Exciting Books
The Ohio State University
Room 200 Ramseyer Hall
29 West Woodruff
Columbus, Ohio 43210-1177

A useful introduction to thematic approaches to children's literature, including science and social studies topics, written by teachers and librarians. A list of back issues is available on request. Subscription: $10 per year for four issues.

Workshop
Heinemann Educational Books, Inc.
70 Court Street
Portsmouth, New Hampshire 03801

A themed annual volume by and for teacher-researchers about children's writing and reading. Includes strategies for using children's literature, special features by children's authors, and author interviews.

The Wright Group
10949 Technology Place
P.O. Box 27780
San Diego, California 92127

A source for "big books" that also offers content-area literature through its Wright Enrichment Reading Program; free catalog.

Yellow Brick Road
P.O. Box 25309
Rochester, New York 14625

A bimonthly newsletter about children's authors and thematic approaches to children's literature. Subscription: $10 per year.

II. Science and Social Studies Resources

Audubon Adventures
613 Riversville Road
Greenwich, Connecticut 06831

A classroom newspaper with activities covering nature, the environment, and ecology. Subscription: $25 per year per classroom (25 copies) for four issues.

Audubon Magazine
950 Third Avenue
New York, New York 10022

A photo and information resource for teachers covering a wide range of topics having to do with the natural world and human life. Subscription: $18.00 per year for six issues.

Cobblestone
28 Main Street
Peterborough, New Hampshire 03458

A themed history magazine for intermediate–middle grade students that has addressed such topics as immigration, computers, American Indians, U.S. elections, and the circus. Back issues are available. Subscription: $15.00 per year for six issues.

Cynergetics
P.O. Box 84
East Windsor, Connecticut 06028

Teacher-developed enrichment programs of books and activities based on content-area themes; free brochure.

Foxfire
The Foxfire Fund
Rabun Gap, Georgia 30568

The original *Foxfire* magazine, written and produced by students at Rabun Gap High School. Subscription: $9 per year for four issues.

Frey Scientific Company
905 Hickory Lane
Mansfield, Ohio 44905

Scientific equipment and specimens; free catalog.

National Audubon Society
613 Riversville Road
Greenwich, Connecticut 06831

Magazines, books, videos, classroom newspapers, ecology workshops, and speakers; free catalogs and brochures.

National Dairy Council
Rosemont, Illinois 60018

Films, pamphlets, posters, and teachers' guides; free catalog.

National Geographic Magazine
17th and M Streets NW
Washington, D.C. 20036

A superior reference: photos, illustrations, and text. Subscription: $18.00 per year for twelve issues.

National Geographic Society
Educational Services
Department 5250
Washington, D.C. 20036

A comprehensive collection of videos, filmstrips and tapes, books with tapes, books, maps, and more; free catalog.

National Geographic World
17th and M Streets NW
Washington, D.C. 20036

A monthly children's magazine exploring nature and the world; excellent photos and text. Subscription: $10.95 per year for twelve issues.

National Wildlife
8925 Leesburg Pike
Vienna, Virginia 22184

Photos and text on wildlife and ecological and environmental issues. Subscription: $12.00 per year for six issues.

National Wildlife Federation
1412 Sixteenth Street N.W.
Washington, D.C. 20036

A source for books, magazines, and videos; free brochure.

Natural History
Central Park West at 79th Street
New York, New York 10024

Published by the American Museum of National History; an excellent photo and information resource for teachers. Subscription: $19.95 per year for twelve issues.

Nature Book Society
Corner of 10th and Mulberry
P.O. Box 10875
Des Moines, Iowa 50380-0875

A collection of resource and picture books, by category; free catalog.

Nature Company
P.O. Box 2310
Berkeley, California 94702

Offers everything from objets d'art and T-shirts to posters, games, and specimens; free catalog.

Owl Magazine
P.O. Box 11314
Des Moines, Iowa 50340

Available in both French and English language editions. A magazine for and about kids and the world around them. Subscription: $12.95 per year for twelve issues.

Ranger Rick's NatureScope
1412 16th Street, NW
Washington, D.C. 20036-2266

Teacher resource for helping children understand and appreciate nature; excellent activities and extensive bibliography. Subscription: $14.00 per year for five issues.

Rent-a-Kit
Boston Children's Museum
300 Congress Street
Boston, Massachusetts 02210

A large variety of materials and resources to rent on many subjects: Pilgrims, China, Eskimos, the Middle Ages, ancient civilizations, etc.; free catalog.

Scienceland
501 Fifth Avenue
New York, New York 10017

Photo resource magazine and excellent teacher resource. Subscription: $24.00 per year for eight issues.

Sierra Club
P.O. Box 7959
San Francisco, California 94120

A source for print and video resources; free brochures.

Smithsonian Magazine
900 Jefferson Drive
Washington, D.C. 20560

Excellent teacher resource and source for photos; covers nature, art, history, humans and their inventions, and interaction with their environment. Subscription; $20.00 per year for twelve issues.

Topics Series
The Bookwright Press
387 Park Avenue South
New York, New York 10016

Collections of books that address a related topic (e.g., great lives, the seasons, great civilizations) for students in the elementary grades; free catalog.

III. Fine Arts Resources

Alarion
P.O. Box 1882
Boulder, Colorado 80306

Multimedia programs in history through art and architecture, grades 4–9;
free catalog.

International Film Bureau, Inc.
332 South Michigan Avenue
Chicago, Illinois 60604

16 mm films, videos, slides, and filmstrips (including some suitable for
primary grades) on art (history and appreciation), artists and their works,
and animation.

The Metropolitan Museum of Art
Fifth Avenue at 82nd Street
New York, New York 10028

Videotapes and slide shows on a variety of art topics; free catalog.

Museum of Fine Arts
465 Huntington Avenue
Boston, Massachusetts 02115

Offers a variety of "Artpacks": fine art reproductions on postcards with
appropriate activities; especially suitable for a learning center; free catalog.

National Gallery of Art
Department of Extension Programs
Publications Service
Washington, D.C. 20565

Free catalogs of art books, posters, art objects, films, and prints.

reading & o'reilly
Box 302
Wilton, Connecticut 06897

Sound filmstrips for primary to high school on art history and appreciation;
an interdisciplinary approach to visual learning; free catalog.

School Arts
The Art Education Magazine for Teachers
Printers Building
Worcester, Massachusetts 01608

An excellent resource for classroom teachers as well as art teachers.

Shorewood Fine Arts Reproductions, Inc.
27 Glen Road
Sandy Hook, Connecticut 06482

Art programs for grades K–12 in many categories, including seasons, ships and the sea, the family adventure, black artists in America, and American history. Prints can be purchased mounted, laminated, or shrink-wrapped.

The University Prints Catalog
21 East Street, P.O. Box 485
Winchester, Massachusetts 01890

A collection of thousands of available art prints in many sizes, both color and black and white; free catalog.

IV. Local Resources

American Field Service

Speakers and resource information about specific countries.

Aquariums

On-site programs, resource libraries, outreach programs.

Architects

Historical architecture, architectual styles, physical requirements of building design for residential, commercial, and governmental purposes.

Artists and Craftspeople

Establish a file of writers, musicians, painters, sculptors, printmakers, photographers, woodworkers, etc., who live in the region and might be approached for on-site visits or as speakers.

Camps

Often stress ecological and environmental issues and offer on-site and outreach programs and print resources.

Chambers of Commerce (Local and State)

Maps, brochures, speakers about local industry, demographics, historical sites, etc.

Children's Museums

On-site and outreach programs aimed at actively involving students in learning about the world around them.

Civil War Roundtables

Speakers, debates, re-creations of battles, and information on local involvement in the Civil War.

Colleges and Universities

Libraries (reference resources, displays, programs, visual aids), speaker's bureaus, community outreach programs, museums, theater productions, bookstores, etc.

Department of Public Works

State and community infrastructure laws, citizen input, development, planning, maintenance, maps.

Experiment in International Living

Speakers, resources and/or references for information about specific countries.

4-H Clubs

Nature, environment, and ecology studies; speakers, books, and outreach programs.

Garden Clubs

Speakers, Junior Garden Club sponsor, local beautification and education efforts, community civic association.

Historical Societies (Local, Regional, and State)

Speakers, displays, outreach programs, books, pamphlets, videos, and reference sources.

Humane Societies

Speakers, field trips, animal safety and community concern, animal control laws.

Libraries (Local and State)

Reference resources, displays and museums, speakers, outreach programs, and audiovisual resources.

Lumber Yards

Forest products, lumber grading and uses, local commerce, community needs.

Meteorologists

Radio and television personalities will often speak to school groups; also, weather maps are available at many military bases.

Nature Conservancies (Local and National)

Speakers on environmental issues, from preservation of land access to endangered environments; field trips to areas under supervision of the conservancy.

Newspapers

Reference resource, writing production, speakers, and on-site visits.

Nurseries, Florists, and Arborists

Plant and tree life, preservation, identification, cultivation, environmental impact, landscaping; speakers and on-site visits.

Planetariums

On-site programs, print resources, speakers, and outreach programs.

Realtors

Land values, historical value of buildings, architecture through community history, growth and control, ownership requirements, and legal requirements.

Research Institutions (Medical, Environmental, etc.)

Research libraries, speakers, visual aids, outreach programs, and print resources.

Safety and Law Agencies

Speakers and on-site visits; law and citizenship responsibilities.

Special Interest Museums

Often located on the site of a historical building or industry; outreach programs and displays, reference resources.

State Commissions on the Arts, History, and Architecture

Speakers, print and visual resources, outreach programs.

State Government

- Libraries
- Departments of Forestry
        Conservation
        Wildlife
        Marine Resources
        Game and Fisheries
        Parks and Recreation

Speakers, print and visual resources, and on-site visits.

Travel Agencies

Speakers, as well as a resource for the names of local residents who have traveled extensively. On-site visits, schedules, posters, transportation studies, planning itineraries, and legal requirements for travel to other countries.

University or State College Extension Services

Outreach programs in almost every area of human endeavor.

Utilities

Water, gas, electric, and phone companies usually have consumer education programs and print and visual resources and allow on-site visits.

Veterinarians

Animal health and care, legal responsibilities, what to do with injured wildlife.

V. Professional Resources: Writing and Reading to Learn

Atwell, Nancie. 1987. *In the Middle: Writing, Reading, and Learning with Adolescents.* Portsmouth, NH: Boynton/Cook.

Includes two chapters and an appendix about using dialogue journals in response to literature, and writing workshop methods that can be adapted for report-writing workshops.

Avery, Carol. 1989. "We Built a Wall." In *Workshop 1: Writing and Literature*, ed. Nancie Atwell. Portsmouth, NH: Heinemann.

A first-grade class reads about, recreates, and writes about the Great Wall of China.

Berthoff, Ann E. 1981. "A Curious Triangle and the Double-Entry Notebook: or, How Theory Can Help Us Teach Reading and Writing." In *The Making of Meaning: Metaphors, Models, and Maxims for Writing Teachers*. Portsmouth, NH: Boynton/Cook.

An exploration of the double-entry journal technique, both how it works and why.

Calkins, Lucy McCormick. 1986. *The Art of Teaching Writing*. Portsmouth, NH: Heinemann.

Includes two extremely useful chapters on learning logs and report writing.

Chittenden, Lynda. 1982. "What If All the Whales Are Gone Before We Become Friends?" In *What's Going On? Language/Learning Episodes in British and American Classrooms, Grades 4–13*, ed. Mary Barr, Pat D'Arcy, and Mary K. Healy. Portsmouth, NH: Boynton/Cook.

A stunning article about a study of marine mammals conducted by a class of nine- and ten-year-olds.

Coulombe, Deborah A. 1984. *The Seaside Naturalist: A Guide to Nature Study at the Seashore*. Englewood Cliffs, NJ: Prentice-Hall.

A great teacher/parent resource for conducting ocean studies with children.

Dialogue
CAL
1118 22nd Street, N.W.
Washington, D. C. 20037

This themed newsletter about dialogue journals carries the news of current research as well as articles and notes from teachers describing their practice. Back issues are available. Subscription: $10.00 per year for three issues.

Emig, Janet. 1983. "Writing as a Mode of Learning." In *The Web of Meaning: Essays on Writing, Teaching, Learning, and Thinking*. Portsmouth, NH: Boynton/Cook.

A benchmark paper about analytic writing as a uniquely powerful, multi-representational way of learning.

Five, Cora, and Martha Rosen. 1985. "Children Re-create History in Their Own Voices." In *Breaking Ground: Teachers Relate Reading and Writing in the Elementary School*, ed. Jane Hansen, Thomas Newkirk, and Donald Graves. Portsmouth, NH: Heinemann.

A librarian and a fifth-grade teacher collaborate on a study of the American Revolution that involves children in reading relevant literature about the period and writing their own literature.

Fulwiler, Toby. December 1980. "Journals Across the Disciplines." *English Journal* 69: 14–19.

A discussion of reasons and methods for incorporating academic journals in every subject area at any level.

Fulwiler, Toby, ed. 1987. *The Journal Book*. Portsmouth, NH: Boynton/Cook.

Forty-two chapters by teachers from grades 1–12, as well as artists, philosophers, counselors, mathematicians, and economists, about the value of journals as tools for speculation, exploration, and critical thought.

Gere, Anne Ruggles, ed. 1985. *Roots in the Sawdust: Writing to Learn Across the Disciplines*. Urbana, IL: National Council of Teachers of English.

A group of secondary teachers from a variety of disciplines explore how, and why, writing fosters learning in math, science, English, social studies, foreign language, philosophy, psychology, and art.

Giacobbe, Mary Ellen. 1986. "Learning to Write and Writing to Learn in the Elementary School." In *The Teaching of Writing: Eighty-fifth Yearbook of the National Society for the Study of Education*, ed. Anthony R. Petrosky and David Bartholomae. Chicago: University of Chicago Press. (Also distributed by NCTE, Urbana, IL.)

An account of fourth-grade teacher Carolyn Currier's approach to report writing, and a close look at one student's process as a researcher and writer.

Graves, Donald H. 1989. *Investigate Nonfiction*. The Reading/Writing Teacher's Companion series. Portsmouth, N.H.: Heinemann.

An extremely useful exploration of how children—and teachers—might read and write the various nonfiction genres and examine the world around them.

Greeley, Patricia E. 1989. "Historical Fiction: The Tie That Binds Reading, Writing, and Social Studies." In *Workshop 1: Writing and Literature*, ed. Nancie Atwell. Portsmouth, NH: Heinemann.

A fifth-grade social studies class writes historical fiction about the westward movement of the 1800s.

Hands On
Foxfire Fund
Rabun Gap, Georgia 30568

A journal for teachers whose students are involved in experiential, community-based projects such as Foxfire. Subscription: $5.00 per year for four issues.

Hansen, Jane. 1987. *When Writers Read.* Portsmouth, NH: Heinemann.

Includes exceptional chapters about reading in the content areas and journals in a reading program.

Macrorie, Ken. 1988. *The I-Search Paper: Revised Edition of* Searching Writing. Portsmouth, NH: Boynton/Cook.

The classic book about using writing to learn. Although designed as a text for secondary students, it is a superb reference for the elementary school teacher who wishes to help children take charge of their searching and writing.

Martin, Nancy, ed. 1984. *Writing Across the Curriculum Pamphlets.* Portsmouth, NH: Boynton/Cook.

A one-volume collection of a series of pamphlets, first published in England in the mid-1970s, about writing as an instrument of learning, reflection, and discovery.

Martin, Nancy, et al. 1976. *Writing and Learning Across the Curriculum 11–16.* Portsmouth, NH: Boynton/Cook.

Emphasizes cooperative learning between students and between the student and teacher, and explores the role of expressive writing in helping children understand new material; the student examples are wonderful.

Matthews, Kathy. 1985. "Beyond the Writing Table." In *Breaking Ground: Teachers Relate Reading and Writing in the Elementary School,* ed. Jane Hansen, Thomas Newkirk, and Donald Graves. Portsmouth, NH: Heinemann.

A discussion of writing across the curriculum in a primary classroom, laying the foundation for writing as a natural complement to everything that students do.

Mitchell, John. 1980. *The Curious Naturalist.* Englewood Cliffs, NJ: Prentice-Hall, in association with the Massachusetts Audubon Society.

Environmental activities to follow the four seasons; an exceptional resource for both parents and teachers.

Moore, Rena Quiroz. 1989. "Fossil Hunters: Relating Reading, Writing, and Science." In *Workshop 1: Writing and Literature,* ed. Nancie Atwell. Portsmouth, NH: Heinemann.

A teacher of grades two and three explores science teaching and learning as processes comparable to writing and reading.

Murray, Donald. 1987. *Write to Learn*. 2d ed. New York: Holt, Rinehart and Winston.

An invaluable text for learning how to generate, organize, clarify, and present information in writing, as well as a source of ideas for minilessons for a report-writing workshop.

Ontario Science Center. 1987. *Science Works*. Reading, MA: Addison-Wesley.

Science experiments for home or classroom.

Rief, Linda. 1985. "Why Can't We Live Like the Monarch Butterfly?" In *Breaking Ground: Teachers Relate Reading and Writing in the Elementary School*, ed. Jane Hansen, Thomas Newkirk, and Donald Graves. Portsmouth, NH: Heinemann.

An account of an eighth-grade study of aging that draws on published literature as well as students' interviews with grandparents and residents of a nursing home. Particularly helpful on interviewing techniques.

Saul, Wendy, and Alan R. Newman. 1986. *Science Fare*. New York: Harper & Row.

One of the best science sourcebooks on the market. Includes resources by topic and describes a range of activities—electronics, astronomy, biology, computers—in full, rich contexts.

Sisson, Edith A. 1982. *Nature with Children of All Ages*. Englewood Cliffs, NJ: Prentice-Hall.

Environmental science activities for all ages and geographical regions; a resource for parents and teachers.

Stein, Sara. 1979. *The Science Book*. New York: Workman Publishing.

A comprehensive science resource book for elementary school teachers.

Wigginton, Eliot. 1986. *Sometimes a Shining Moment*. Garden City, NY: Anchor Books.

An inspiring, personal account of the Foxfire experiment; includes the Foxfire I curriculum.

Wilde, Jack. 1988. "The Written Report: Old Wine in New Bottles." In *Understanding Writing: Ways of Observing, Learning, and Teaching*, 2d ed., ed. Thomas Newkirk and Nancie Atwell. Portsmouth, NH: Heinemann.

A fifth-grade teacher who emphasized craft in the writing of reports explores his students' processes as they compose in a range of genres about animals.